AGRICULTURE CROPS AND FOOD SECURITY

ENV BOOKS SERIES

AGRICULTURE CROPS AND FOOD SECURITY

Editors

Dr. Pawan Kumar 'Bharti'
Society for Environment, Health, Awareness of Nutrition & Toxicology (SEHAT)
1775, Sohan Ganj, Near Clock Tower
Delhi - 110 007 (India)
E-mail: gurupawanbharti@rediffmail.com

&

Dr. Alka Chauhan
Society for Environment, Health, Awareness of Nutrition & Toxicology (SEHAT)
1775, Sohan Ganj, Near Clock Tower
Delhi - 110 007 (India)

DPH

DISCOVERY PUBLISHING HOUSE PVT. LTD.
INDIA

Published by:

Namit Wasan

DISCOVERY PUBLISHING HOUSE PVT. LTD.
4383/4B, Ansari Road, Darya Ganj
New Delhi-110 002 (India)
Phone : +91-11-23279245, 43596064-65
Fax : +91-11-23253475
E-mail : discoverypublishinghouse@gmail.com
namitwasan9@gmail.com
sales@discoverypublishinggroup.com
web : www.discoverypublishinggroup.com

***First Edition:* 2017**

ISBN: 978-93-5056-881-1

Agriculture Crops and Food Security

Printed at:
Infinity Imaging Systems
Delhi

ENV Books Series, India

Calls descriptive and error free chapters for upcoming volumes of books on various environmental issues. Send your manuscripts to envbooks@gmail.com

Founding Editor (Editor-in-Chief)

Dr. Pawan Kumar 'Bharti'
Society for Environment, Health, Awareness of Nutrition & Toxicology (SEHAT-India)
1775, Sohanganj, Near Clock Tower, Delhi-7, (India)
E-mail:*gurupawanbharti@rediffmail.com*

Other Important Titles by Editor-in-Chief:

1. **Advances in Biotechnology and Ecological Sciences**
   Bharti, P.K., Chauhan, A. and Ray, J. (eds.)
   (ISBN: 978-93-5056-358-8).
2. **Advances in Agriculture and Ecology**
   Bharti, P.K.; Chauhan, A. and Ezeaku Peter Ikemefuna (eds.)
   (ISBN: 978-93-5056-362-5).
3. **Agriculture and Environmental Biotechnology**
   Bharti, P.K. and Chauhan, A. (eds.)
   (ISBN: 978-93-5056-479-0).
4. **Agriculture Development and Sustainable Environment**
   Ray, J. and Bharti, P.K. (eds.)
   (ISBN: 978-93-5056-759-3).
5. **Agriculture Ecology and Environment**
   Bharti, P.K. and Olubukola O. Babalola (eds.)
   (ISBN: 978-93-5056-480-6).
6. **Agriculture Ecology, Sustainable Development and Agribusiness Management**
   Mehta Piyush; Sharma Pankaj; and 'Bharti' P.K. (eds.)
   (ISBN: 978-93-5056-851-4).
7. **Agriculture, Environment and Nano-science**
   Bharti, Pawan K. (ed.)
   (ISBN: 978-93-5056-760-5).
8. **Agricultural Practices and Crop Disease Control**
   Chauhan Alka and Sharma Anubhuti (eds.)
   (ISBN: 978-93-5056-859-0).

9. **Agro-biodiversity:** ***Conservation and Sustainable Development***
Sharma, Pankaj; Singh, Narayan; and Bharti, P.K. (eds.)
(ISBN: 978-93-505-782-1).

10. **Agro-forestry and Climate Change**
Bharti, Pawan K. and Singh, Narayan (eds.)
(ISBN: 978-93-5056-514-8).

11. **Agro-forestry and Sustainable Agriculture**
Sharma, Pankaj; Bharti, P.K. (eds.)
(ISBN: 978-93-5056-786-9).

12. **Air Pollution and Ecosystem Health**
Swami Abhishek and Bharti, P.K. (eds.)
(ISBN: 978-93-5056-877-4).

13. **Aquaculture and Fisheries Environment**
Gupta, S.K. and Pawan K. Bharti (eds.)
(ISBN: 978-93-5056-408-0).

14. **Aquatic Biodiversity and Pollution**
Bharti, P.K.; Chauhan, A. and Kaoud, H.A.H. (eds.)
(ISBN: 978-93-5056-359-5).

15. **Aquatic Ecology and Biotechnology**
Bharti, P.K. and Zaki, M.S.A. (eds.)
(ISBN: 978-93-5056-451-6).

16. **Aquatic Environment and Toxicology**
Bharti, Pawan K. (ed.)
(ISBN: 978-93-5056-236-9).

17. **Biodiversity, Biotechnology and Environmental Conservation**
Bharti, P.K. and Bhandari, G. (eds.)
(ISBN: 978-93-5056-750-0).

18. **Biodiversity, Biotechnology and Pollution Control**
Bharti, P.K. and Chauhan, Alka (eds.)
(ISBN: 978-93-5056-887-3).

19. **Biodiversity of Aquatic Ecosystem:** ***Significance, Threat and Conservation*** **(2013)**
Bharti, P.K. and Kaoud, H.A.H. (eds.)
(ISBN: 978-93-5056-297-0).

20. **Biological Diversity and Ecology**
Arya, M.K.; Bharti, P.K. and Ritesh Joshi (eds.)
(ISBN: 978-93-5056-785-2).

21. **Bioremediation and Microbial Biotechnology**
Gupta, Sandeep; and Bharti, P.K. (eds.)
(ISBN: 978-93-5056-783-8).

22. **Biotechnological Approaches and Water Ecosystem**
Zaki, M.S.A.; and Bharti, P.K. (eds.)
(ISBN: 978-93-5056-779-1).

23. **Biotechnology, Agro-ecology and Environment**
Chauhan, Avnish and Bharti, P.K. (eds.)
(ISBN: 978-93-5056-757-9).

24. **Biotechnology and Environmental Management**
Arya Arun; Maheswari Raaz K., & Bharti, P.K (eds.)
(ISBN: 978-93-5056-862-0).

25. **Clean Technologies and Environmental Protection**
Chauhan, A.; Sharma, S. and Bharti, P.K. (eds.)
(ISBN: 978-93-5056-731-9).

26. **Climate Change and Agriculture**
Bharti, P.K. and Chauhan, Avnish (eds.)
(ISBN: 978-93-5056-148-5).

27. **Climate Change and Biodiversity**
Bharti, P.K. and Chauhan, Avnish (eds.)
(ISBN: 978-93-5056-360-1).

28. **Climate Change, Disaster Management and Environment**
Chauhan, Alka; Bharti, P.K. (eds.)
(ISBN: 978-93-5056-784-5).

29. **Conservation and Cultivation of Medicinal Plants**
Bharti, P.K. and Singh Narayan (eds.)
(ISBN: 978-93-5056-740-1).

30. **Crop Productivity and Plant Disease Management**
Chauhan, Alka; Bharti, P.K. and Sadana, Deepti (eds.)
(ISBN: 978-93-5056-791-3).

31. **Eco-toxicology and Eco-technology**
Bharti, P.K. and Zaki, M. (eds.)
(ISBN: 978-93-5056-313-7).

32. **Environmental Biotechnology and Application**
Bharti, P.K. and Chauhan, Avnish (eds.)
(ISBN: 978-93-5056-262-8).

33. **Environmental Conservation and Biotechnology**
Chauhan, A. and P.K. Bharti (eds.)
(ISBN: 978-93-5056-512-4).

34. **Environmental Health and Problems**
Bharti, P.K. and Gajananda, Kh. (eds.)
(ISBN: 978-93-5056-263-5).

35. **Environmental Pollution and Biodiversity**
Bharti, P.K.; Chauhan, Avnish and Kumar, P. (eds.)
(ISBN: 978-93-5056-149-2).

36. **E-Waste and Environmental Issues**
Bhalla, Resham and Bharti, P.K. (eds.)
(ISBN: 978-93-5056-886-6).

37. **Farming Techniques and Crop Production**
Chauhan Alka; Sharma Anubhuti; Ray Jaswant and 'Bharti' P.K. (eds.)
(ISBN: 978-93-5056-855-2).

38. **Fisheries and Toxicology**
Zaki, M.S.A.; Bharti, P.K. and Chauhan, A. (eds.)
(ISBN: 978-93-5056-452-3).

39. **Fish Habitat and Aquaculture**
Bharti, P.K.; Gupta Kr. Sanjay (eds.)
(ISBN: 978-93-5056-744-9).

40. **Forest and Biodiversity Conservation**
Chauhan Alka; Bharti, P.K. (eds.)
(ISBN: 978-93-5056-873-6).

41. **Food Processing, Management and Nanotechnology**
Chauhan, Avnish; Bharti, P.K. (eds.)
(ISBN: 978-93-5056-796-8).

42. **Freshwater Ecosystem and Xenobiotics**
Bharti, P.K.; Zaki, M. and Chauhan, A. (eds.)
(ISBN: 978-93-5056-299-4).

43. **Geospatial Technology and Water Management**
Chauhan, Alka; Bharti, P.K. (eds.)
(ISBN: 978-93-5056-885-9).

44. **Heavy Metals and Metalloids in Biosphere:** ***Impacts & Assessment***
Chauhan, Avnish, Gupta, Sandeep; and Bharti, P.K. (eds.)
(ISBN: 978-93-5056-860-6).

45. **Land Reclamation, Soil Quality and Agriculture**
Bharti, P.K. and Chauhan, Alka (eds.)
(ISBN: 978-93-5056-882-8).

46. **Limnology and Aquatic Science**
Sharma, S., and Bharti, P.K. (eds.)
(ISBN: 978-93-5056-735-7).

47. **Medicinal and Nutritional Values of Plants**
Chauhan, Alka; Bharti, P.K. (eds.)
(ISBN: 978-93-5056-883-5).

48. **Medicinal Plants:** ***Distribution, Utilization and Significance***
Sharma, P.; Bharti, P.K. and Narayan Singh (eds.)
(ISBN: 978-93-5056-734-0).

49. **Microbial Applications and Environment**
Bharti, Pawan K. (ed.)
(ISBN: 978-93-5056-515-5).

50. **Microbial Ecology and Habitat**
Bharti, Pawan K. (ed.)
(ISBN: 978-93-5056-514-8).

51. **Microbial Environment and Bioremediation**
Chauhan Alka; K. Rathoure Ashok; and K Maheshwari Raaz (eds.)
(ISBN: 978-93-5056-856-9).

52. **Microbiological and Pharmacological Aspects of Biodiversity**
Sharma Pankaj; Sharma Gautam Neha and Sharma Pankaj (eds.)
(ISBN: 978-93-5056-878-1).

53. **Natural Ecosystem and Climate Change**
Bharti, P.K., and Kh. Gajananda (ed.)
(ISBN: 978-93-5056-745-6).

54. **Pest Management and Agro-Techniques**
Biswas, Asim; Bharti, P.K., Chauhan, Avnish (eds.)
(ISBN: 978-93-5056-794-4).

55. **Plant Biotechnology and Industrial Applications**
Chauhan, Alka; Bharti, P.K. (eds.)
(ISBN: 978-93-5056-884-2).

56. **Prakriti me Aushadhi (*in Hindi*)**
Singh, J.R.; Bharti, P.K. and Bharti, B.
(ISBN: 978-93-5056-200-0).

57. **Seed Technology, Plant Growth and Cropping System**
Tyagi, P.K. and Bharti, P.K. (eds.)
(ISBN: 978-93-5056-738-8).

58. **Seed Treatment, Plant Heath and Agro-technology**
Chauhan, A. and Bharti, P.K. (eds.)
(ISBN: 978-93-5056-810-1).

59. **Soil Characteristics and Agro-ecology**
Avnish Chauhan and Bharti, P.K. (eds.)
(ISBN: 978-93-5056-758-6).

60. **Soil Contamination and Conservation**
Ezeaku, P.I. and Bharti, P.K. (eds.)
(ISBN: 978-93-5056-737-1).

61. **Soil Quality and Contamination**
Bharti, P.K. and Chauhan, Avnish (eds.)
(ISBN: 978-93-5056-361-8).

62. **Sustainable Aquaculture Management**
Gupta, S.K.; Bharti, P.K (eds.)
(ISBN: 978-93-5056-797-5).

63. **Waste Disposal and Management**
Bharti, P.K.; Tabassum, B. and Bajaj, P. (eds.)
(ISBN: 978-93-5056-729-6).

64. **Waste Generation and Utilization**
Bajaj Priya; Tabassum, B., and Bharti, P.K. (eds.)
(ISBN: 978-93-5056-792-0).
65. **Waste Management and Environmental Health**
Tabassum, B., Bajaj Priya, and Bharti, P.K. (eds.)
(ISBN: 978-93-5056-777-7).
66. **Water Resources:** ***Mapping Monitoring and Management***
Tyagi, P.K., Chauhan, Avnish and Bharti, P.K. (eds.)
(ISBN: 978-93-5056-861-3).
67. **Water Resources and Agriculture**
Bharti, P.K. and Ezeaku Peter Ikemefuna (eds.)
(ISBN: 978-93-5056-481-3).
68. **Waste Resources Management:** ***Monitoring and Assessment***
Gupta, Sandeep and Bharti, P.K. (eds.)
(ISBN: 978-93-5056-799-9).

Preface

Industrialization and commercialization gradually changed this landscape as farm operation and ownership transitioned to larger corporations. Technological advances, new farming equipment and innovative cultivation techniques allowed commercial farms to decrease labor needs while increasing the overall productivity of the land. This specialization also meant that larger farms with higher productive capacities, increased access to capital, and better transportation networks could more effectively supply consumers in an expanding economy. The adequacy of food supply in a particular area or country can be affected by climatological, economic, and even political factors. The food currently produced worldwide is more than sufficient to provide adequate nutrition to the global population; yet, in many countries, a significant number of people still suffer from hunger and/or malnutrition.

The present book updates the subject content of agriculture crops, impact of climate and other factors, food supply, food security, food varieties and the influence of environmental factors on agriculture crops. Thanks are due to publisher and contributors from various institutions and universities. The book will be helpful for the researchers, academia working in the field of agriculture crops, impact of climate and other factors, food supply, food security, food varieties and the influence of environmental factors on agriculture crops.

Editors
(envbooks@gmail.com)

Contents

Introduction

Agriculture is an important sector of the economy. When food-service and other agriculture-related industries are included, the agricultural and food sectors contribute significantly to the gross domestic product.

Agriculture and fisheries are highly dependent on the climate. Increases in temperature and carbon dioxide (CO_2) can increase some crop yields in some places. But to realize these benefits, nutrient levels, soil moisture, water availability, and other conditions must also be met. Changes in the frequency and severity of droughts and floods could pose challenges for farmers and ranchers and threaten food safety. Meanwhile, warmer water temperatures are likely to cause the habitat ranges of many fish and shellfish species to shift, which could disrupt ecosystems. Overall, climate change could make it more difficult to grow crops, raise animals and catch fish in the same ways and same places as we have done in the past. The effects of climate change also need to be considered along with other evolving factors that affect agricultural production, such as changes in farming practices and technology.

Crops and Temperature

Many untested assumptions lie behind efforts to project global warming's potential influence on crops. In addition to the magnitude and pace of change, the stage of growth during which a crop is exposed to drought or heat is important. When a crop is flowering or fruiting, it is extremely sensitive to changes in temperature and moisture; during other stages of the growth cycle, plants are more tolerant.

Moreover, temperature and seasonal rainfall patterns vary from year-to-year and region-to-region, regardless of long-term trends in climate. Temperature and rainfall changes induced by climate change likely will interact with atmospheric gases, fertilizers, insects, plant pathogens, weeds and the soil's organic matter to produce unanticipated responses.

Other factors:

- Ultraviolet Radiation
- Carbon Dioxide
- Pest Attack

Agricultural Technologies

Several technologies may help farmers reduce the anticipated adverse impacts from global warming. In addition, yields for some crops may increase, especially in Africa. Beneficial technologies include:

Conservation

The high rate of soil erosion reflects the urgency of stemming soil loss, which is as threatening to sustained levels of food production as projected changes in climate. North America and Africa lose 16 to 30 tons of soil per hectare each year, and substantial amounts of nitrogen and other vital nutrients are washed or blown away with that soil.

Furthermore, optimum soil organic matter, topsoil depth, water-holding capacity and soil biota all are reduced as soil erodes. Rainfall's beneficial impacts are reduced too due to increases in water runoff and reductions in the soil's water-holding capacity. Taken together or separately, these factors limit the soil's productivity and, as a result, can reduce crop yields from 15 to 30 percent.

When sound soil and water conservation practices are followed, erosion rates can be reduced to about one ton per hectare per year, which is approximately the rate at which soil reforms under normal agricultural conditions. Adopting such practices would increase crop yields 2 to 15 percent in North America and 5 to 15 percent in Africa.

Improving Crop Varieties

Some crop varieties have greater tolerance for moisture stress than current dominant crops and could be tested as substitutes for commonly used varieties. For example, switching from spring to winter wheat in Canada has been suggested as a practical way to deal with increased moisture stress. If a crop such as corn can no longer be grown in a region because of low rainfall, crops such as sorghum, millet, cassava, sweet potato, or wheat, which have lower moisture requirements, could be substituted. However, the yield in kilograms of food produced per hectare would be lower because substitute crops usually produce less harvestable food than corn. They also may be less nutritious. Plant breeding is expected to improve yields about 1 percent during the next half century. Biotechnology also could be used to develop new crop varieties that require slightly less water, but success will be difficult because drought tolerance is a multigenic character, and basic photosynthesis requires enormous amounts of water.

Crop Rotations

A return to crop rotations would substantially reduce soil erosion and water runoff and improve the control of insects, disease, and weeds. They are sound agricultural practices that should be widely used in agriculture.

Improved Pest Control

Because insects, diseases, and weeds destroy about 35 percent of potential crop production worldwide, use of appropriate technologies to reduce pest losses would increase crop yields. In addition to the prudent application of pesticides, increased use of nonchemical pest controls would help minimize crop losses.

Nonchemical controls include crop rotations, biological controls, altering planting dates and fertilizer and irrigation applications and soil management and tillage. These technologies could help minimize projected pest losses and thereby help maintain crop yields.

Irrigation

Irrigation could substitute for reduced rainfall, but only if abundant water and energy resources are available. Excessive groundwater withdrawal is a serious problem in the western United States, northern China and parts of India. Salinization and waterlogging of soil are other serious problems associated with irrigation.

All these factors are likely to limit the use of irrigation, even in the face of water shortages for agriculture. World net irrigated area per capita has been declining since 1978.

Other Technologies

Increasing soil organic matter, effectively using livestock wastes, increasing crop diversity, ridge-planting and developing wind breaks could reduce the negative impacts of climate change on agriculture.

Changes in Crop Yields

Individual crops vary in their response to climate change, however, making generalizations difficult. A crop-by-crop and region-by-region analysis is needed. However, moisture is vital in all crop production and less moisture is certain to be a major limiting factor in North America. Also, heat stress may be a problem for crops such as corn and potatoes.

Industrialization and commercialization gradually changed this landscape as farm operation and ownership transitioned to larger corporations. Technological advances, new farming equipment and innovative cultivation techniques allowed commercial farms to decrease labor needs while increasing the overall productivity of the land. This specialization also meant that larger farms with higher productive capacities, increased access to capital and better transportation networks could more effectively supply consumers in an expanding economy.

The adequacy of food supply in a particular area or country can be affected by climatological, economic and even political factors. The food currently produced worldwide is more than sufficient to provide adequate nutrition to the global population; yet, in many countries, a significant number of people still suffer from hunger and/or malnutrition. In order to protect the domestic agricultural sector, many countries turn to using subsidies and tariffs. However, while wealthier countries, including the U.S. and members of the European Union, can afford large subsidies to ensure the financial stability of their farming sectors, it makes it extremely difficult for farmers in developing countries to compete on the world market.

Industrialized nations—and even some developing countries—are achieving a quality of life unparalleled in human history. The movement from rural areas to cities, more sedentary lifestyles with less required physical labor and readily available processed convenience foods are all contributing factors to what some have termed a worldwide? obesity epidemic? In the last 20 years, there has been an unprecedented global increase in the number of individuals who are overweight. According to the Centers for Disease Control, an estimated 64 percent of adults in the U.S. are overweight or obese. Even more troubling is, during that same time, the number of children who are overweight has nearly doubled.

However, developing countries, primarily in Sub-Saharan Africa and South Asia, face the biggest challenges over nutritional deficiencies and famine. Many populations obtain as much as 90 percent of their diet from grains, which lack vital nutrients and can lead to deficiency. It is also difficult to estimate the actual scope of poverty and hunger in the world because governments are rarely motivated to inquire into the fate of those for whom they have not provided. And, despite the wide publicity given to famines, they continue to decrease.

It is now recognised that the combined impact of extreme weather and pest outbreaks, both in terms of pest damage and vectors of disease, could be catastrophic for the Asia's agricultural sector. Adaptation and mitigation are thus approaches which are being increasingly adopted, often in combinations as Integrated Pest Management.

However, the growing concentration of agricultural production in small holdings farmed by older, predominantly female, farmers with low levels of literacy and education, is leading to an agricultural population which does not respond well to adaptation measures.

Globally, there are an estimated 450 million small-scale farms, supporting a population of roughly 2.2 billion people and representing 85% of the world's farms. Our key research question will address the adaptation to environmental change, brought on by both climate change and land use changes, requiring modern adaptive methods of farming at a time when the farming population is ageing.

The specific case we shall explore will be the impact of changing insect populations and the perceived need to move to modern agricultural methods in order to address this changing pest environment with an increasingly ageing uneducated farming population.

References

https://www.epa.gov/climate-impacts/climate-impacts-agriculture-and-food-supply

http://www.ciesin.org/docs/004-138/004-138.html

https://enviroliteracy.org/food/food-production-supply/

http://www.futureoffood.ox.ac.uk/project/implications-food-production-adaptation-environmental-change-ageing-agricultural-sector-case

Agriculture Crops and Food Security
Edited by: Dr. Pawan Kumar 'Bharti' and Alka Chauhan
ISBN: 978-93-5056-881-1
Edition: 2017
Published by: Discovery Publishing House Pvt. Ltd., New Delhi (India)

1

Effect of Agricultural Remedies on Environment and Global Warming Security

[1]Rohit Bhati and [2]Neeraj Choudhary

ABSTRACT

Due to limitless desire of today's fast life and unsustainable development, our environment is being damaged at alarming rates. The negative impacts of these environmental damages are either being faced by many parts of world or likely to appear in near future in the form of several climatic catastrophes. This is the hi time for every human being of the earth to avoid excess energy utilization at every corner of our life and to led the foundation of evergreen, sustainable and controlled development so that our future alongwith several other living beings of this beautiful earth will be safe. The role of agriculture and forest sectors in mitigating the global warming is of paramount importance due to its carbon capture and storage capacity. The necessary modifications in our cropping/farming practices should be incorporated so as to minimize the production of GHG and capture and long term storage of these GHG into various global mass from the atmosphere. Further, every nation has to work very hard with honesty in the future to contain the greatest challenge of global warming.

INTRODUCTION

The phenomenon of increasing average temperature of the Earth's near-surface air and oceans is known as Global warming. The increase in the average global temperature started since the middle of twentieth century (with industrialization) and is projected to continue in the future at an alarming rate due to indiscriminate energy consumption by industrialized world and resultant massive emission of green house gases. Global surface temperature increased by 0.74) 0.18°C during past 100 years ending in 2005. The last 24 years have been hottest in the 20th century and year 2006 was found as hottest in the available records since 1856. According to the Intergovernmental Panel on Climate Change (IPCC-2007), most of the temperature increase since the

[1] Department of Entomology, SVPUA&T, Meerut, U.P., India-250110
[2] Department of Microbiology, JVWU, Jaipur, Rajasthan, India-303007

mid-twentieth century is very likely due to the increase in anthropogenic greenhouse gases (GHG) concentration such as carbon dioxide (CO_2), methane (CH_4), nitrous oxide (N_2O) and chloroflurocarbons (CFCs). Several climate model projections indicate that global surface temperature will likely increase further by 1.1-6.4°C during the twenty-first century. Although most studies focus on the period up to 2100, warming is expected to continue for more than a thousand years even if greenhouse gas levels are stabilized. This is very alarming situation for the entire humanity and if sufficient steps are not taken immediately to mitigate the global warming at each and every level of human activity, the whole of the world is bound to suffer from a great catastrofe of changing climate and their negative impacts in the future. The trailors of the effect of global warming are being faced by many parts of the world in the form of unexpected changes in weather conditions. Increasing global temperature will cause a rise in sea levels and will change the amount and pattern of precipitation, likely expansion of the subtropical desert regions. Other likely effects include increases in the intensity of extreme weather events, changes in agricultural yields, modifications of trade routes, glacier retreat, species extinctions and increases in the ranges of disease vectors and ultimately the increased incidence of many human and animal diseases.

MAJOR EFFECTS OF GLOBAL WARMING

1. Melting of glaciers of mountains will lead to dryness of major rivers and drinking water shortage and Antarctic region glacier retreating is resulting in the sea level rise.
2. Extreme weather events–unexpected folds, droughts, summers, pattern and distribution of precipitations, etc.
3. The depletion of ozone layer at Antarctica and Glacier Retreat.
4. Possible acidification of sea water.
5. Huge disturbance in several ecosystems.
6. Possible expansion of subtropical desert area.
7. Extinction of certain species and loss of Biodiversity (danger of extinction for 20-30% species).
8. Loss of agricultural production in Southern hemisphere and long-term effect on agricultural productivity.
9. Increased incidence of vector borne diseases in humans, animals and crops.

The Green House Effect

Green house effect is the process by which absorption and emission of infrared radiation by atmospheric gases (i.e. CO_2, CH_4, N_2O CFCs, etc.) warm the planet's lower atmosphere and surface. Existence of the greenhouse effect as such is not disputed. The question is instead how the strength of the greenhouse effect changes when human activity increases the atmospheric concentrations of particular greenhouse gas. Human activities related to unsustainable development since the industrial revolution have increased the atmospheric concentration of various greenhouse gases, leading to increased radiative forcing from CO_2, methane, tropospheric ozone, CFCs and nitrous oxide. The atmospheric concentrations of CO_2 and methane have increased by 36 per cent and 148 per cent respectively since the beginning of the industrial revolution in the mid-1700s. Fossil fuel burning has produced approximately three-quarters of the increase in CO_2 from human activity over the past 20 years. Most of the rest is due to land-use changes, particularly deforestation. Carbondioxide concentrations are expected to continue to rise due to continued burning of fossil fuels and land-use changes. The rate of rise will depend on certain economic, sociological, technological, and natural developments. The IPCC Special Report on Emissions Scenarios gives a wide range of future CO_2 scenarios, ranging from 541 to 970 ppm by the year 2100 from the present level of around 392 ppm (Subrahmanyam, 2011). Fossil fuel reserves are sufficient to reach this level and continue emissions past 2100 if coaltar sands or methane clathrates are extensively exploited.

Global Warming and Agriculture

Food is the first requirement of human beings and deforestation followed by agriculture to fulfill increased demand of food grains for exploding human population are the oldest causes of global warming. According to Paleo-climatologist William Ruddiman, the human influence on the global climate began around 8,000 years ago with the start of deforestation to provide land for agriculture. A lot of energy is utilized by agriculture sectors which results in the massive emission of greenhouse gases. According to the IPCC (2007) the share of agriculture sector in total anthropogenic greenhouse gas emissions was 13.5 per cent in the year 2004. In agriculture, the use of energy begins with land preparation and continues till the storage and processing of the product. The estimated amounts of CO_2 production from different common agricultural activities are given in Table 1.1. The need for more food production in the future for exploding human population will likely to further increase the greenhouse gases emissions via agriculture.

Table 1.1: The Estimated Amount of CO_2 from Different Common Agricultural Activities

S. No.	Agricultural activities/inputs	CO_2 emission(kg carbon/ha)
1.	Tillage(general)	2-20
2.	Sowing by planter or seed drill	2-4
3.	Spraying pesticides	1-1.40

4.	Lifting irrigation water and sprinkler irrigation 25 cm water depth 50 cm water depth	129±98 258±195
5.	Conventional tillage	35.3
6.	Chisel till or minimum till	7.9
7.	Zero till	5.8
8.	Harvesting through combine machine	6-12
9.	Fertilizer production (a) N_2Ob (b) P_2O_5c (c) K_2O	0.9-1.8 carbon equivalent/kg 0.1-0.3 carbon equivalent/kg 0.1-0.2 carbon equivalent/kg
10.	Pesticide production (a) Herbicides (b) Insecticides (c) Fungicides	6.3 carbon equivalent/kg 5.1 carbon equivalent/kg 3.9 carbon equivalent/kg
CO_2	4380 kg	

Source: Bhanu and Singh (2008); Lal (2004)

Weeds are the greatest biological enemy of crops causing huge losses in quality and quantity of agricultural produce through competition with crops for nutrients, solar light, water and space and also by acting as carriers for many plant pathogens. In this way weeds directly or indirectly enhances the energy utilization for their management and also by utilizing valuable resources like water, nutrients and pesticides, etc., and ultimately contributes to greater greenhouse gas emissions. Besides contributing to global warming, agriculture sector has the greatest opportunities for containing global warming by harvesting and conserving atmospheric CO_2 through plant species (via photosynthesis). Hence, our present agricultural systems can be remodeled for maximum harvesting of atmospheric CO_2 by incorporating various agri-horti-silvicultural systems. However, due to a living-dynamic ecosystem, the components of our agriculture system are at greater risk to the catastrophic effects of the global warming. The possible effects of changing climate on various agricultural and allied sectors are given as below:

Impact on Food Production and Livelihood Security

The food production systems and livelihood will more likely to be adversely affected by the changing climate. If, satisfactory steps have not been taken, the global agricultural potential could fall by 5-20 per cent by 2080. By the same time the food demands of exploding population will increase much more as compared to present. Most of the developing countries falling in Africa and

Asia will experience major losses in the agricultural productivity. India will be a major sufferer of the threats of global warming (Kalra, 2012). There will be increase in food grain prices in 2050 by 90 per cent for wheat, 12 per cent for rice and 35 per cent for maize (Subrahmanyam, 2011). Thus, the food security of the world will be adversely affected particularly of low income groups.

CROP PRODUCTIVITY

The climate change may affect crop production in many ways: it may affect productivity, quantity and quality of produce, changes in resources (water, nutrient, labour, etc.) use efficiency, nutrient mineralization and cycling, soil drainage/erosion and nutrient loss, reduction of agro-biodiversity (particularly of beneficial organisms), shrinking of cultivated area, hydraulic amenities, attack of weeds, plant pathogens and vector borne diseases, insect-pests and efficacy of pest management practices. The shortening of crop growing periods, decreased water availability due to higher evapotranspiration and poor vernalization of temperate cereals are likely effects of global warming which could reduce the crop productivity. Crop productivity is projected to increase slightly at mid to high altitudes when local mean temperature increases up to 1-3°C depending upon the crop and beyond this productivity will decrease. The lower altitudes specially the tropical dry regions will face decreased crop productivity even at small increase in local temperature. The average world's crop production is projected to increase at increasing temperature range of 1-3°C, but beyond this food production will decrease. Due to increased temperature and unexpected weather changes, the irrigated wheat yields will be reduced by around 30 per cent and irrigated rice yields by 15 per cent in developing countries (Subrahmanyam, 2011). However, Rao (2011) documented more than 30 per cent decline in crop yield in Indian sub-continent by 2050 due to increasing global temperature. In countries like India global warming resulted into late onset and early ending of winter season which is very dangerous for wheat productivity. In a study by Kushwaha *et al.* (2012) from Pantnagar, Uttarakhand (India), a reduction of 5-10 per cent in wheat yields was recorded for each degree rise in air temperature and reduced winter rains during the crop season. However, only 0.5°C increase in winter temperature caused 10 per cent reduction in wheat yield in the state of Punjab (Sinha and Swaminathan, 1991). This emphasizes that, how the potential productivity of our leading food crops like wheat is at danger due to global warming. The productivity of rice-wheat, wheat based, rice-rice and other rice based systems are at risk due to changing climate. These cropping systems are primary determinant of Indian food security. The rising CO_2 concentration may increase yield substantially through enhanced photosynthesis and will improve water use efficiency but the effects of CO_2 on crops is dependent upon the magnitude of changes in environmental temperature (Pal *et al.*, 2011).

Changing Climate and Nutrient Cycling

Due to increase in CO_2 concentration in the atmosphere there is possibility of increased biological nitrogen fixation and nodule size in legumes (Bahuguna and Pal, 2011). In general, it is postulated that, the mineralization of nutrients in the soil will be enhanced at higher temperature and CO_2 concentration. The demand of nitrogen was found to be enhanced in wheat due to moderate increase in nitrogen use efficiency (16%), enhanced utilization of native organic-N (hence 16 per cent loss in total soil organic-N) and increased physiological efficacy of N-utilization (14%). Higher C:N ratio of wheat and rice residue due increased atmospheric CO_2 will cause lower decomposition rates and thus supplementing carbon sequestration in soil. The demand of phosphorus may also be increased due to increased P-use efficiency and greater mobilization of P under increased CO_2 and temperature (Purkayastha, 2011).

Changing Climate and Crop Protection

Other than crop production factors, crop protection is going to be greatly affected by the changing climate. Changes in temperature, precipitation, rising CO_2 concentration have potential consequences on crop-weed interactions and thus could affect crop productivity. Since weeds have greater genetic diversity and physiological plasticity and hence better adaptation potential than the crops, they will readily adapt to changing climate as compared to crop and could compete with crops with greater potential. There may be possible reduction in the weed control efficacy of herbicides as reported by Naidu (2011) in case of glyphosate, isoproturon, clodinafop, 2,4-D and sulfosulfuron on *Chenopodium album, Phalaris minor, Avenafatua, Amaranthusviridis* and *Lathyrussativus* respectively. Similar to weeds, the attack of insects-pests and diseases is expected to increase with rising global temperature. Temperature is the key determinant in the regulation of life history pattern of all the insects. The insect-pest attack may be directly affected by climate change by affecting the habitat range, migration behaviour, over-wintering, interspecific interactions, population growth of pest or indirectly by affecting the growth and resistance of host plant. The life cycle of many insects will be shorter due to increasing temperature and hence there will be more and more number of pest generations and resultant increase in crop losses. The temperature sensitive resistance of host to pest may be broken down by high temperature. In many cases increased CO_2 in the air will lead to reduced nitrogen content in the leaves (increased C:N ratio). Therefore, a herbivore including insect-pests must depend upon increased compensatory feeding for fulfilling its nitrogen (protein) requirements as reported in case of *Neodiprionlecontei* (Deka *et al.*, 2011). The defoliating insects are expected to increase leaf consumption by 30 per cent whereas phloem-sucking pests will likely shorten their generation time. Further the efficacy of pesticides can also be modified due to high temperature, CO_2 and precipitation patterns. Increased CO_2 could cause the thickening of epicuticular wax layer of the host and thus reduced uptake of pesticides and its efficacy (Chander, 2011). The degradation and residual effect of pesticides can also be affected by increased temperature. Many of the crop diseases will become more severe due to increase in temperature and environmental humidity.

Vulnerability of Tree and Fruit Crops

In case of fruit trees altered timing of bud breaking, and flowering phenology could have important impacts on production due to spring frost damage, reduced pollination and fruit setting (Paul *et al.*, 2011). Global warming will affect flowering behaviour of many tree and fruit species and thus affect the fruit development and seed dispersal in many ways. Decreased winter chilling of many fruit species will be devastating for many tree/fruit based industries/ sectors. Many fruit and nut trees are more sensitive to temperature changes due to their heat accumulation limits and chilling hour requirements. Thus the productivity of several cool season fruits like grape, walnut, avocados, stone and pome fruits could be decreased to a greater extent. The most threatened tree species due to global warming are alpine and sub-alpine trees which have no place to move as temperature rises. The productivity of cold loving conifers and pines will be reduced to a greater extent. The increased risk of wildfires is another big problem for forest ecosystem.

LIVE-STOCK AND FORAGE PRODUCTION

Increased CO_2 in the atmosphere can decrease the forage quality of pastures and rangelands because of decreased nitrogen and protein content. The rising temperature and erratic precipitation may affect major rangelands of the world in short and mid terms. Other aspects like CO_2 fertilization, invasive species and land use changes may also have significant effects on the productivity of rangelands. Animal husbandry sector is a major producer of methane (1/5 of total) which is second most important green house gas after the CO_2. Among animals cattles are more efficient producer of methane than the other ruminants. The likely decrease of protein in forage due to increased CO_2 fertilization, increasing attack of vector borne diseases and other parasites, livestock land use changes will definitely have various consequences on the productivity of animal sector. The catastrophic effects of global warming on the animal sector could affect the livelihood of millions of peoples engaged in this sector. More particularly, the food, nutrition and livelihood security of small and marginal farming depending greatly on livestock sector will be at greater risk due to unexpected disturbances in this sector. In general, the changing climate affects livestock sector four ways:

- By affecting forage and feed grain availability and prices,
- By affecting livestock pastures and forage crop production and quality,

- Increased attack of diseases and parasites, and
- Directly affecting the animal health, growth, reproduction and other physiological functions.

The overall effect on livestock may be in the form of altered mortality rates, feed conversion rates, rate of gain, milk production, conception rates, appetite and susceptibility to pathogens. The food borne zoonoses may increase due to temperature rise and this will likely enhance the use of veterinary drugs. The Rift valley fever disease caused by *rift valleyfever virus* (RVFV) is a mosquito transmitted human and animal viral disease which is shifting its distribution in Africa due to climate change. Prolonged transmission cycle of animal vectors and their expansion to cooler areas will further accelerate the disease spread (Mohammad and Awan, 2012).

EFFECT ON AQUACULTURE AND FISHERIES SECTOR

Unlike most of terrestrial animals, all aquatic animals for human consumption are poikilothermic, meaning their body temperatures vary with the ambient temperature. Any changes in habitat temperatures will significantly influence their metabolism and, hence, growth rate, total production, reproduction seasonality and possibly reproductive efficacy and susceptibility to diseases and toxins. The marine and fresh water aquaculture is going to be affected at a greater extent by the global warming. The increasing mean sea level due to glacier retreat and acidification of sea water along with increasing temperature could cause severe disturbances in marine ecosystem. Climate change is also modifying the fresh water species. Global warming is affecting the seasonality of biological processes, altering species composition, and food web in both marine and fresh water ecosystem and this can cause unpredictable consequences for fish production. The increased rate of eutrophication can have negative effects on freshwater aquaculture. The problem of heavy metal may be accelerated due to methylation of mercury and its subsequent accumulation in fishes.

Fisheries

The impacts of physical and biological changes on fisheries communities will be variable. Both negative and positive impacts could be foreseen, their strength depending on the vulnerability of each community, the combination of potential impacts (sensitivity and exposure) and adaptive capacity. Impacts would be felt through changes in capture, production and marketing costs, changes in sales prices and possible increases in risks of damage or loss of infrastructure, fishing tools and housing. Fishery-dependent communities may also face increased vulnerability in terms of less stable livelihoods, decreases in availability or quality of fish for food, and safety risks due to fishing in harsher weather conditions and further from their landing sites. Decrease in calcification caused due to acidification of seawater affects organisms like corals, foraminifera, echinoderms, crustaceans, and mollusks. These calcifiers span the food chain from autotrophs to heterotrophs and directly affect the growth and reproduction of fish as well as the plankton on which they rely for food. Thermohaline circulation occurring due to differences in salinity, temperature and wind patterns, provide warm waters with rich source of nutrients. Global warming could shutdown or slow down of the thermohaline circulation. This could result in mortality of marine creatures, reduction of biodiversity and could affect migration of species.

Rise in sea level will have adverse impact on the low lying coastal habitats such as densely settled delta and small islands, Estuaries, mud flats, mangroves, coral reefs and coastal wetlands. Many species of commercially important fish breeding and raising their young ones in these habitats will be most vulnerable. Increased coastal erosion and changes in current pattern will have adverse effects on coastal ecosystem. Freshwater fishery will also feel the pressure because of climate change through reduced availability of water due to increased water extraction for other competing activities. Biological productivity of the freshwater ecosystem will be affected in the water stress scenario. With rise in lake and stream temperatures, species will either die or migrate to habitats that are more favourable. Cold-water freshwater fish populations (trout, whitefish, and grayling) will be at receiving end of the adverse impact in many lakes and streams due to declining water levels, flow and reductions in nutrient loading and recycling.

Aquaculture

Impacts of changing climate on aquaculture could be positive or negative and might be due to direct and indirect impacts on the natural resources aquaculture requires, namely water, land, seed, feed and energy. As fisheries provide significant feed and seed inputs, the impacts of climate change on them will also, in turn, affect the productivity and profitability of aquaculture systems. Vulnerability of aquaculture-based communities will stem from their resource dependency and exposure to extreme weather events. Climatic changes could increase physiological stress on cultured stock. This would not only affect productivity but also increase vulnerability to diseases and, in turn, impose higher risks and reduce returns to farmers. Interactions of fisheries and aquaculture subsectors could create other impacts. For example, extreme weather events could result in escapes of farmed stock and contribute to reductions in genetic diversity of the wild stock, affecting biodiversity more widely. Warming of water temperature will require greater attention to possible dissolved oxygen level. Warming could introduce disease organisms or exotic or undesired species. Species that may already be at their upper tolerance level may find it difficult to adapt to changing environment, which will have negative impact on their existence. Coastal aquaculture facilities may have to consider about the impact of sea level rise on facilities, like submergence, contaminant loads from nearby waste sites etc. These impacts will be combined with other aspects affecting adaptive capabilities, such as the increased pressure that ever larger coastal populations place on resources; any political, institutional and management rigidity that negatively impacts on communities' adaptive strategies; deficiencies in monitoring and early-warning systems or in emergency and risk planning; as well as other non-climate factors such as poverty, inequality, food insecurity, conflict and disease. However, new opportunities and positive impacts emerging from such areas as changes in species and new markets also could be part of future changes. Warming will mean longer culture period and increased rate of biological processes and production. So far, these opportunities are not well understood but, nevertheless, are possible. A community's ability to benefit also will depend on its adaptive capacity.

EFFECTS ON BIODIVERSITY

Our various needs such as food, feed, fibre, fuel, shelter, medicines, etc. depend upon biological diversity of the earth. Species diversity and genetic richness also decide several ecosystem functions of various habitats. Primary food production, nutrient recycling, natural pest control and bioremediation are some of the important ecosystem functions. The rich agro-biodiversity enhances population of natural enemies and their effectiveness towards natural control of pests by:

- Providing alternative hosts/pray at times of pest's host scarcity;
- Providing food base to adult predators, parasitoids and to microbial antagonists;
- Sustaining acceptable pest population to ensure continuous survival of their natural enemies;
- Providing shelter for overwintering, nesting and other activities.

The extinction on certain species and loss of biodiversity is among the most serious effects of global warming. Due to 2.5°C increase in average global temperature above the pre-industrial levels, 20-30 per cent of all plant and animal species will be at high risk of extinction (IPCC, 2007).

IMPACT ON WATER AVAILABILITY

Water is a key resource in any kind of agriculture and also an invaluable input for our daily life. Climate change will likely affect the rainfall (pattern and distribution), evaporation, runoff and soil moisture storage. Many of the perennial rivers like Ganga and Yamuna in India will be at risk of drying due to glacier retreat of high mountains. This emphasizes the effect of changing climate on hydro-electric and irrigation projects dependent upon these type of rivers. Hence the water availability for agriculture and daily life as well will be a greatest challenge posed by the global warming.

COPING UP WITH GLOBAL WARMING

General Mitigation Options of Global Warming (as per IPCC, 2007 Guidelines)

- Carbon-dioxide-capture and storage
- Bio-energy crops
- Land use changes and management
- Bio-mass electricity and energy through unconventional sources
- Hydropower and Geothermal energy
- Green buildings and other green technologies

Social Ways of Containing Global Warming

- Population control and reduced energy utilization
- Simple life style
- Discouraged consumerism

FIGHTING WITH CHANGING CLIMATE AND REMODELLING OF OUR EXISTING FARMING SYSTEMS AND AGRICULTURE

Keeping in view the target of developments, food and nutrition security, increasing energy needs of exploding population, it will be impossible to either reduce the present level emission or near future emission of green house gases. But, the devoted technological interventions in all sectors of development can reduce the rate of emission and resultant temperature increase. The agricultural and farming practices can be changed/modified keeping in view the various adaptive and mitigation measures of global warming recommended for agriculture and allied sectors. There are two ways to cope up with negative effects of global warming. These are:

A. Adaptive Measures

This signifies various adaptation measures in every fields of life according to the changing climate. Various adaptation measures through different sectors are viewed here:

CROP PRODUCTION

The adaptation measures at farm level can be made for planting and harvesting dates, crop rotations, mixed cropping, catch cropping, improved crop varieties, improved fertilizer management, irrigation use efficiency and good tillage practices. Followings are the some important suggestions for formulating the adaptations measures in the crop sector:

- Searching, evaluation and use of temperature and drought tolerant verities of crops particularly in case of winter season crops
- Development of CO_2 responsive and O_3 tolerant germplasms of crops
- Screening, evaluation and use of resistant/tolerant/smothering crop varieties to increased attack of weeds/pests and plant pathogens. It is also important to search out the resistant crop cultivars to be effective at higher temperatures
- Appropriate tillage, irrigation, mulching and other crop management practices for conserving the soil moisture
- Modifying the cropping practices for higher recourses use efficiency Development of pest management systems (including pesticides) effective under higher temperature
- Alterations in dates of sowing to break the host-pest synchrony. More attention to preventive measures of pest/weeds and disease control
- Precise pest-risk analysis and reorienting our pest control programmes
- Development of pesticides effective at higher temperatures and with lower doses
- Development of reliable medium range weather forecasting models for modifying our cropping systems and practices as per changing weather
- Temperature tolerant strains of natural enemies and biological control agents of pests and pathogens should be evolved for effective pests control under the changing climate
- Conservation of biodiversity in agro-ecosystem to improve natural pest control and productivity
- Major emphasis on water saving technologies and rainwater harvesting
- Modification of crop simulation/forecasting models, early warning systems/expert systems according to the changing climate
- Bioprospecting of genes for greater tolerance to various abiotic stresses
- Development and use of fruit varieties with lower chilling requirement and searching new management strategies for breaking the dormancy during insufficient winter chilling
- Exploring the possibilities for expansion of fruit crops like wine grape, almonds, table grapes, oranges, walnut and avocadoes into cooler regions and further impact studies
- Preparation of national action plan to execute adaptations measures of global warming in a holistic way

ADAPTATION STRATEGIES FOR LIVESTOCK SECTOR

The major adaptation measures in case of livestock sector are provisions of shading (tree and other shades), sprinklers, improved air flow and cooling system, lesser crowding, improved diets, careful handling, breeding new animal breeds adaptive under changing climate and improved vaccinations and other preventive measures of pest/disease and vector control.

ADAPTATION STRATEGIES FOR FISHERIES

There is a need for implementation of adaptive holistic, integrated and participatory approaches to fisheries management, as required for an ecosystem approach. Responses to direct impacts of extreme events on fisheries infrastructure and communities are likely to be more effective if they are anticipatory, as part of long-term integrated management planning. Some of the potential adaptation measures in fisheries are described in Table 1.2.

Table 1.2: Potential Adaptation Measures in Fisheries

Possible Impact of climate change on Fisheries	Potential adaptation measures
Reduced Yield	Access higher value markets/shifting targeted species
	Re-building Fish stock and improving fish governance
	Increase effort
	Reduce costs to increase efficiency
	Diversify livelihoods
Increased variability of Yield	Diversify livelihood portfolio
	Design insurance schemes
Change in distribution of Fisheries	Migration of fishing effort/Strategies and processing/ Distribution facilities
Reduced Profitability	Exit Fishery
Vulnerability of infrastructure and communities to flooding, sea level rise	Rehabilitate infrastructure/Disaster response
Integrated Coastal Zone management	Setting up early warning systems
Increased dangers of Fishing	Setting up of weather warning system
	Investment in improved vessel stability/safety/ communication
Influx of New Fishers	Support local management institutions/co-operatives, Diversify livelihood

Source: FAO (2008).

ADAPTATION STRATEGIES FOR AQUACULTURE

Improved management and better aquaculture practices would be the best and most immediate form of adaptation, providing a sound basis for production that could accommodate possible impacts. Adaptations include changing to less carnivorous species, genetic improvements, feed source diversification, better formulation, quality control and management (Table 1.3).

Table 1.3: Potential Adaptation Measures in Aquaculture

Climate change Element	Impacts on Aquaculture	Adaptive measures
Warming	Raising of temperature above optimal tolerancelevel of farmed species causing stress and relatedadverse impacts	Use of better feeds, avoiding handling stress, selectivebreeding and genetic improvements for higher temperature tolerance etc.
	Increase in growth, Higher production	Increase in feed input; Adjust market and harvest schedules
	Increase virulence of dormant pathogens andincidence of new diseases	Management measures to reduce stress in farmed animal, set up bio-security measures, monitor to reduce health risk, Improvement in diagnostics and treatment measures, Genetically improved variety for higher disease resistance.
	Limitation on fish meal and fish oil supplies/price	Alternative to fish meal and fish oil, development of new form of feed management, genetic improvement for alternative feeds, shift to non-carnivorous species, culture of bivalves and sea weeds, etc.
Seal level rise and changes in circulation of water currents	Intrusion of salt water	Shift stenohaline species up stream, introduce euryhalinespecies in its place.
	Loss of agricultural land	Provide alternative livelihoods throughaquaculture,capacitybuilding and developing infrastructure.
	Reduced catch from coastal fisheries, depletion ofnatural seed stock	Greater use of hatchery seed, protection of nursery habitatsand natural breeding grounds,
	Reduced options for aquaculture feeds, incomeloss to fishers	Develop/use formulated feed; develop alternative livelihoods for suppliers
	Increase of harmful algal blooms (HAB's)	Improve monitoring and early warning systems
Acidification	Impact on calcareous shell formation/deposition	Adapt production and handling techniques, Move production zones

Water stress and drought conditions	Limitation of freshwater abstraction	Improve water use efficiency, encourage non-consumptiveuse of water in aquaculture, multiple use of water, etc.
	Change in water retention period (Reduction in inland system and increase in coastal lagoons)	Use of fast growing fishes for culture, increase efficacy ofwater sharing with primary users, e.g. irrigation in paddyfield
	Reduced availability of wild seeds	Shift to hatchery reared seeds, improve seed quality andproduction efficiency
Extreme weather events	Destruction of facilities, loss of stock, businessloss, mass escape of stock with potential to impact biodiversity	Encouragement for individual or cluster insurance, improve farm design to minimize damage, loss and prevent mass escape, advocate use of indigenous species to minimize impact on biodiversity, use of sterile stock in farming systems

Source: FAO (2008)

B. Mitigation Measures

These measures are aimed to save the energy from all fields of developments and ensure lesser emission of GHS. These are:

AGRICULTURE AND FORESTRY SECTORS

Agriculture is a cause as well as solution for global warming problem. Agriculture is responsible for about 32 per cent of world's GHG emission (IPCC, 2007). Each ton of carbon lost from soil adds about 3.7 tons of CO_2 in the air. Whereas, every ton increase in soil organic carbon (SOC) sequester 3.7 tons of CO from the atmosphere. Hence, the well planned aforestation, resource conservation technologies, bio-fuels and bio-energy crops, improved crop management practices, agro-forestry and carbon sequestration technologies have great potential for capturing and long term storage of CO_2 into SOC pool and timber biomass and lesser emission of GHG. The important mitigation options of global warming through agriculture and allied sectors are described here:

(*i*) **Aforestation and Agro-forestry:** Intensive region specific aforestation programmes according to the climate change projections will capture and store large amount of CO_2 from atmosphere into the timbers and tree logs. Any burning of fuel wood will be a renewable energy source. Though there are lesser chances for any wider increase in the area of forest due to other land use and compulsion of increasing food production from more or less static agricultural land (about 142 Mha.). Hence, the incorporation of the tree and fruit crop species into various agricultural systems like agri-silviculture, agri-horticulture, agri-silvi-horti system, agri-silvi-horti-pastoral systems etc. could be a major strategy capture and sequester large amount of CO_2 into the biosphere reserves for longer time. Further these systems will fulfill basic human needs like fuel, food, feed, fodder, fibre (5Fs) and ensure livelihood security of the farming communities.

(*ii*) **Biofuels and Bioenergy Crops:** Any replacement of petroleum with biofuels of plant origin will be a direct contribution in reducing the overall emission of GHG. Since, in biofuels atmospheric CO_2 is first captured in vegetations, hence its further burning is simply the recycling of atmospheric CO_2. New potential and high output biofuel crops must be searched out and used at wider scale. The conversion of low fertile soil, underutilized and degraded lands in biofuel production belts will be a win-win situation for coping up with global warming. These biofuel belts along with replacing the fossil fuels, could generate employments, increase earnings and upgrade the life status of local area peoples and also help in increasing carbon sequestration and the productivity of soil (McGarry, 2009).

(*iii*) **Biogas Production:** The production and use of methane gas (CH_4) from animal manures and other wastes would be a sustainable option for reducing the GHG emission into the air and preventing from various respiratory ailments caused by smokes due to burning of fuelwood and dry-animal-dung-fuel. This can also solve the problem of cooking gas shortage up to a great extent. The small and marginal farming communities are the potential beneficiaries of biogas technology. This technology can also ensure the production of high quality organic manure as a supplementary product for crop production and a sustainable option for the management of crop/livestock residues.

(*iv*) **Carbon Sequestration:** Carbon sequestration refers to the transfer of atmospheric CO_2 into other long lived global pools which can include oceanic, pedologic, geological and biotic strata and thus there is net decrease in the atmospheric CO_2. Carbon sequestration through various land use and agricultural management systems has greatest potential to mitigate global warming (IPCC, 2007; Verchot and Singh, 2009). The carbon sequestration potential through agricultural systems lies in the fact that the global soil holds more amount of organic carbon (1,100Gt) while atmosphere (750Gt) and terrestrial biosphere (560 Gt) holds far lesser organic carbon. Long and short term strategies of carbon sequestration through improved agricultural management system can mitigate the problem to a greater extent, improves soil quality, and productivity (Tariyal and Malkania, 2012). Conservation tillage, grazing, fertility management through earthwarms and organic farming and land conservation practices exhibit a great potential for improving SOC. Increased area under agroforestry and forests would be a best option for conserving atmospheric CO_2 into long lived timber masses.

(v) **Resource conservation technologies:** These include the technologies and agricultural practices which saves the resources like time, labour, money, water and energy, increases resources use efficiency (water, nutrients, labour etc.), increases SOC, soil productivity and finally ensures environmental sustainability. Wider adaptability of these practices in agriculture will result into the lower emission of GHG.

These are described as below:

(a) ***Site specific nutrient management (SSNM):*** It includes the location specific and need based nutrient supply system, background knowledge of the nutrient status of soil, use of organic manures and biofertilizers, use of appropriate type, method and time of fertilizer application, use of colour chart and other sensitive techniques for applying the splits of fertilizers, use of efficient nitrification inhibitors to check the N_2O emission from the soil, recovery of applied nutrients and their residues in soil. The overall aim of all these conservation techniques is to increase the nutrient use efficiency, avoid nutrient losses and ultimately to minimize the emission of GHG like N_2O and CH_4.

(b) ***Minimum tillage:*** It has been proved with sufficient evidences that minimum tillage practices i.e. zero-till seeding of wheat and other crops, minimum tillage, bed planting, direct seeding etc. along with efficient weed management techniques saves considerable amount of energy, labour, time and money on these operations and also reduce the emission of green house gases. The zero-tilled wheat and direct seeded rice are good example of minimum tillage systems with almost similar yields of conventional sowing/tillage systems. Reduced tillage in combination with crop residue retention can increase SOC, reduces soil erosion, and improves soil structure and stability.

(c) ***Water management:*** Rain water harvesting, water conservation through mulching/improved tillage systems and appropriate irrigation scheduling and reduced evapotranspiration losses in agricultural system can help in reduced GHG emission and in other ways saves huge energy expenses on lifting the water. Irrigation management in case of rice has the great potential to reduce the emission of CH_4 and other GHG

as proved with aerobic rice. Reduced tillage in combination with crop residue retention can increase SOC, reduces soil erosion, and improves soil structure and stability. Waterlogged paddy fields are major source of CH_4 emission due to extreme methanogenesis. The aerobic rice culture with intermittent irrigation can reduce methane emission up to 40 per cent as compared to flooding. Further incorporation of rice straw (decomposed) into the soil before transplanting reduces methane emission up to 49 per cent as compared to rice straw amended as such (Misra *et al.*, 2012).

(d) ***Biointensive, highly productive resource efficient cropping systems:*** The resource efficient, highly intensive cropping systems based on crop rotation, nutrient recycling, and executed through cropping systems and tillage management could be a potential means to improve overall system productivity, increase SOC and lowers the emission of GHG.

(e) ***Sound weeds/pests and disease management technologies:*** Effective weeds, pests and disease management can play important role in mitigation of global warming through saving of unwanted energy expenditure on manufacturing, transport and application of pesticides and also reducing the crop losses and increasing the productivity. IPCC (2007) especially emphasized the weed management in crops as these pests could cause the severe reduction in crop yield by competing for nutrients, water, space, light and by hosting and spreading several types of pests and diseases. Bio-intensive integrated weeds, pests and disease management with intelligent negative/positive forecasting systems would be a good practice to lessen the emission of GHG. Preventive pest management practices, i.e. seed treatment, resistant varieties, soil solarization, etc. are more sustainable options.

(f) ***Organic farming:*** The organic inputs used into organic farming can result up to 55 per cent greater humic carbon into the soil. The lower rate of carbon mineralization in the organically managed soil as compared to fertilizer added soils is the main region for increased humic carbon. Moreover, improved soil structure and physical/chemical environments increases the overall productivity and ultimately results into lesser emission of GHG. Use of biosolids, green manures, green wastes and biochar into organically managed soils greatly contributes to soil organic carbon of more stable forms.

LIVESTOCK SECTOR

The dietary manipulation, livestock management (animal numbers, feed quality, health and productivity, dung management etc.) and rumen manipulation for reduced methane production are some of the general mitigation options for livestock sectors. Increasing the productivity of animals, feed quality improvement with various treatments and additives, balance feeding with low fibre diet, concentrate supplementation of feed, inclusion of legumes in feed, mineral supplementation to reduce gas production, long chain fatty acid supplementation, collection and capture of methane and proper management of dung to reduce N_2O are general recommendations to reduce GHG emission from animals sector.

FISHERIES AND AQUACULTURE SECTOR

Fisheries Sector

Some of the possible mitigation measures, which can be undertaken in fisheries sector for limiting GHG emission and improving aquatic ecosystem through enhanced resilience to withstand external shocks, are as follows:

- Eliminating inefficient fleet structure
- Improving fisheries management
- Reducing post-harvest losses
- Waste recycling
- More efficient vessels and gears for reduced fuel usage
- Safeguarding stock and improving resilience to climate change

Aquaculture Sector

- Developing low-carbon aquaculture production systems
- Policy support with respect to climate change mitigation measures such as certification, encourage transparent measures of mitigation
- Focus areas would be Increase water and energy efficiency

Rural/agricultural Women and Global Warming

Women play a vital role in rural and agriculture sectors particularly in the developing countries. Under the changing climatic scenarios, these women are bound to face the catastrophic effects of rising temperatures and odd weather conditions. Moreover, social obligations on type of clothing and other safety measures further exaggerates the problems and making farm women more vulnerable to the bad effect of global warming. Women contribute as human labour right from land cleaning and preparation to sowing/transplanting, weeding, interculture, collection of feedstocks and care of livestocks, harvesting, grading and up to storage and preparation of food. Many a times, the agricultural farm women are affected by heat shocks, dehydration, skin cancers, pesticide poisonings etc. due to drudgery during transplanting, weeding, interculture, livestock's feed collection and harvesting making their conditions more heartbreaking. Higher level of technological interventions in agriculture, farm mechanization, job oriented professional education, increased productivity and profitability of farm, increased attention on women health, safety and equity issues are some of the suggestions for preparedness of farm women to cope up with bad effects of global warming. Kienzle *et al.* (2009) reported about 60 per cent saving in farm labour during land cleaning, preparation, planting and weeding due to adoption of conservation agriculture practices.

REFERENCES

Anand, A. and Nagarajan, S. (2011). Impact of Climate Change on Quality of Cereals and Oilseed Crops. *In*: Climate Change: Impacts and Adaptations in Crop Plants (Eds. M.P. Singh; S. Khetarpal; R. Pandey and P. Kumar). Today and Tomorrow's Printers & Pub. New Delhi-110 012, pp. 33-53.

Bhanu, C. and Singh, P.K. (2008). Weed Management and Global Warming. *In*: A Manual on Advances in Weed Managements (J.G. Varshney; P.K. Singh and A. Dixit Eds.). NRCWS, Jabalpur, India, pp. 152-155.

Bisht, B.S.; Singh, V.; Melkania, U.; Srivastava, R.K. and Nautiyal, N. (2012). Climate Change and Agriculture: Emerging Scenarios and Adaptation Strategies. Biotech Books, New Delhi, p. 331.

Chander, S. (2011). Simulation of Effect of Biotic Stresses on Crop Productivity under Climate Change Scenario. *In*: Climate Change: Impacts and Adaptations in Crop Plants (Eds. M.P. Singh; S. Khetarpal; R. Pandey and P. Kumar). Today and Tomorrow's Printers & Pub. New Delhi, pp. 283-299.

Datta, M.; Singh, N.P. and Daschaudhary, D. (2008). Climate Change and Food Security. New India Pub. Agency, New Delhi, p. 342.

Deka, S.; Barthakur, S. and Pandey, R. (2011). Poon Insect Pest Dynamics. *In*: Climate Change: Impacts and Adaptations in Crop Plants (Eds. M.P. Singh; S. Khetarpal; R. Pandey and P. Kumar). Today and Tomorrow's Printers & Pub. New Delhi, pp. 301-312.

FAO (2008). Climate Change for Fisheries and Aquaculture: Technical Background Document from the Expert Consultation Held on 7 to 9 April 2008, FAO, Rome. (No. HLC/08/BAK/6).

Goddard, T.; Haugen-Kozyra, K. and Ridge, A. (2009). Conservation Agriculture Protocols for Green House Gas Offsets in a Working Carbon Market. *In*: Lead Papers, Session 3.1: Climate Change. 4th World Congress on Conservation Agriculture, 4-7 Feb. 2009, New Delhi, India, pp. 341-350.

IPCC (2007). Climate Change 2007: Synthesis report. www.ipcc.ch/

Kalra, K. (2012). Food Production in Peril: Concerns and Challenges of Global Warming. *In*: Climate Change and Agriculture: Emerging Scenarios and Adaptation Strategies (Eds. B.S. Bisht; V. Singh; U. Melkania; R.K. Srivastava and N. Nautiyal). Biotech Books, New Delhi, pp. 214-230.

Kienzle, J.; Berger, A.; Sims, B. and Apina, T. (2009). Conservation Agriculture for Drudgery Alleviation in SSA. *In*: Lead Papers, Session 4.2: Equity Issues (Employment, Drudgery and Regional Disparities etc.). 4th World Congress on Conservation Agriculture, 4-7 Feb. 2009, New Delhi, India, pp. 445-454.

Kumar, N. and Agarwaal, P.K. (2011). Climate Change Research in Agriculture: Role of Crop Simulation Models. *In*: Climate Change: Impacts and Adaptations in Crop Plants (Eds. M.P. Singh; S. Khetarpal; R. Pandey and P. Kumar). Today and Tomorrow's Printers & Pub. New Delhi, pp. 1-16.

Kushwaha, H.S.; Rani, M.; Kumar, A. and Mehra, M. (2012). Climate Change and Its Impact on Productivity of Rice and Wheat: A Case of *tarai* Area of Uttarakhand. *In*: Climate Change and Agriculture: Emerging Scenarios and Adaptation Strategies (Eds. B.S. Bisht; V. Singh; U. Melkania; R.K. Srivastava and N. Nautiyal). Biotech Books, New Delhi, pp. 22-39.

Lal, R. (2004). Agricultural Activities and the Global Carbon Cycle. *Nutr. Cycling Agroecosyst.* 70:103–116.

McGarry, D. (2009). Mitigating Climate Change and Better Ensuring Agriculture's Adaptation for Impending Climate Change Through Conservation Agriculture. *In*: Lead Papers, Session 3.1: Climate Change. 4th World Congress on Conservation Agriculture, 4-7 Feb. 2009, New Delhi, India, pp. 362-372.

Misra, A.K.; Bharadwaj, V. and Rastogi, A. (2012). Greenhouse Gas Emission from Agricultural Fields: Making Agriculture Truly Environment Friendly. *In*: Climate Change and Agriculture: Emerging Scenarios and Adaptation Strategies (Eds. B.S. Bisht; V. Singh; U. Melkania; R.K. Srivastava and N. Nautiyal). Biotech Books, New Delhi, pp. 1-12.

Mohammed, A.S. and Awan, K.D. (2012). Global Climate Change and Its Impact on Livestock Production: A Threat to Livestock Dependent Economies. *In*: Climate Change and Agriculture: Emerging Scenarios and Adaptation Strategies (Eds. B.S. Bisht; V. Singh; U. Melkania; R.K. Srivastava and N. Nautiyal). Biotech Books, New Delhi, pp. 122-162.

Naidu, V.S.G.R. (2011). Impact of Elevated CO_2 and Temperature on Crop-weed Interaction. *In*: Climate Change: Impacts and Adaptations in Crop Plants (Eds. M.P. Singh; S. Khetarpal; R. Pandey and P. Kumar). Today and Tomorrow's Printers & Pub. New Delhi, pp. 157-168.

Natu, P.S.; Pandey, R. and Ghildiyal, M.C.(2011). Climate Change Impacts on Rice Productivity. *In*: Climate Change: Impacts and Adaptations in Crop Plants (Eds. M.P. Singh; S. Khetarpal; R. Pandey and P. Kumar). Today and Tomorrow's Printers & Pub. New Delhi, pp. 85-101.

Pathak, H. (2009). Green House Gas Mitigation in Rice-wheat System with Resource Conservation Technologies. *In*: Lead Papers, Session 3.1: Climate Change. 4th World Congress on Conservation Agriculture, 4-7 Feb. 2009, New Delhi, India, pp. 373-377.

Paul, V.; Pandey, R. and Singh, A. (2011).Vulnerability of Trees and Fruit Crops to Climate Change. *In*: Climate Change: Impacts and Adaptations in Crop Plants (Eds. M.P. Singh; S. Khetarpal; R. Pandey and P. Kumar). Today and Tomorrow's Printers & Pub. New Delhi, pp. 169-186.

Puranic, H.V. and Gupta, A.K. (2012). Impact of Climate Change on Agriculture: Adopting Some Adaptation Measures. *In*: Climate Change and Agriculture: Emerging Scenarios and Adaptation Strategies (Eds. B.S. Bisht; V. Singh; U. Melkania; R.K. Srivastava and N. Nautiyal). Biotech Books, New Delhi, pp. 13-21.

Purkayastha, T.J. (2011). Nutrient Dynamics in Rhizosphere under Impending Climate Change. *In*: Climate Change: Impacts and Adaptations in Crop Plants (Eds. M.P.

Singh; S. Khetarpal; R. Pandey and P. Kumar). Today and Tomorrow's Printers & Pub. New Delhi, pp. 267-282.

Reed, D. (2007). Economic and Social Benefits of Soil Carbon Management: Policy Implications and Recommondations. *In*: Soil Carbon Management: Economic, Environmental and Social Benefits. (Eds) J.A. Kimble; C.W. Rice; D. Reed; S. Mooney; R. F. Follett and R. Lal., CRC Press (Taylor & Francis Group LLC), Boca Raton, pp. 13-43.

Singh, L.; Singh, P.; Khanday, B. A. and Chand, S. (2012). Factors for Climate Change: Efforts to Overcome Global Warming Impact on Agricultural Production System and Livelihood. *In*: Climate Change and Agriculture: Emerging Scenarios and Adaptation Strategies (Eds. B.S. Bisht; V. Singh; U. Melkania; R.K. Srivastava and N. Nautiyal). Biotech Books, New Delhi, pp. 66-97.

Subrahmanyam, D.; Voleti, S.R. and Sailaja, B. (2011). Climate Change Impacts on Rice Productivity. *In*: Climate Change: Impacts and Adaptations in Crop Plants (Eds. M.P. Singh; S. Khetarpal; R. Pandey and P. Kumar). Today and Tomorrow's Printers & Pub. New Delhi, pp. 143-155.

Taryal, K. and Melkania, U. (2012). Agriculture's Potential to Combat Climate Change: A Review of the Evidence. *In*: Climate Change and Agriculture: Emerging Scenarios and Adaptation Strategies (Eds. B.S. Bisht; V. Singh; U. Melkania; R.K. Srivastava and N. Nautiyal). Biotech Books, New Delhi, pp. 290-312.

Verchot, L.V. and Singh, V.P. (2009). Carbon Sequestration Opportunities with Small Holder Communities: Forestry, Agriculture and Agro-forestry. *In*: Lead Papers, Session 3.1: Climate Change. 4th World Congress on Conservation Agriculture, 4-7 Feb. 2009, New Delhi, India, pp. 351-360.

Agriculture Crops and Food Security
Edited by: Dr. Pawan Kumar 'Bharti' and Alka Chauhan
ISBN: 978-93-5056-881-1
Edition: 2017
Published by: Discovery Publishing House Pvt. Ltd., New Delhi (India)

2 Solar Radiation and Crop Growth

[1]Pulak Kumar Patra, [1&2]Suman Samanta,
[2]SaonBanerjee, [2]Asis Mukherjee

ABSTRACT

Sunshine is important in plant growth because the heat and the light required by all growing plants are supplied by solar radiation. The quality and the quantity of the sun-light transmitted to growing plants are both dependent upon atmospheric conditions, as well as upon the season of the year. They vary from place to place and from month to month. Because solar radiation furnishes the required energy for certain chemical activities within growing plants, as well as promotes evaporation from the foliage, they play an important role in crop growth and productivity. Thus availability of solar radiation data is crucial for agricultural management practices. The present paper deals with different components of solar radiation, their estimation techniques. The significance of solar radiation in crop growth is discussed with special reference to rice and potato.

INTRODUCTION

Sun is the prime force which drives all the physical and biological processes in the earth. Solar radiation (SR) is the set of electromagnetic radiation emitted by the Sun due to nuclear fusion in it. The electromagnetic spectrum striking the Earth's atmosphere spans a range of 100 nm (Ultraviolet) to about 1 mm (Infrared). The Sun also emits gamma and X-rays as a result of solar flare and solar corona respectively. The availability of surface incoming solar radiation observations is necessary for applications such as evapotranspiration estimation or plant growth and developmental and yield simulation models.

Extraterrestrial radiation is the intensity (power) of the SR at the top of earth's atmosphere and usually calculated as a complex function of latitude (radians), day of the year, solar declination angle (radians) and solar constant. Solar constant (sc) is the amount of solar energy per unit time, at the mean distance of the earth from the sun, received on a unit area of a surface normal to

[1] Dept. of Environmental Studies, Visva-Bharati, Santiniketan, West Bengal
[2] AICRP on Agrometeorology, BCKV, Kalyani: 741235, Nadia, West Bengal.

the sun (perpendicular to the direction of propagation of the radiation) outside the atmosphere. World Radiometric Centre has recommended the SC value as 1367 W m^{-2} for estimation of SR and evaluation of empirical correlations across the. SC is extremely important for GSR estimation since its 0.1% change can significantly influence the earth's atmosphere, as well as the surface albedo (Pelkowski, 2009).

The atmosphere acts as a filter to the bands of solar spectrum, and at its different layers as solar radiation passes through it to the Earth's surface, so that only a fraction of it reaches the surface. The atmosphere absorbs part of the radiation, some directly reflects back to space, and the rest to the Earth, and then it is irradiated. Sunlight in space at the top of Earth's atmosphere at a power of 1367 watts/m^2 is composed (by total energy) of about 50% infrared light, 40% visible light, and 10% ultraviolet light. At ground level this decreases to about 1120–1000 watts/m^2 and by energy fractions to 44% visible light, 3% ultraviolet (with the Sun at the zenith, but less at other angles), and the remainder infrared. Once the incoming solar radiation moves through the atmosphere, its intensity is reduced by attenuation (the combined effect of absorption and scattering) by atmospheric gases (particularly ozone and water vapor) and aerosols (clouds and particulate matter). Reflection (*i.e.,* albedo) in the atmosphere and on the surface is also responsible for reduction of the radiant flux density from the solar constant. However, sometimes radiation reaching the Earth's surface can be higher in magnitude compared with its corresponding ideal cloud free sky (De Miguel, 2011). These events/ phenomena are called *radiation enhancements* being able to produce surface solar levels higher than their extraterrestrial value (Anton, 2012).

Accurate information/estimation/knowledge of incoming Global Solar Radiation (GSR) is of particular importance for solar energy based technologies, hydrological systems, photosynthesis/biological processes, air-sea interaction etc. However, solar radiation is an infrequently measured meteorological variable, compared to temperature and rainfall. There are very few meteorological stations that measure global solar radiation, especially in developing countries. Daily solar radiation data is required by most models that simulate crop growth because growth is primarily based on the photosynthetic processes which involve the utilization of radiation and its conversion to chemical energy. Thus solar radiation is becoming increasingly appreciated because of its influence on living matter and the feasibility of its application for useful purposes. The components of solar radiation and their estimation techniques along with significance in crop growth are discussed below.

COMPONENTS OF SOLAR RADIATION

Solar radiation on the earth can be classified as:

Direct radiation: This radiation comes directly from the sun without any change in its direction. This type of radiation is characterized by projecting defined shadow onto the objects that intersect.

Diffuse radiation: This radiation comes from all over the atmosphere as a result of reflection and scattering by clouds, particles in the atmosphere, dust, mountains, trees, buildings, the ground itself, and so on. On a clear day with a clear sky, the direct radiation is predominant above the diffuse radiation. But during cloudy sky, there could be a small component of direct radiation and a substantial component of diffuse radiation.

Net Radiation

Earth's net radiation (R_n), sometimes called net flux, is the difference between incoming and outgoing radiation at the top of the atmosphere. It is the most important component to understand and estimates the earth's surface energy balance. Earth's net radiation varies throughout the year because of year-wise variation of earth-sun distance and solar angle (varies 6% between January and July). The earth possesses a net gain of energybetween 40° N and 40° S but the pole-ward of 40° N and 40° S there is a net loss of radiation. Net radiation can be positive, negative, or zero. Net radiation is positive when there is more incoming radiation than outgoing radiation. This condition found during the day time when the sun is out and the air temperature is the warmest. At night, net radiation is usually a negative value as there is no incoming solar radiation and net longwave is dominated by the outgoing terrestrial longwave flux. Net radiation is zero when the incoming and outgoing components are in perfect balance, which doesn't occur too often. This also explains why the warmest part of the year is in July/August, not on 21 June during the summer solstice. Radiation energy comes in to the system when sunlight penetrates the top of the atmosphere. R_n at the mid-canopy and top of the canopy, which attained the peak value at solar noon, was dependent on plant height, leaf area index (LAI) and crop growth stage. Net radiation (R_n) is also a key parameter in computing reference evapotranspiration and is a driving force in many other physical and biological processes (Rosenberg *et al.*, 1983).

Photosynthetically Active Radiation (PAR)

Photosynthetically Active Radiation (PAR) is the amount of light available for photosynthesis, which is light in the 400 to 700 nanometer wavelength range. PAR changes seasonally and varies depending on the latitude and time of day. Levels are greatest during the summer at mid-day. Factors that reduce the amount of PAR available to plants include anything that reduces sunlight, such as cloud cover, shading by trees, and buildings. Air pollution also affects PAR by filtering out the amount of sunlight that can reach plants. Chameides *et al.*, (1999) concluded that the air pollution in China, which reduces ground radiation, would have a large negative impact on Chinese agricultural production. But Cohan *et al.*, (2002) suggested that if the diffuse radiation increase from aerosols was considered, the impact of pollution on Chinese agriculture is not as serious as Chameides *et al.*, (1999) estimated. Some researchers suggested that the increase in aerosols from human activities and tropical clouds, which decrease PAR, would inhibit the photosynthesis of vegetation (Graham *et al.*, 2003). But Stanhill and Cohen, (2001) observed that there was no evidence that any alteration in radiation affects agriculture, even though solar radiation on Earth has decreased about 20% in the past 50 years. Another study suggested that, though aerosols can reduce the direct solar radiation at the Earth's surface, they can also increase the amount of diffuse solar radiation, which plays a more significant role in vegetation photosynthesis, especially for dense vegetation (Gu *et al.*, 2003).

Availability of this portion of the spectrum controls the photosynthesis process in green leaf (Ross and Sulev, 2000). This portion of the radiation spectrum is extremely important as it serves as the sole energy source for photosynthesis in plant to provide the living organisms food, fibres, etc. (Myers, 2005). Degree of exposure to PAR determines the capacity of plant to produce biomass and its partitioning within the plant consequentially determines the crop yield (Vander Werf, 1996). Green vegetation can absorb up to 95% of the incident PAR, the bulk of which is converted into latent and sensible heat. Only a small fraction (<5%) is consumed in photochemical processes in which CO_2 is assimilated as organic carbon (Myneni and Ganapol, 1992). Therefore, the amount of PAR absorbed by green vegetation (APAR) not only influences the net primary productivity and the carbon cycle but also affects the exchange of energy and water between the atmosphere and the land surface. A strong relationship exists between PAR and shortwave irradiance. Britton and Dodd (1976) studied that the proportion of PAR changed with intensity of incident irradiance and length of photoperiod.

PAR is a key variable in a wide range of eco-physiological models. PAR has been used in estimates of leaf photosynthesis (Alados and Alados-Arboledas, 1999), productivity of agricultural crops and forests (Nojd and Hari, 2001) and the radiation intercepted by the canopy (Zhang *et al.*, 2000).

The magnitude and variation of PAR that reaches vegetation are important factors controlling the photosynthesis rate of terrestrial ecosystems, and affect directly growth, development and health of all plants. PAR also affects the exchange of material and energy between the land surface and atmosphere, and therefore is a key parameter in photosynthesis and carbon cycle models (Liu *et al.*, 2004). Monteith *et al.*, 1972 found that net primary production under non-stressed conditions is linearly related to the amount of PAR that is absorbed by the green foliage. Based on this relationship the well-known Monteith equation was established. Abbate *et al.* (1997) demonstrated that intercepted PAR (IPAR) is the main factor for determining crop growth in wheat.

Several Carbon cycle models have also been developed by some scientist. Prince *et al.* (1995) developed Global Production Efficiency Model (GLO-PEM) which assumes the gross primary productivity (GPP) is related to PAR, FPAR (Fraction of Photosynthetically Active Radiation), maximum light use efficiency, air temperature, soil moisture and vapor pressure. In Carnegie-Ames-Stanford Approach (CASA) model, solar irradiance is used to calculate NPP (Potter *et al.*, 1993). Vegetation Photosynthesis Model (VPM), developed by Xiao *et al.* (2004), the vegetation canopy consists of two different components, i.e., photosynthetically active vegetation (PAV; mostly green leaves) and non-photosynthetic vegetation (NPV; mostly senescent foliage, branches and stems). VPM also takes into account temperature, leaf age and other parameters.

MEASUREMENT TECHNIQUES OF SR COMPONENTS

Estimation of Global Solar Radiation

In India, availability of daily SR data is also very scarce because large scale measurements are only carried out by the IMD at 45 radiation observatories with data loggers at four of these stations. For example, in West Bengal, India Meteorological Department is able to provide SR data only for Kolkata station. Hence, the researchers from all over the world have to rely on different indirect approaches for estimation of global radiation i.e., estimation of GSR from other meteorological parameters.

Measurements of solar radiation may be direct or indirect:

Direct methods: The traditional way or direct methods of knowing the amount of GSR in a particular region is to install GSR measuring device (pyranometer/pyrheliometer) at as many locations as possible in the region of interest and look after their day-to-day maintenance and recording, which is a very costly exercise (Teke, 2014). A thermoelectric pyranometer with a shading ring is used for measurement of diffuse radiation. Inverted pyranometers and sunphotometers are used for measuring reflected solar irradiance and solar spectral irradiance and turbidity respectively. The sensor of a Pyranometer has a horizontal radiation-sensing surface that absorbs solar radiation energy from the whole sky and transforms this energy into heat. Global solar radiation can be ascertained by measuring this heat energy. Most pyranometers in general use are now the thermopile type, although bimetallic pyranometers are occasionally found.

Empirical equations for deriving SR: In the absence of direct measurement techniques, some indirect approaches including theoretical models and satellite imageries have become the desired tools to predict and estimate the GSR of a place using some meteorological parameters such as temperature, BSS, rainfall, cloud cover etc.These models use historical meteorological data of the location under study. Empirical models are classified in three categories: sunshine-based models, temperature-based models and cloud-based models (Muneer *et al.*, 2007). Some researchers used the sunshine duration, others used the relative humidity and temperature (Layi, 1994), while others used the number of rainy days, sunshine hours and a factor that depends on latitude and altitude (Chiemeka, 2008). But according to some researchers, SR data calculated from sunshine duration achieves highest degree of precision for agricultural and hydrological studies (Sahin, 2007). This fact is strongly supported by Akpabio and Etuk (2003) and Li *et al.* (2011) who used bright sunshine duration for GSR estimation at various sites of Nigeria and China respectively.

Development of empirical correlations was started in the early 20th Century when Kimball (1919) presented a graphical relationship between BSS and GSR data from several locations in the USA. Chineke, (2008) tested the Hargreaves model over tropical Africa to estimate the global solar radiation. A number of correlations which include more meteorological parameters such as latitude, ambient temperature, the total precipitation, relative and specific humidity, the elevation, amount of cloud cover etc. have been developed by different works (Winslow *et al.*, 2001). Amongthe existing correlations, the following relation is widely accepted modified form of the Angstrom-type regression equation, relating the clear sky GSR to BSS duration. Angstrom (1924) first proposed the equation and then modified by (Prescott, 1940 and Page, 1961) to its present form and presented as:

$$H/H_0 = a + b(^n/_N)$$

Where,

H = Incoming daily global solar radiation (MJ m^{-2} day^{-1})

H_0 = Daily extra-terrestrial radiation (MJ m^{-2} day^{-1})

a and b = Empirical constants

n = Bright sunshine hours per day (hr)

N = Astronomical day length (hr)

Where the Astronomical day length N is calculated by the following formula

$$N = \frac{2}{15}\cos^{-1}[-\tan(\phi) * \tan(\delta)]$$

Where,

ϕ = latitude in degree

δ = Solar declination angle in degree

H_0 is determined using equation defined by Castellvi (2001) as

$$H_0 = 37.6\,[1 + 0.033\cos(0.0172k)]\,[\omega\sin(\phi)\sin(\delta) + \sin(\omega)\cos(\phi)\cos(\delta)]$$

Here,

I_{SC} = solar constant in MJ m^{-2}

ω = sunset hour angle in radian = arccos [– tan(ϕ) tan(δ)]

k = Julian day

A new set of constants for an Angstrom-type equation was obtained to estimate GSR at Lucknow, India (Singh *et al.*, 1996).

GSR has a good relation with sunshine duration and thus most of the scientists prepared/proposed empirical models based on BSS. But along with Pyranometer, sunshine recorders are also not available or not in functional mood/condition in most of the observatories. Therefore, other parameters including maximum and minimum temperature, rainfall, cloud cover etc. which, are frequently measured and monitored, can be used to calculate solar radiation values for such locations with reasonable accuracies. A new type of correlation was developed by Bakirchi (2009) using BSS for Turkey.

Estimation of Net Radiation

A net radiometer is a type of actino meter used to measure net radiation at the Earth's surface in meteorological applications. The name net radiometer reflects the fact that it is supposed to measure incoming minus upwelling radiation. It is most commonly used in the field of eco-physiology.

Rao *et al.*, (1980) found that the percentage of net to total radiation was found to be greatest during the growing season and minimal when the surface vegetation cover was dry.

Net radiation and global solar radiation pattern was studied on bare soil, short gram, winter wheat and barley to determine their variations diurnally as well as changing canopy architecture and growth stages (Rodskyer, 1978).

Allen *et al.*, (2005) describe the net radiation (Rn) is the key variable in hydrological studies. Measured net radiation data are rarely available and are often subject to error due to equipment calibration or failure. In addition, point measurements of net radiation do not represent the diversity of the regional net radiation values which are needed for large scale evapotranspiration mapping. They observed that when R_n estimated from relationships employed in the equation of Penman, is found to be greater than the values of net radiation that are measured. Since the net short-wave (solar) radiation is well estimated when derived from Penman relationships, the problem is identified as an overestimate of the net long-wave radiation and primarily as an underestimate of the outgoing long-wave radiation from the surface of the Earth.

Estimation of PAR

Generally a quantum sensor, it may be point or line, is used to measure the PAR in and above the canopy. PAR is generally expressed in quantum flux (μmol m^{-2} Sec^{-1}) whereas GSR and R_n are expressed in energy flux (W m^{-2} Sec^{-1}). But, due to the non-availability of PAR measurement facilities in most places across the world, this parameter is often calculated indirectly based on its relationship with SR. Moon (1940) analysed the spectral distribution of incoming SR at places of low altitudes. At sea level, when sun was more than 30^0 above horizon, then 44% to 45% of incoming SR is PAR. Monteith (1973), suggested that the PAR can be taken as half of the total SR in the tropics as well in temperate latitude. According to McCree (1966), PAR value reaches its peak (48% of SR) when sky is covered with cloud. But many researchers have found that PAR percentage is not constant, but vary according to location, season, sky clearness, sky brightness and atmospheric depth for the solar beam, relative BSS duration and water vapour pressure, altitude, day length etc. (Li *et al.*, 2010). But Anderson, (1966) depicted that radiation measurements are invalid because radiation is measured with artificial surfaces that differ from the photosynthetically active elements with respect to size, structure, arrangement and directional distribution.

Nowadays, estimation of PAR from remote sensing data has become the preferential choice. Alados *et al.*, (2000) have estimated the photosynthetically active radiation from measurements of global solar radiation with good results. Broesamle *et al.*, (2001) explained that if we could obtain an estimation of solar photosynthetically active solar irradiance from satellite images there would be much more information available as geostationary satellite data cover wide area and have an adequate temporal frequency.

Compared with traditional observation and interpolation methods, remote sensing techniques are more convenient and are a promising approach to obtain the spatial distribution of PAR. PAR can be retrieved from satellite data using knowledge of atmosphere radiation transfer and remote sensing inversion techniques. Frouin and Gautier (1990) obtained PAR from remote sensing data by revised the method of Gautier *et al.* (1980) by replacing solar radiation wavelength range with PAR wavelength range.

Fraction of PAR is usually related to remotely sensed vegetation indices, which are combinations of visible and near-infrared satellite measurements. Determination of downwelling PAR from satellite data requires knowledge of the atmosphere, clouds and surface, cloud properties being the most critical. In contrast, the PAR absorbed at the surface by the vegetation-soil complex can be retrieved much more easily.

The method of estimation of constant solar irradiance (R_s) is subject to errors arising from the influence of climate temporal and spatial variations on the ratio between PAR and R_s (Zhang *et al.*, 2000). PAR can also be estimated from R_s associated with other variables commonly measured in meteorological stations, such as dew point temperature (Alados *et al.*, 1996), air temperature and precipitation (Nojd and Hari, 2001) and the clearness index (by the ratio between global and extraterrestrial solar radiation) (Tsubo and Walker, 2002).

RADIATION USE EFFICIENCY (RUE) OFCROPS

Crop communities exert a strong influence over their local microenvironment. One of the most important factors that influence plants development is the solar radiation intercepted by the crop. The solar radiation brings energy to the metabolic process of the plants. Photosynthesis is a chemical process that converts carbon dioxide into organic compounds, especially sugars, using the energy from sunlight. A part of this, solar energy is used in the evaporation process inside the different organs of the plants, and also in the transpiration process through the stomas.

Plants intercept both direct and diffuse sunlight. The upper leaves receive both types of radiation, while the lower leaves intercept a small portion of direct radiation. Diffuse radiation therefore, becomes more significant in the lower leaves due to radiation transmitted and reflected from the leaves and the soil surface. In the interception of light by a canopy, difference between the solar incident radiation and reflected radiation by the soil surface, is a determining factor in crop development and provides the energy needed for fundamental physiological processes such as photosynthesis and transpiration (Villalobos *et al.*, 2002).

Crop productivity is determined by above-ground total dry matter (ATDM) accumulation along with its partitioning to various parts of plants (Van der werf, 1996). ATDM and crop growth rates are dependent on the ability of the crop canopy to (*a*) either the interception of photosynthetically active radiation (IPAR) which is function of leaf area index (LAI) and crop canopy architecture or (*b*) conversion of IPAR to ATDM, i.e., radiation use efficiency (RUE) (Sinclair and Muchow, 1999). Teixeira *et al.* (2008) explained that solar radiation is the main energy contributing in production through photosynthesis but efficient light conversion for high fodder is advantageous to contribute for yield. Greater surface area or canopy volume of a variety may contribute higher in resource capturing i.e. solar light and CO_2 resulting faster biomass production. The radiation use efficiency (RUE) approach that relates dry mass accumulation with the amount of intercepted PAR (Kiniry, 1999).

Light is the primary source of photosynthesis and higher production is subjected to the maximum light interception by the crop canopy (Brown *et al.*, 2006). Light conversion to chemical energy depends on leaf area, rate of radiation interception and crop photosynthetic rate (Stewart *et al.*, 2003). Temperature, solar radiation, and rainfall influence crop yield by directly affecting the physiological processes involved in grain production, and indirectly through diseases and insects. According to Hubik, (1993), solar radiation (SR) is one of the main factors influencing biomass and yield production and its quality beside other factors associated with prolonged Radiation in the phase of stem elongation and grain filling. While low intensity of SR during grain filling phase negatively influences grain yield (Lekes, 1984).

Fisher (1985) found a good relation regarding how solar radiation and temperature influence the number of kernel formulation in wheat crops and found that solar irradiance and temperature had great influence on grain yield of rice. It was observed that 77% shading had a greater adverse effect when applied to the ripening stage (Islam and Morison, 1992). Puri *et al.*(1988) studied the effects of temperature and solar radiation in the production of grain yield of Barley, wheat and triticale. It was found that the dry matter accumulation, leaf area development and radiant energy interception were strongly correlated with each other (Coulson, 1985). The effect of canopy structure on light interception, growth, yield and quality of wheat was reviewed to find out their correlation (Chahal *et al.*, 1994).

It is a fact that that all portion of SR is not beneficial for crop growth. Some portion of it may stunt or inhibit the crop growth and its yield. A high level of UV-B radiation has deleterious effects on growth of plants, photosynthesis activity, flowering and crop yield (Singh, 1994).

SOLAR RADIATION AND RICE GROWTH

Normally rice is water loving crop and requires a mean temperature range of 17 to 33°C. Good rice production is associated with exposure to the light of optimum intensity, quality and duration during different phenological stages. Duration of reproductive stage as well as solar radiation (SR) and temperature prevailing during the stage govern the grain growth process of rice (Bastidas *et al.*, 2008). The Solar radiation requirements of a rice crop differ from one growth stage to another. Shading during the vegetative stage slightly affects the yield and yield components. But shading during the reproductive and ripening stage have pronounced negative effect on the number of spikelet and its filling procedure (Yoshida and Parao, 1976). All portion of incoming solar radiation is not good for crops. UV-B radiation adversely affects the crop yield by reducing leaf areas and crop heights (Liu *et al.*, 2013).High level of solar radiation in June in combination with high temperatures and a high saturation deficit can cause marked reduction of tillers (Chmielewski and Kohn, 1998).

During ripening, shading markedly reduces grain yield because of a spurt in spikelet sterility (Yoshida, 1981). In both the tropics and the temperate region, productivity, or rice yield per hectare, is primarily determined by the level of incident solar radiation.

Based on experiments in Texas, Stansel (1975) suggested that the rice plant's most critical period of solar energy requirement is from panicle initiation until about 10 days before maturity. In the tropics, the correlation between solar radiation for the 45 day period before harvest (from panicle initiation to crop maturity) and grain yield, plotted by harvest month, was highly significant. Earlier experiments indicated a strong correlation between grain yield and solar radiation during the last 30 days of crop growth (Moomaw *et al.*, 1967).

Subsequent IRRI research indicated that the increase in dry matter between panicle initiation and harvest was highly correlated with grain yield (De Datta *et al.*, 1968).

With irrigation, the dry season rice yields in the tropics (11t/ha reported at IRRI) should be similar to those reported by Best (1962) for the temperate region (12.5 t/ha). However, the grain yields obtained during the wet season are lower that those in the dry season because of the lower level of solar radiation received during the grain filling and ripening stages.

Grain yield in rice significantly decreased in all varieties due to low light exposure. Percentage of filled spikelets was more affected than 1000 grain weight (Islam *et al.*, 1989). Shading the rice crop artificially to 50% of normal light intensity from panicle initiation to maturity, the number of tillers, number of filled spikelets and yield decreased from 456 to 396/m^2, from 27.8 to 11.3/m^2 and from 4.78 to 2.48 t/ha respectively (Hussain *et al.*, 1989).

Dey *et al.* (1989) reported that low light (50% sunlight) from 40 days after planting to flowering reduced the total dry matter production of early maturing varieties of rice (Swarnaprobha & Ratna) by 43% at flowering in both dry and wet seasons by decreasing photosynthetic rate. Low light decreased the number of panicle and grains/m^2 and increased spikelets sterility. Shading also delayed heading date by 2-3 days except in the late maturing varieties of rice (Sangpungbyeo and Bongkwangbyeo) culm length and percentage spikelets sterility increased but number of spikelets/plant and ripening ratio decreased due to shading (Kim *et al.*, 1991). The reduction of grain yield due to decrease in incident solar radiation and its utilization efficiency was assessed by Reddy *et al.* (1995).

Under no stressed conditions (i.e., with adequate water and nutrient supply), cumulative dry matter is linearly related to the amount of solar radiation or PAR intercepted by the crop canopy and the slope of this regression is known as radiation use efficiency (Soltani *et al.*, 2006). RUE appears to be a more conservative (i.e., less variable) attribute compared to LAI or IPAR (Sinclair, 1993). RUE is generally used in many crop growth models to estimate total above-ground biomass and crop yields (Curt *et al.*, 1998). According to O'Connell *et al.* (2004), RUE levels vary with plant species, climatic conditions, measuring method and plant characteristics. But, despite these differences, many species sustain very consistent RUE values throughout the duration of the cropping season (Park *et al.*, 2005). Due to the variation in RUE observed in different rice cultivars, they have different growth rates and yields (Curt *et al.*, 1998). In addition to LAI values, accurate and good values of K are vital for simulating light interception and RUE.

POTATO GROWTH AND RADIATION

Potato (*Solenumtuberosum* L.) is a member of nightshade family (Solanaceae) and one of the major food crop in the world and by far the most important vegetable crop in terms of quantities produced and consumed worldwide (FAO, 2005). Bowen (2003) reported that production of potato is exceeded only by wheat, rice and maize in world for human consumption. The crop grows best in cold temperature but frost-free seasons and does not perform well in heat (Haverkort and Verhagen, 2008). At global level, India ranks third (after China and Russia) in potato acreage covering 2.02 million Ha land and stand second (only after China) in tuber production, producing 46.4 million tons per annum (FAO, 2014). More than 85% of potato area is confined to Indo-Gangetic Plains (IGP), where it is grown post monsoon to winter season (November to February) with irrigation facilities and contributes more than 80% to the total tuber production of the country(Pandey and Kang, 2003). Climatic parameters including solar radiation, temperature, rainfall, etc., along with soil moisture status determine the distribution of potato. Effect of latitude, seasonal mean air temperature (ranging from 13.8 to 19.9°C), solar radiation (ranging from 12.0 to 21.3 MJ $m^{-2}day^{-1}$), humidity, soil moisture and atmospheric CO_2 concentrations on tuber production has been studied by Temmerman *et al.* (2002) in a European condition.

Stuttle *et al.* (1996) observed that tuber yield improvements might be obtained by increasing the net daily photosynthetically active radiation (PAR) through higher solar irradiance or longer photoperiod. Photoperiods control the tuber production by maintaining the balance between gibberellic acid and abscisic acid secretion in plant (Dwelle, 1985). He also delineated the fact that the top leaves of a potato canopy could not absorb more than 1200 $\mu E\ m^{-2}\ s^{-1}$ and should allow the remaining light to pass to the lower canopy. Gawronska and Dwelle (1989) concluded that the reduction in total biomass is associated with low intensity light. They also observed that under low light condition tubers are of irregular shape and small in size compare to high light where the percentage of biomass partitioned to the tubers is higher. Studies also revealed that dry matter accumulation of crops including potato grown under non-limiting conditions is directly related to the amount of intercepted radiation (Van der Zaag and Doornbos, 1987). Cumulative seasonal PAR was calculated as the product of incident PAR and PAR interception on a daily basis summed upto harvest. Thus, growth rate of agricultural crops can be linearly related to intercepted PAR when soil water is adequate (Gallagher and Biscoe, 1978). In Philippines, Demagante *et al.* (1996) reported 740, 900 and 945 MJ m^{-2} radiation interception (RI) for early, medium and late maturing potato cultivars respectively. Whereas, in Netherlands RI varied from 1180 to 1435 MJ m^{-2} for different varieties in different seasons (Haverkort *et al.*, 1991). Hence, the accurate determination and clear understanding of the PAR components are required for many applications specially for different crop simulation models (Frouin and Pinker, 1995).

Spitters *et al.* (1988) observed that different species have their own growth rate depending on their specific RUE. Bangemann *et al.* (2014) observed that the RUE values estimated under 'Ditta' variety were 2.28 g MJ^{-1} and 2.55 g MJ^{-1} in the year 2006 and 2007 respectively. It has been observed that dry matter production increased with elevation and altitude because of increase in RUE values. Studying the performance of potato at three elevations, Manrique *et al.* (1991) reported an increase in RUE varies with altitude values from 2.20 g MJ^{-1} at 91 m elevation to 2.80 g MJ^{-1} at 1097 m. RUE values may also vary greatly among locations. Kinir *et al.* (1989) reported similar variability in RUE values but for grain crops. According to Haverkart and Harris (1986), RUE values of potato dry matter varied from 0.64 to 1.42 gm MJ^{-1} for a single cultivar. Though according to some researchers, large variation in RUE values is an indicator of the fact that crop growth is not solely dependent on radiation interception but also on soil and other climatic factors (Kiniry *et al.*, 1990). However, Sinclair and Muchow (1999) reported that RUE can be influenced by many factors including some abiotic stresses like water stress (Biscoe *et al.*, 1979) and nutritional deficiency (Muchow and Sinclair, 1994).

CONCLUSION

RUE levels vary with plant species, climatic conditions, measuring method and plant characteristics. But, despite these differences, many species sustain very consistent RUE values throughout the duration of the cropping season (Park *et al.*, 2005). Due to the variation in RUE observed in different rice cultivars, they have different growth rates and yields (Curt *et al.*, 1998). In addition to LAI values, accurate and good values of K are vital for simulating light interception and RUE

REFERENCES

Abbate, P.E., Andrade, F.H., Culot, J.P. and Bindraban, P.S. 1997. Grain Yield in Wheat: Effects of Rradiation during Spike Growth Period. *Field Crops Res.* 54: 245–257.

Akpabio, L.E. and Etuk, S.E. 2003. Relationship between Global Solar Radiation and Sunshine Duration for Onne, Nigeria. *Turkish Journal of Physics*. 27:161-167.

Alados, I. and Alados-Arboledas, L. 1999. Validation of an Empirical Model for Photosynthetically Active Radiation. *Int. J. Climatol.*19:1145–1152.

Alados, I., Foyo-Moreno, I. and Alados-Arboledas, L. 1996. Photosynthetically Active Radiation: Measurements and Modelling. *Agric. For.Meteorol.* 78: 121–131.

Anderson, M.C. 1966. Some Problems of Simple Characterization of the Light Climate in Plant Communities. *In* Light as an Ecological Factor. Eds. R. Bainbridge, G.C. Evans and O. Rackham. Blackwell Science Publishers, Oxford, pp. 77–90.

Angstrom, A. 1924. Solar and Terrestrial Radiation. *Quarterly Journal of the Royal Meteorological Society*. 50(210): 121-125.

Antón, M., Alados-Arboledas, L., Guerrero-Rascado, J.L., Costa, M.J., Chiu, J.C. and Olmo, F.J. 2012. Experimental and Modeled UV Erythemal Irradiance under Overcast Conditions: the Role of Cloud Optical Depth. *Atmospheric Chemistry and Physics*. 12: 11723–11732.

Bakirci K. 2009. Models of Solar Radiation with Hours of Bright Sunshine: A Review. Renewable *Sustainable Energy Review*. 13: 2580–2588.

Bangemann, L. W., Sieling, K. and Kage, H., 2014. The Effect of Nitrogen and Late Blight on Crop Growth, Solar Radiation Interception and Yield of Two Potato Cultivars. *Field Crops Res*. 155: 56–66.

Bastidas, A.M., Setiyono, T.D., Dobermann, A., Cassman, K.G., Elmore, R.W. and Graef, G.L. 2008. Soybean Sowing Date: The Vegetative, Reproductive and Agronomic Impacts. *Crop. Sci*. 48: 727–740.

Best, R. 1962. Production Factors in the Tropics. *Neth.J. Agric. Sci*.,10 (Spec. issue): 347-353.

Bowen, W.T. 2003. Water Productivity and Potato Cultivation. In J.W. Kijne, R. Barker and D. Molden (eds.) Water Productivity in Agriculture: Limits and Opportunities for Improvement. CAB International 2003, pp. 229-238.

Britton, C M. and Dodd, J.D. 1976. Relationships of Photosynthetically Active Radiation and Shortwave Irradiance. *Agric. Meteorol*. 17: 1 – 7.

Brown, H.E., Moot, D.J. and Teixeira, E.I. (2006). Radiation Use Efficiency and Biomass Partitioning of Lucerne (*M. sativa* L.) in a Temperate Climate. *European J. Agron*, 25: 319 327.

Castellvi, F. 2001. A New Simple Method for Estimating Monthly and Daily Solar Radiation. Performance and Comparison with Other Methods at Lleida (NE Spain); A Semiarid Climate. Theor. Appl. Climatol. 69, 231-238.

Chameides, W.L., Yu, H., Liu, S.C., Bergin, M., Zhou, X. and Mearns, L. 1999. Case Study of the Effects of Atmospheric Aerosols and Regional Haze on Agriculture: An Opportunity to Enhance Crop Yields in China through Emission Controls. Proceedings of the National Academy of Sciences. 96: 13626"13633.

Chiemeka, I.U. 2008. Estimation of Solar Radiation at Uturu, Nigeria. *International Journal of Physical Sciences*, 3: 126-30.

Chineke, T.C. 2008. Equations for Estimating Global Solar Radiation in Data Sparse Regions. Renew *Energy*. 33(4): 827-831.

Chmielewski, F.M. and Kohn, W. 1998. Impact of Weather on Yield Components of Spring Cereals over 30 Years. *Agric For Meteorol* 96(1-3): 49-58.

Cohan, D.S., Xu, J., Greenwald, R., Bergin, M.H. and Chameides, W.L. 2002. Impact of Atmospheric Aerosol Light Scattering and Absorption on Terrestrial Net Primary Productivity. *Global Biogeochemical Cycles*.16(4): 1090.

Curt, M.D., Fernandez, J. and Martinez, M. 1998. Productivity and Radiation Use Efficiency of Sweet Sorghum (Sorghum bicolor L.) Moench) cv. Keller in Central Spain. *Biomass Bioenergy*. 14: 169-178.

De Datta, S.K., A. C. Taura and Balaoing, S. M. 1968. Effect of Plant Type and Nitrogen Leel on the Growth Characteristics and Grain Yield of Indica Rice in the Tropics. *Agron. J*.60: 645-647.

De Miguel, A., Roman, R., Bilbao, J. and Mateos, D. 2011. Evolution of Erythemal and Total Shortwave Solar Radiation in Valladolid Spain: Effects of Atmospheric Factors. *Journal of Atmopheric Solar-Terrestrial Physics*. 73: 578–586.

Demagante, A.L., Harris, P.M. and Van der Zaag, P. 1996. Variation among Clonal Lines of Potato in Response to Irrigation Regimes in an Isohyperthermic Environment. *Field Crops Res*. 47: 191-200.

Dey, S.K., Singh, V.P. and Murty, K.S. 1989. Effect of Low Light at Different Stages of Development on Growth and Yield of Rice. *Indian J. Plant Physiol*., 32(1): 74-77.

Dwelle, R.B. 1985. Photosynthesis and Photoassimilate Partitioning. In P.H. Li (ed.) Potato Physiology. Academic Press Inc., Orlando, FL. pp. 35-58.

FAO, 2005. FAOSTAT Agricultural Data. Agricultural Production, Crops, Primary. Available at http://faostat.fao.org/faostat/collections?subset=agriculture United Nations Food and Agriculture Organization.

Frouin, R. and Pinker, R.T. 1995. Estimating Photosynthetically Active Radiation (PAR) at the Earth's Surface from Satellite Observations. *Remote Sensing of Environment*. 51: 98–107.

Gallagher, J.N. and Biscoe, P.V. 1978. Radiation Absorption, Growth and Yield of Cereals. J. *Agric. Sci. Camb*. 91: 47–60.

Gawronska, H. and Dwelle, R.B. 1989. Partitioning of Photoassimilates by Potato Plants (Solanum tuberosum L.) as Influenced by Irradiance I. Partitioning Patterns in Cultivar Russet Burbank Grown under High and Low Irradiance. *Am. Potato J*. 66: 201-213.

Graham, E.A., Mulkey, S.S., Kitajima, K., Phillips, N.G. and Wright, S.J. 2003. Cloud Cover Limits Net CO_2 Uptake and Growth of a Rainforest Tree during Tropical Rainy Seasons. Proceedings of the National Academy of Sciences. 100(2): 572"576.

Gu, L., Baldocchi, D.D., Wofsy, S.C., Munger, J.W., Michalsky, J.J. and Urbanski, S.P. 2003. Response of a Deciduous Forest to the Mount Pinatubo Eruption. *Enhanced Photosynthesis Science*. 299: 2035"2038.

Haverkort, A.J. and Harris, P.M. 1986. Conversion Coefficients between Intercepted Solar Radiation and Tuber Yields of Potato Crops under Tropical Highland Conditions. *Potato Res*. 29: 529-533.

Haverkort, A.J. and Verhagen, A. 2008. Climate Change and its Repercussions for the Potato Supply Chain. *Potato Research*. 51(3-4): 223-237. http://dx.doi.org/10.1007/s11540-008-9107-0

Haverkort, A.J., Fasan, T. and Van de Waart, M. 1991. The Influence of Cyst Nematodes and Drought on Potato Growth. 2. Effects on Plant Water Relations Under Semi Controlled Conditions. *Netherlands Journal of Plant Pathology*. 97: 162-170.

Hubik, E. 1993. Effect of Weather Conditions on Development of Yield-Forming Components of Spring Barley. *Plant Production*. 8: 723-734.

Hussain, I S.A., Urs, Y.S.V. and Herle, P.S. 1989. Effect of Light on the Chaffiness and Yield in Phalguna Rice Variety in Dakshina Kannada. *Current Research*. 17(4): 48-49.

Islam, M. S. and Morison, J.I.L. 1992. Influence of Solar Radiation and Temperature in Irrigated Rice Grain Yield in Bangladesh. *Field Crops Res*. 30 (1-2): 13 – 28.

Islam, M.S. and Haque, M.Z. 1989. Adaptability of Rice Varieties to Low Light Intensity. (Pub) International Rice Research Newsletter. 14(2): 11-12.

Kim, K.S., Kim, S.K., Hich, B.L. and Yoon, K.M. 1991. Effect of Shading at Heading Stage on Yield Components in Rice. *Korean J. Crop Sci*.,36(2): 127-33.

Kimball, H.H. 1919. Variations in the Total and Luminous Solar Radiation with Geographical Position in the United States. *Mon. Weather Rev*. 47(11): 769-793.

Kiniry, J.R. 1999. Response to Questions Raised by Sinclair and Muchow. *Field Crops Res*. 62:245-247.

Kiniry, J.R., Jones, C.A., O'toole, J.C., Blanchet, R., Cabelguenne, M. and Spanel, D.A. 1989. Radiation-use Efficiency in Biomass Accumulation Prior to Grain Filling for Five Grain-crop Species. *Field Crops Res*. 20: 51–64.

Layi, F. 1994. Evaluation of Global and Diffuse Solar Irradiation in Ibadan from Specific Humidity and Relative Sunshine. *International Journal of Ambient Energy*. 15(2): 95-98.

Lekes, J., Benada, J., Bruckner, F., Kopecky, M., Minarik, F., Prikryl, K., Vonka, Z. and Zenisceva. L. 1984. Jecmen, (Monograph in Czech), SZN Prague. p. 307.

Li, H., Ma, W., Lian, Y., Wang, X. and Zhao, L. 2011. Global Solar Radiation Estimation with Sunshine Duration in Tibet. China. *Renewable Energy*. 36(11): 3141-3145.

Li, R., Zhao, L. and Ding, Y.J. 2010. Monthly Ratios of PAR to Global Solar Radiation Measured at Northern Tibetan Plateau, China. *Solar Energy*. 84: 964–973.

Liu, B., Liu, X., Li, Y. and Herbert, S.J. 2013. Effects of Enhanced UV-B Radiation on Seed Growth Characteristics and Yield Components in Soybean. *Field Crops Res*. 154: 158–163.

Manrique, L.A., Kiniry, J.R., Hodges, T. and Axness, D.S. 1991. Dry Matter Production and Radiation Interception of Potato. *Crop Science*. 31: 1044-1049.

McCree, K.J. 1966. A Solarimeter for Measuring Photosynthetically Active Radiation. *Agricultural Meteorology*. 3: 353-366.

Monteith, J.L. 1972. Solar Radiation and Productivity in Tropical Ecosystems. *J. Appl. Ecol.* 9: 747–766.

Moon, P. 1940. Proposed Standard Solar-radiation Curves for Engineering Use. *J. Frankl. Inst*. 230: 583–617.

Muchow, R.C. and Sinclair, T.R. 1994. Nitrogen Response of Leaf Photosynthesis and Canopy Radiation use Efficiency in Field Grown Maize and Sorgham. *Crop Science*. 9: 721-727.

Muneer, T., Younes, S. and Munawwar, S. 2007. Discourses on Solar Radiation Modeling. *Renewable and Sustainable Energy Reviews*. 11(4):551–602.

Myers, D.R. 2005. Solar Radiation Modeling and Measurements for Renewable Energy Applications: Data and Model Quality. *Energy*. 30: 1517-1531.

Myneni, R.B. and Ganapol, B.D. 1992. Remote Sensing of Vegetation Canopy Photosynthetic and Stomatal Conductance Efficiencies. *Remote Sens. Environ*. 42: 217-238.

Nojd, P. and Hari, P. 2001. Instantaneous PAR Estimated using Long Records of Daily Temperature and Rainfall. *Agric. For. Meteorol*. 109: 47–59.

O'Connell, M.G., O'Leary, G.J., Whitfield, D.M. and Connor, D.J. 2004. Interception of Photosynthetically Active Radiation and Radiation-use Efficiency of Wheat, Field Pea and Mustard in a Semi-arid Environment. *Field Crops Res*. 85: 111–124.

Page, J. K. 1961. The Estimation of Monthly Mean Values of Daily Total Short Wave Radiation on Vertical and Inclined Surfaces from Sun Shine Records for Latitudes 40^0N-40^0S. *Proceedings of the United Nations Conference on New Sources of Energy*. 98(4): 378-390.

Park, S.E., Robertson, M. and Inman-Bamber, N.G. 2005. Decline in the Growth of a Sugarcane Crop with Age under High Input Conditions. *Field Crops Res*. 92: 305–320.

Pelkowski, J. 2009. A Physical Rationale for Generalized Ångström-Prescott Regression. *Sol. Energy*. 83(7): 955-963.

Potter, C.S., Randerson, J.T. and Field, C.B. 1993. Terrestrial Ecosystem Production: A Process Model Based on Global Satellite and Surface Data. *Global Biogeoch. Cycle*.7: 811–842.

Prescott, J.A. 1940. Evaporation from a Water Surface in Relation to Solar Radiation. *Tran. R. Soc. S. Austr.* 64, 114–118.

Puri, Y.P., Qudlsel, C.O., Niller, M.F., Bughott, K.G., Jan, C.C. and De Pacc. C. 1988. Barley, Wheat and Triticale Grain Yield in Relation to Solar Radiation and Heat Units. *Crop Science*. 25 (6): 893–900.

Reddy, Y. A. N., Prasad, T. G. and Kumar, M. U. 1995. Constraints in Bio Productivity of High and Low LAI Types of Rice during Wet Seasons. *Indian J. Plant Physiol*., 38(2): 173-174.

Rodskyer, N. 1978. Net and Solar Radiation over Bare Soil, Short Grass, Winter Wheat and Barley, Sweed. *J. Agric. Res.* 8(4): 195–201.

Rosenberg, N.J., Blad, B.L. and Verma, S.B. 1983. Microclimate—The Biological Environment, Wiley, New York.

Ross, J. and Sulev, M. 2000. Sources of Errors in Measurements of PAR. *Agric. For. Meteorol.* 100: 103–125.

Sahin, A.D. 2007. A New Formulation for Solar Irradiation and Sunshine Duration Estimation. *International Journal of Energy Research.* 31(2): 109-118.

Sinclair, T.R. 1993. Crop Yield Potential and Fairy Tales. In: Buxton, T.R., Shibles, D.R., Forsberg, R., Blad, R.A., Asay, B.L., Paulsen, K.H., Wilson, R.F. (Eds.), International Crop Science I. Crop Science Society of America, Madison, WI. pp. 707–711.

Sinclair, T.R. and Muchow, R.C. 1999. Radiation use Efficiency. *Advances in Agronomy.* **61**: 215-265.

Singh, A. 1994. Effects of Enhanced UV-B Radiation on Higher Plants. *Trop. Ecol.* **35**: 321–47.

Singh, O.P., Srivastava, S.K. and Gaur, A. 1996. Empirical Relationship to Estimate Global Radiation from Hours of Sunshine. *Energy Convers. Manage.* 37: 501-504.

Skeiker, K. 2006. Correlation of Global Solar Radiation with Common Geographical and Meteorological Parameters for Damascus Province, Syria. *Energy Conversion and Management.* **47**: 331-345.

Soltani, A., Robertson, M.J., Rahemi-Karizaki, A., Poorreze, J. and Zarei, H. 2006. Modeling Biomass Accumulation and Partitioning in Chickpea (*cicerarietinum*L.). *J. Agron. Crop Sci.* 192: 379-389.

Stanhill, G. and Cohen, S. 2001. Global Dimming: A Review of the Evidence for a Widespread and Significant Reduction in Global Radiation with Discussion of Its Probable Causes and Possible Agricultural Consequences. *Agric. For. Meteorol.***107:** 255-278.

Stansel, J.W. 1975. Effective Utilization of Sunlight. Texas Agricultural Experiment Station in Co-operation with the U. S. Department of Agriculture. Six Decades of Rice Research in Texas. *Res. Monogr.* 4: 43-50.

Stewart, D.W., Costa, C., Dwyer, L.M., Smith, D.L., Hamilton, R.I. and Ma, B.L. 2003. Canopy Structure, Light Interception and Photosynthesis in Maize. *Agron. J.* **95**: 1465-1474.

Stuttle, G.W., Yorio, N.C. and Wheeler, R.M. 1996. Interacting Effects of Photoperiod and Photosynthetic Photon Flux on Net Carbon Assimilation and Starch Accumulation in Potato Leaves. *Journal of the American Society of Horticultural Science.* 121: 264-268.

Teixeira, E.I., Moot, D.J. and Brown, H.E. 2008. Defoliation Frequency and Season Affected Radiation use Efficiency and Dry Matter Partitioning to Roots of Lucerne (*M. sativa* L.) Crops. *European J. Agron.* 28: 103-111.

Teke, A. and BaakYildirim, H. 2014. Estimating the Monthly Global Solar Radiation for Eastern Mediterranean. *Journal of Energy Conversion and Management.*

Temmerman, L.D., Wolf, J., Colls, J., Bindi, M., Fangmeier, A., Finnan, J., Ojanpera, K. and Pleijel, H. 2002. Effect of Climatic Conditions on Tuber Yield (Solanum tuberosum L.) in the European 'CHIP' Experiments. *Eur. J. Agron.* 17: 243-255.

Tsubo, M. and Walker, S. 2002. A Model of Radiation Interception and use by A Maize-Bean Intercrop Canopy. *Agric. For. Meteorol.***110**: 203– 215.

Van der Werf, A. 1996. Growth Analysis and Photoassimilate Portioning. In: Photoassimilate Distribution in Plants and Crops: (Eds.): E. Zamski, A. Schaffer, Source-Sink Relationship. Marcel Dekker Inc., New York, pp. 1-20.

Van der Zaag, D.E. and Doornbos, J.H. 1987. An Attempt to Explain Differences in the Yielding Ability of Potato Cultivars Based on Differences in Cumulative Eight Interception, Utilization Efficiency of Foliage and Harvest Index. *Potato Res*. 30: 551–568.

Winslow, J.C. 2001. A Globally Applicable Model of Daily Solar Irradiance Estimated from Air Temperature and Precipitation Data, Ecological Modelling.

Xiao, X., Zhang, Q. and Braswell, B. (2004). Modeling Gross Primary Production of Temperate Deciduous Broadleaf Forest using Satellite Images and Climate Data. *Remote Sens Environment*, 91: 256–270

Yoshida, S. 1981. Fundamentals of Rice Crop Science. Los Banos (Philippines): International Rice Research Institute. p. 269.

Yoshida, S. and Parao, F.T. 1976. Climatic Influence on Yield and Yield Components of Lowland Rice in the Tropics. In Climate and Rice International Rice Research Institute, Los Banos, Laguna. Philippines, pp. 471-494.

Zhang, X., Zhang, Y. and Zhoub, Y. 2000. Measuring and Modeling Photosynthetically Active Radiation in Tibet Plateau during April–October. *Agric. For. Meteorol*. 102: 207–212.

Agriculture Crops and Food Security
Edited by: Dr. Pawan Kumar 'Bharti' and Alka Chauhan
ISBN: 978-93-5056-881-1
Edition: 2017
Published by: Discovery Publishing House Pvt. Ltd., New Delhi (India)

3

Value Added Processing of Potato

[1]Sukhpreet Kaur, [1]Poonam Aggarwal

INTRODUCTION

Potato (*Solanumtuberosum L.*) popularly known as "The king of vegetables" has emerged as fourth most important food crop in the world after rice, wheat and maize. Potato contains carbohydrates, proteins, minerals, dietary fiber and negligible amount of fat. Apart from being a significant source of starch, potatoes are considered as a potential antioxidant source in human nutrition. Polyphenols, ascorbic acid and carotenoids are the major bioactive compounds known in potato for their antioxidant, anti-inflammatory and antimicrobial properties. Research has shown that their consumption can prevent many of the chronic diseases associated with cancer, inflammation, atherosclerosis and ageing caused by free radicals and oxygen. So potato can be utilized for production of functional foods. Potato production has significantly increased in recent years in many developing countries, particularly India, making it to the position of second largest potato producing country in the world. Despite the increasing production, bulk of the crop incurs heavy post harvest losses due to its perishable nature and inadequate storage facilities in our country. Thus, processing of potatoes has considerable potential to reduce post-harvest losses and to generate income through the manufacture of value-added food products.This chapter provides an overview of potato production, composition including physicochemical and bioactive attributes and processing: quality requirements, storage methods and value addition processing of potato.

POTATO PRODUCTION AND DISTRIBUTION

Potato is widely grown and is the world's single most important non cereal crop with an important role in food security. It is the third most important food crop in the world after wheat and rice in terms of human consumption. The total world potato production is estimated at 385.30 million tons in 2014 (FAO STAT 2015). The world potato sector is undergoing major changes. Earlier,

[1] Department of Food Science and Technology, Punjab Agricultural University, Ludhiana-141004, Punjab, India.

most potatoes were grown and consumed in Europe, North America and other countries. Since then, potato production and demand has significantly increased in recent years in many countries, particularly Asia where it has become more important as a food and industrial crop. According to FAO reports, for the first time in the year 2005, the developing world's potato production exceeded that of the devolved world. China is now the largest potato producer with a production of approximately 96 million tons followed by India and Russian Federation (FAO STAT 2015).

Over the past decade, the productivity of potato in India has registered a noticeable increase (Table 3.1). India produced 45.34 million tons of potato in the year 2013-14 (FAO STAT 2015), making it to the position of world's second largest potato producing country in the world after China. Indo Gangetic plains, where the crop is harvested during February-march, contribute to about 90% of the total potato production in India (Marwaha *et al.* 2004). The major potato producing states include Uttar Pradesh, Gujarat, West Bengal, Bihar and Punjab (Saxena and Mathur 2013). Punjab is the hub of seed potato of India with a production of 26 lakh metric tons in the year 2012-13 (Kaur and Aggarwal 2014a).

Table 3.1: Year Wise Production of Potato in India

Year	Production (million tons)
2000-01	24.71
2001-02	22.49
2002-03	24.45
2003-04	23.16
2004-05	27.92
2005-06	28.78
2006-07	29.17
2007-08	28.59
2008-09	34.65
2009-10	34.39
2010-11	36.57
2011-12	42.34
2012-13	41.48
2013-14	45.34

Source: (FAO STAT 2015)

Status of Potato Processing

Processing is a fast growing sector in potato world economy. In USA and European countries, processing industry absorbs about 55-60% of annual potato production. However, in India, processing of potatoes constitutes only about 6% of total annual production (Marwaha *et al.* 2010). The growth of potato processing industry in India is hampered mainly due inadequate storage facilities and non-availability of suitable potato varieties throughout the year. All potatoes varieties grown in the country are not suitable for processing. The suitability of a variety for a particular process depends upon its physic-chemical composition such as the dry matter content and reducing sugars (Bons and Kaur 2009). Based on this fact, potato varieties are divided into two categories viz. table and processing purpose. Table varieties are the commonly grown potato varieties which are used for table purpose only. Due to their low dry matter content and high reducing sugars, these are rendered unfit for processing. Whereas commercial potato varieties are cultivated for processing purpose. These varieties have high dry matter content and low reducing sugar content. High dry matter and low reducing sugars are required for obtaining higher recoveries and a desirable color in the finished potato products.

KufriJyoti, KufriPukhraj, KufriBadshah and KufriLauvkar are the main table potato varieties for the Indo-Gangetic plains. Kufri Chipsana-1, developed and released by Central Potato Research Institute, CPRI remains the most desirable Indian potato variety for processing (Pandey *et al.* 2009). Among the exotic varieties, Atlantic, Lady rosette, Shepody, Kennebec and Santana are the most suitable varieties for diverse forms of processing. Exotic varieties having desirable processing quality traits are nowadays successfully grown in India. Some of the important Indian and exotic potato varieties suitable for different products are listed in Table 3.2.

Table 3.2: Indian and Exotic Potato Varieties for Different Processed Products

Category	Processed product
Indian varieties (Processing purpose)	
Kufri Chipsona-1	Potato chips, flakes, French fries, potato specialty products
KufriFrysona	French fries
KufriChandramukhi	Potato chips, flakes and potato specialty products
Indian varieties (Table Purpose)	
KufriJyoti	-
KufriPukhraj	-
KufriBadshah	-
KufriLauvkar	-
KufriPushkar	-
Exotic varieties (Processing purpose)	
Kennebec	French fries
Innovator	French fries
Santana	French fries
Shepody	French fries
Kennebec	French fries
Lady Rosette	Potato chips, flakes, potato specialty products

With increasing potato production throughout the country and inappropriate storage facilities of potatoes, there exist greater proportions of wastage. Under such circumstances, the post harvest processing of the perishable raw potato tubers into value added products helps to extend the storage life, solve the problem of storage and increase the supply of potatoes in off seasons (Marwaha 1997; Misra and Kulshrestha 2003).

COMPOSITION OF POTATO

Potato is a highly nutritive vegetable and has variousphysico-chemical and bioactive characters. Physico-chemical attributes of potatoinclude moisture, total solids, sugars, starch, protein, fiber, vitamins and minerals whereas bioactive characters include ascorbic acid content, total phenolic content and antioxidant activity.

Physico-chemical Composition

Potato is a nutritive vegetable, containing high amount of carbohydrates, vitamins, minerals, dietary fiber and good quality protein (Kaur *et al.* 2012). Potato protein content has an excellent biological value of 90-100 (Camire *et al.* 2009). In addition, potato has negligible fat and is a good source of several B vitamins and potassium. Vitamin C content of potato is low but potato can be considered as a significant source of this vitamin due to its high consumption levels (Ezekiel *et al.* 2013). Freshly harvested potatoes contain approximately 80% water and 20% dry matter. Starch accounts for 60-80% of the total dry matter content (Table 3.3).

Table 3.3: Composition of Potato (g/100g)

Constituent	Quantity
Dry Matter	23.70
Starch	17.50
Reducing Sugars	0.30
Crude fibre	0.71
Total Nitrogen	0.32
Crude protein (Total nitrogen × 6.25)	2.00
Lipids	0.12
Ash	1.10
Organic acids	0.60
Ascorbic acid (mg)	15.0-25.0
Phenolic compounds (mg)	30.0

Source: Lisinska and Leszcynski (1989)

A wide varietal variation has been observed among proximate composition of different potato cultivars (Khan *et al.* 1997; Marwaha 1997; Marwaha *et al.* 2009). Kaur and Aggarwal (2014b) evaluated fourteen potato cultivars including 11 Indian cultivars and 3 exotic cultivars for processing quality characteristics including specific gravity, dry matter, reducing sugars, starch, protein and ash content. All the physic-chemical attributes were affected by cultivars. Among the Indian cultivars, Kufri Chipsona-1 and among the exotic cultivars, FC-3, Lady rosette and Atlantic were rated as the best varieties for processing into chips since these contained highest amount of specific gravity, dry matter content and lowest amount of reducing sugars. On the other hand, commonly grown cultivated varieties such as KufiPukhraj, KufriBadshah and Kufri Jyoti were considered unfit for processing (Table 3.4).

Many researchers have established a positive correlation between tuber dry matter content and specific gravity (Marwaha *et al.* 2010, Abbas *et al.* 2011; Ganga *et al.* 2013; Kaur and Aggarwal 2014).

Table 3.4: Processing and Nutritional Quality Attributes of Different Potato Cultivars

S.No.	Cultivar	Specific gravity	Dry matter (%)	Reducing sugars(%)	Total sugars (%)	Starch (%)	Protein (%)	Ash (%)
1	Kufri Chipsona-1	1.096	24.31	0.06	0.12	18.50	5.20	1.12
2	Kufri Chandramukhi	1.095	24.30	0.18	0.30	18.10	4.50	2.09
3	Kufri Pukhraj	1.052	15.31	0.54	0.77	12.00	3.53	1.73
4	Kufri Chipsona-3	1.097	22.30	0.18	0.32	15.20	2.80	0.70
5	Kufri Badshah	1.066	18.30	0.38	0.46	13.20	1.40	0.98
6	1533	1.082	21.20	0.20	0.30	13.90	2.85	1.01
7	Kufri Lauvkar	1.080	21.10	0.22	0.32	14.20	2.00	0.98
8	KufriJyoti	1.066	18.20	0.38	0.41	12.80	1.82	0.95
9	Super	1.045	14.70	0.28	0.43	11.81	1.82	1.12
10	Kufri Khyati	1.042	14.30	0.30	0.50	12.80	1.61	1.08
11	Kufri Pushkar	1.040	14.06	0.30	0.40	12.31	1.34	0.98
12	FC-3	1.085	21.93	0.08	0.16	14.50	2.80	0.89
13	Atlantic	1.094	23.90	0.07	0.12	15.90	2.90	1.12
14	Lady Rosette	1.095	24.00	0.06	0.14	16.00	1.81	0.70

Source: Kaur and Aggarwal (2014b)

Bioactive (phytochemical) Composition

Besides being a rich source of energy (starch), potato also contain some health promoting compounds such as phenolic acids, ascorbic acid and carotenoids (Ezekiel *et al.* 2013). These compounds are commonly described as antioxidants (Gumul *et al.* 2011). These phytochemicals are known for their antioxidant, anti-inflammatory and antimicrobial properties (Lachman and Hamouz 2005). The scavenging activity of these compounds is mainly due to their redox properties, which allow them to act as reducing agents, hydrogen donors, and singlet oxygen quenchers (Babbar *et al.* 2011). Research has shown that their consumption can prevent many of the chronic diseases associated with cancer, atherosclerosis and ageing caused by free radicals and oxygen (Brown 2005; Han *et al.* 2007; Kasper *et al.* 2013). Potatoes are a major contributor to dietary phytochemical concentrations due to consumption levels. The antioxidant activity of potatoes has been identified to be higher than other vegetables, including onion, carrot and bell pepper (Al-Saikhan *et al.* 1995).

The bioactive composition among different potato cultivars varies depending upon the variety, growing location and method of extraction. The antioxidant activity of extracts from 36 vegetables including potato was evaluated by using a model system consisting of β-carotene and linoleic acid by Kaur and Kapoor (2002). The total phenolics of the extracts were determined spectrophotometrically according to the Folin-Ciocalteu procedure. The authors placed potato in the medium category containing phenolic content between 100 and 200 mg catechol/100 g. The anti-oxidant activity of potato expressed as per percent inhibition of oxidation ranged 62.3% in ethanol extract and 62.5% in water extract, respectively. Anti-oxidant activity correlated significantly and positively with total phenolics ($r^2 = 0.6578$, $P < 0.05$).

The antioxidant activity (AA) and total phenolic content (TPC) of native Chilean potatoes were determined by Ah-Hen *et al.* 2012. Twelve potato landrace clones collected from established cultivations on Chiloe Island and Valdivia were selected. TPC and AA were compared with two commercial varieties, Shepody and Desirée. TPC was determined by the Folin-Ciocalteu method and β-carotene bleaching was used to compare AA. The TPC varied in the peeled potato samples from 191 to 1864 mg 100 g-1 DM meanwhile these parameters varied from 345 to 2852 mg 100 g-1 DM in unpeeled samples. Antioxidant activity was higher in unpeeled potatoes, and was the highest in the unpeeled NG-6 or 'Bruja' native potato. The commercial var.Shepody showed pro-oxidant activity and had a relatively lower TPC. Results also indicated a higher concentration of total phenolics in the periderm of the colored native Chilean potatoes. Purple or red fleshed local potato cultivar from four districts of Manipur were evaluated for their total phenolic, protein, carbohydrate and lipid contents (Lokendrajit *et al.* 2013). The total phenolic content in the four districts was found to be very high i.e. 256-270 mg per 100g of the dry weight. Significant differences were found between the purple or red fleshed and other varieties. There was not much variation in the fat content in the local cultivar and other varieties whereas the protein content was more than the average of the other genotype. The protein content in the four districts ranged between 8.12-8.9%.

Kaur and Aggarwal (2014c) studied the bioactive composition (ascorbic acid, total phenolic content and antioxidant activities) of Indian potato cultivars. Kufri Pukhraj was considered the best cultivar for direct consumption since it contained highest amount of ascorbic acid (19.42 mg/100g), total phenolic content (68.20 mg/100g) and DPPH radical scavenging activity (67.3%). In contrast, Kufri Chipsona-1 most commonly used processing cultivar displayed lowest amount of total phenolics (31.30 mgGAE/100g) and total antioxidant activity (28.80%). The authors also suggested a high degree correlation between total antioxidant activity and phenolic content indicating that these bioactive compounds contribute to the total antioxidant activity of potato. Total antioxidant activity of different Indian potato cultivars is shown in Fig. 3.1.

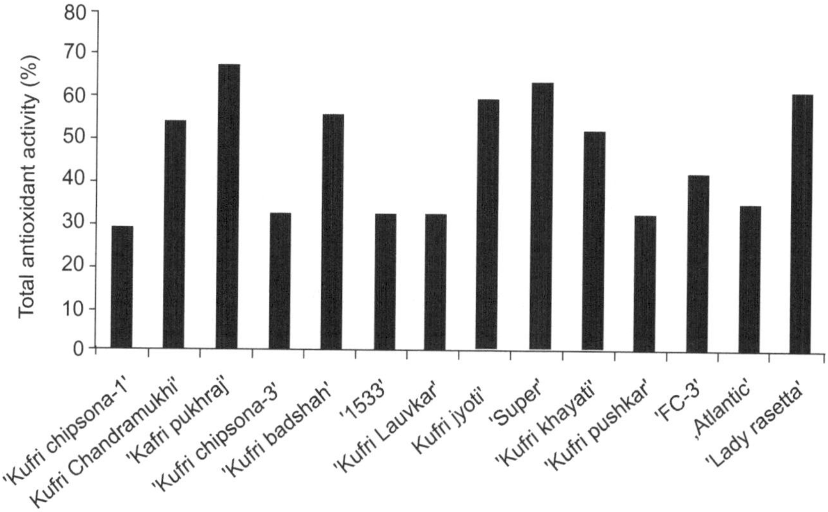

Fig. 3.1: Total Antioxidant activity of different potato cultivars (Kaur and Aggarwal 2014c)

DESIRABLE QUALITY REQUIREMENTS FOR PROCESSING

For processing quality, potatoes must possess certain minimum morphological and biochemical quality attributes.

Morphological Attributes

Morphological attributes include length, shape and depth of eyes. Different length specifications are required for different potato products. For example, oblong to long tubers are required for French fries whereas round medium sized tubers are required for chips. For canning, small tubers of round to oval shape are preferred. For potato flakes and potato specialty products, the requirement of shape is not very strict. Potato tubers with shallow eyes are preferred for most of the processed products as these results in lower peeling losses. In order to achieve higher yields, peeling loss should not be more than 7%.

Biochemical Characteristics

Biochemical parameters desirable to attain quality product include dry matter and reducing sugars content. The potato processing industry is primarily concerned with the quality (color) and yield of processed products.

Reducing sugars

The color of the fried products is the most important visual quality criterion, which is influenced by quantities of reducing sugars (mainly glucose) in tubers because they induce a non enzymatic Millard reaction with free amino acids, forming unacceptable brown-to black-pigmented products (Matsuura-Endo *et al.*, 2006; Kaur *et al.*, 2012). For processing, reducing sugars up to 0.15% fresh weight is considered acceptable (Marwaha *et al.*, 2010). Besides contributing to color and flavor, Millard reaction is suggested as the major mechanism of Acrylamide (a suspected human carcinogen)formation in fried potato products, most notably potato chips and French fries (Amrein *et al.*, 2003; Marwaha *et al.*, 2010). The crucial precursors of this reaction for fried potatoes are glucose, fructose and amino acids. These precursors occur naturally in potatoes; the levels differ between varieties. Recently, much attention has been given on diminishing or eliminating acrylamide precursors to reduce acrylamide and oil content in fried potato products such as raw material (e.g. selection of proper cultivars and storage conditions), pre-treatments (e.g. soaking, blanching, use of organic acids), process optimization (e.g. temperature profile, frying time, moisture profile in product) and post frying operations. Reducing acrylamide levels while maintaining product quality (flavor, color, texture, safety, etc.) in commercial fried potato production is a crucial challenge for the food industry.

Dry matter content

A potato is made up of 2 main components: water and solids. Water represents approximately 80% of a potato's weight and solids make up the remaining 20%. Potato solids vary in potatoes from 17% to 25%, but potato processing industry typically uses potato varieties with 19-22% solids. Yield is greatly affected by the total solid content. High dry matter content is positively correlated with mealiness, crispness and higher yield (Abbas *et al.* 2011) and negatively correlated with oil uptake by fried potato products (Ablong *et al.* 2009; Kaur *et al.* 2016). For estimation of dry matter content, the industry usually determines the specific gravity of potatoes because both specific gravity and tuber solids are found to be correlated. Kaur and Aggarwal (2014b) established a strong correlation between both specific gravity and tuber solids. Potato cultivars having high specific gravity displayed higher total solids while low dry matter was observed in cultivars with low specific gravity (Table 3.4). Potato tuber quality required for different processed products is given in Table 3.5.

Table 3.5: Quality Requirements of Potato for Different Processed Products

Quality characteristics	Chips	French fries	Flakes	Specialty products
Morphological				
Characteristics				
Shape	Round	Oblong	Round to oval	No particular shape desired
Length(mm)	50-70	>50	>35	>35
Eyes	Shallow	Shallow	Shallow	Shallow
Bio-chemical				
Characteristics				
Specific gravity	>1.075	>1.075	>1.075	>1.070
Total Solids	>19	>19	>19	18.5
Reducing sugars(%)	0.05	<0.15	<0.10	<0.25
Enzymatic discoloration	Nil	Nil	Nil	Nil
After cooking darkening	Nil	Nil	Nil	Nil

POTATO STORAGE METHODS

Most of the potato crop of the country is harvested during winters i.e. January-February from the Indo-Gangetic plains, comprising the states of Punjab, Haryana, UP, Bihar and West Bengal, where the harvest is followed by sudden rise in temperatures. Under these conditions, a perishable commodity like potato cannot be stored without refrigeration. About 15% of the total produce is used for table consumption within 2 to 3 months of the harvest and the remaining part is stored for use during rest of the year or for seed purpose. In India, only 30% of potato can be stored in cold storages due to capacity limitations and remaining quantity is stored under ambient conditions (Joshi and Nath 2002). Good storage should maintain tubers in their marketable conditions by preventing accumulation of sugars, spoilage by pathogens (rotting) and by preventing sprout growth.

Storage at 2-4°C

Low-temperature storage at 2-4°C leads to increased reducing sugars (glucose and fructose) due to conversion of starch into sucrose by sucrose synthetase and sucrose phosphate synthetase (Pressey 1970). Sucrose is hydrolyzed into glucose and fructose by enzyme invertase due to decreased activity of invertase inhibitor at low temperature (Shekhar *et al.* 1979). These potatoes are unfit for processing as high level of reducing sugars participates in Millard reaction and causes browning after frying (Fig. 3.2). Marketing of these potatoes again is a problem due to their poor keeping quality once they are removed from the cold store. So potatoes for processing purpose are stored at 10±1°C. Low temperature storage is considered ideal for seed potatoes to maintain them in the right physiological age till the next planting season.

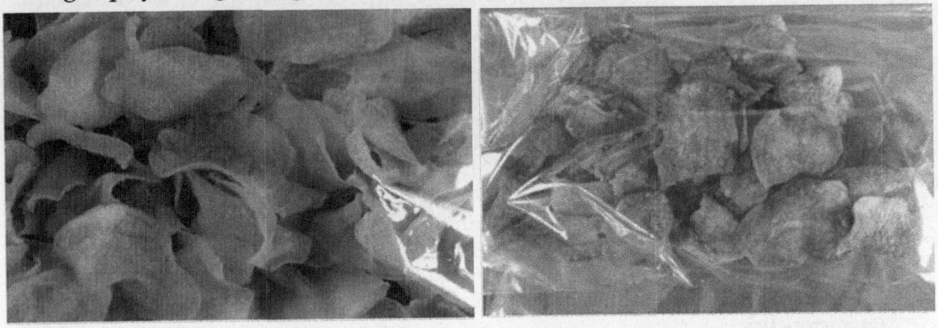

Fig. 3.2: Potato chips prepared from cultivar Kufri Chipsona-1 stored at 10±1°C and 2°C

Storage at 10 ± 1°C

High temperature storage, although suitable for processing, but has its own limitations as it causes shrinkages, rottage and sprouting. Sprouting is a major cause of losses in stored potatoes. Not only does it reduce the number of marketable potatoes but intense evaporation of water from sprout surface also reduce the weight of remaining tuber (Singh *et al.* 2009). Therefore, sprout suppressant is used to check sprout growth. Isoprophyl-N-3-chlorophenyl carbamate (CIPC) has been commonly used as a treatment agent on potatoes at 10±1°C in cold storage. The first dose of CIPC @ 40 ml per ton is applied as fog in cold store with a fogging machine (Fig. 3.3) at the initiation of sprouting (chitting). Potatoes are again given 2nd treatment of CIPC @ 40 ml per ton after 60 days of the first fogging (Mahajan *et al.* 2008). The use of CIPC could also help save energy because temperatures during storage can be higher.

Fig. 3.3: CIPC fogging in cold storage

Processed Potato Products

Kaur *et al.* 2012 evaluated the effects of temperature on storage stability and processing quality of CIPC treated potato cultivars Kufri Chipsona-1 and Kufri Pukhraj stored at 2 or 11°C and approximately 90% relative humidity (RH). Postharvest application of CIPC (40 mL·Mt^{-1} twice) was effective in checking sprouting and maintaining low reducing sugar levels in 'Kufri Chipsona-1' tubers stored at 11°C, approximately 90% RH up to 6 months. French fries and chips prepared from 'Kufri Chipsona-1' had lower moisture content, oil uptake and higher yield than from 'Kufri Pukhraj'. French fries and chips prepared from potatoes stored at 2°C had higher moisture content and oil uptake; those from potatoes stored at 11°C had lower values. 'Kufri Chipsona-1' was best for processing into French fries and chips and potato products were found to be highly acceptable for up to 6 months of storage.

PROCESSING OF POTATO INTO VALUE ADDED PRODUCTS

The processed potato products can be categorized as:

- Commercial potato products
  - ➢ Potato chips
  - ➢ Frozen French fries and other frozen products
  - ➢ Potato Flakes
- Indigenous potato products
- *Dehydrated products*
  - ➢ Potato flour
  - ➢ *Aloowari*
  - ➢ *Aloopapad*
  - ➢ Dehydrated chips
- Fried Potato Products
  - ➢ *Aloobhujia*
  - ➢ *Aloochakli*
- Dehydrated Potato premix
- Canned potato products
  - ➢ Potato cubes
  - ➢ Curried potato

COMMERCIAL POTATO PRODUCTS

Potato processing industry mainly comprises of four segments; potato chips, French fries, potato flakes and same dehydrated and frozen snacks. Potato chips are the most common and popular processed product and at present constitute 85% of salty snack business and account for over 60% of the total potato processing capacity of the industry (Marwaha *et al.* 2010; Pandey *et al.* 2009). The quantity of French fries consumed is much less compared to potato chips but with the opening of fast food restaurants, consumption of French fries is increasing in India and its demand is expected to grow in near future. For French fries, Nearly 60-70% of total world output is shared among US, Canada and Netherland. Lack of suitable potato varieties and refrigerated storage/transport are factors responsible for lower popularity of frozen fries in India, despite their nutritional/dietary advantages over chips.

Potato flakes are the most popular form of dehydrated potato products. Pressing cooked potato mash onto a steam-heated drum, which dries the mash and forms a sheet that can be ground to the required consistency, makes dehydrated potato flakes. In Indian market, potato flakes remains the most important raw material for snack industry mainly for making aloobhujia. Its use in household level is low due to lack of awareness. In perfect contrast to the prevalent trend in India, the major consumer of potato flakes worldwide are domestic and household consumers. Their Popularity is due to their convenience, acceptable quality retaining the original flavor of potato, and ease of reconstitution. The main uses of potato flakes are; 1. As main ingredient in mashed potatoes and fabricated chips, 2. As a thickener in sauces and gravies, 3. As an raw ingredient in making savory snacks, 4. As an ingredient for formed products such as burger, alootikki, patties.

Potato processing industry in India is on the threshold of rapid growth. Therefore, processing is essential for the expansion of potato industry in India. Some important processed potato products are discussed below:

Potato chips

The potatoes are washed and then cut into slices of $\frac{1}{16th}-\frac{1}{18th}$ of an inch thickness using a rotary hand slicer. The slices so obtained are immediately

Washing

↓

Peeling

↓

Slicing

(slice thickness = $\frac{1}{16th}$ to $\frac{1}{18th}$ of an inch)

↓

Surface drying

↓

Frying

(180°C for ≤ 2 min)

↓

Packaging

Fig. 3.4: Flow diagram for preparation of potato chips

dipped in plain water to prevent enzymatic darkening. The surface moisture of slices is removed with the help of muslin cloth and then fried in refined oil in a fryer. Chips are fried at a high temperature (180°C) for 2 min (Kaur and Aggarwal 2014a). The fried chips are then drained and taken out (Fig. 3.4).

French fries

The potatoes are washed and then peeled and trimmed to remove defective portions. Peeled potatoes are cut into 10 mm thick sticks. The sticks are blanched

Washing

↓

Steam peeling

↓

Slicing

(Thickness of sticks = 10 mm)

↓

1st Blanching

(82°C/3 min)

↓

2nd Blanching

(70°C/8 min)

↓

Belt drying

(70°C/8 min)

↓

Par-frying

(180°C/40 sec)

↓

Removal of excess oil by shaking

↓

Cooling

↓

Freezing

↓

Packaging

↓

Final Frying

(180°C/5 min)

Fig. 3.5: Flow diagram for preparation of French fries

for 3 min at 82°C in water to inactivate the enzymes and then at 70°C for 8 min for removal of some of the sugars in the surface layers of the sticks, resulting in French fries of uniform color (Kaur *et al.* 2012). The sticks are then drained free of water. Blanched sticks are passed in a belt dryer at 50°C for about 8-9mins to remove as much as surface moisture of sticks. The dried potato sticks are then par-fried in refined oil for 40 sec at 180°C. Fried sticks are then pre-cooled to 2-4°C and then frozen at –18°C. Final frying is done at 180°C for 5 min (Fig. 3.5).

Potato flakes

Potato after washing, are steamed peeled for few seconds. Peeled potatoes are cut into 10 mm thick slices with a mechanical cutter. Potato slices are blanched in a screw blancher at 65-67°C for 15-20 min. Blanching results in inactivation of enzymes and gelatinizes the starch. Blanched slices are then cooled. Cooling

Washing

↓

Steam Peeling

↓

Slicing
(Thickness of sticks = 10 mm)

↓

Blanching
(82°C/10 min)

↓

Cooling
(10°C/20 min)

↓

Cooking
(Steam at 100°C/25-35 min)

↓

Mashing
(180°C/40 sec)

↓

Drum drying

↓

Flaking

↓

Packaging

Fig. 3.6: Flow diagram for preparation of Potato flakes

is required to create retrogradation, which refers to potato cells becoming firm again after the initial blanching stage. Retrogradation is required to prevent cells from rupturing during cooking and drying (Lamberti *et al.* 2004). Ruptured cells result in a poor sheet of potato flake, as well as undesired sticky textures when the product is reconstitutedby the end-user. After cooling, product is fed to a steam heated belt cooker at 98-99°C for 25-30 min. Immediately following cooking, mashing of the cooked potato is done with a ricer mixer to allow a good mixture of additive solutions. Additives, which improve texture and to extend the shelf life, are added to the mash before the drying process. Typical additives are a dilute solution of sodium meta bisulfite (to slow non-enzymatic browning), and an emulsion of monoglyceride emulsifier (containing antioxidants and various chelating agents). The mash is then fed through a series rollers, which transfer a thin layer of mash on to a steam heated drum. The sheet of driedpotato flake is removed from the drum at the rear of the machine by a blade that runs the full length of the drum. The dried potato film is broken into small pieces in a pre-breaker before packaging (Fig. 3.6).

INDIGENOUS POTATO PRODUCTS

India is second largest producer of potato but due to inadequacies in its post harvest handling, storage and non-availability of suitable varieties, this resourceful crop suffers heavy losses. Therefore, it is essential that potato consumption be increased to sustain the increase in production. The high price of processed potato products viz. chips and French fries in comparison to cereal-based processed products is an important factor limiting their consumption by a majority of Indian population with low-income levels (Pandey *et al.* 2005). To make processed products available to a large section of the population at an affordable price, there is a need to develop indigenous technologies for the production of inexpensive potato products such as which are easy to prepare and can be produced at a cottage industry level. Indigenous potato products include traditional potato products such as dehydrated (papad, wari, chips), fried (bhujia, chakli) and some frozen potato snacks, developed using low cost technologies. These products are easy to prepare and can be scaled up for commercial ventures by unemployed rural youths and village women.

Dehydrated Products

Potato is one of the commonly used vegetables and is staple diet for a large number of people in the world but main disadvantage of the crop is that it is seasonal and bulky production of crop has short life (Misra and Kulshrestha 2003). Lack of sufficient storage facilities result in crop deterioration as post harvest time advances. Dehydration of bumper perishable crop seems to be convenient alternative for long term storage and could serve as means to ensure availability of potatoes in different forms throughout the year. Potato can be processed into various indigenous dehydrated products such as wari, papad, flour and chips which have promising future due to their long shelf life and diverse uses. Dehydrated productsare easy to prepare, require no costly machinery for manufacture and have a longer shelf life.

Potato flour

Potato is a perishable commodity and fresh potatoes are available only for 2-3 months in a year and have to be stored for use in off-season. Potatoes can be processed into dehydrated flour, which is nutritive, more stable and less bulky than fresh potato tubers. Potato flour can be prepared when potatoes are cheap and used in the off season when potato prices are high. Average compostion of potato flour is presented in Table 3.6.

Table 3.6: Composition of potato flour (g /100 g)

Constituent	Quantity
Carbohydrates	79.9
Protein	8.0
Fat	0.10
Moisture	8.0
Calcium (mg)	33.0
Iron (mg)	17.0
Ascorbic acid (mg)	19.0
Thiamin (mg)	0.4.0
Riboflavin (mg)	0.10
Niacin (mg)	3.40

Source: Willard and Hix (1987)

For preparation of potato flour, potatoes are washed, peeled and cut into 2-3 mm thick slices with a rotary hand slicer. The cut potato slices are immersed in water to prevent enzymatic browning. The slices are cooked in boiling water containing 0.25% potassium metabisulphite for 10 minutes (Marwahaand Sandhu 2003). Boiled potato slices are cooled and dried overnight in a hot air cabinet drier (40-50°C) by spreading as a thin film. Dried slices are ground in electric grinder and then powdered in cyclotec mill to fine powder (Kaur and Aggarwal 2015a). Potato flour is packed in polythene bags, kept in air tight container and stored at room temperature till further use (Fig. 3.7).

Raw potato tubers

↓

Peeling

↓

Slicing with rotary hand slicer (2-3 mm thick slices)

↓

Blanching ofpotato slices in 0.25% potassium metabisulphite solution to inhibit enzymatic and non-enzymatic browning

(100°C/6 minutes)

↓

Cooling

↓

Loading in trays

↓

Drying in hot air cabinet drier (50°C/5 hours)

↓

Coarse grinding

↓

Fine grinding in cyclotec mill (0.5 mm mesh size)

↓

Potato flour

↓

Packaging

Fig. 3.7: Flow chart for the preparation of potato flour

Effect of storage on the nutritional value of potato flour prepared from Indian and exotic cultivars stored for six months at room and refrigerated temperatures was studied by Marwaha and Sandhu (2003) and Misra and Kulshrestha (2003a). The authors concluded that potato flour could be stored safely for six months, both at room and refrigerated temperatures, without adversely affecting most nutritional components.

Potato flour prepared from three potato varieties were stored for 6 months at room temperature and refrigerated temperature and subjected to microbial analysis at 0, 3 and 6 month storage, to evaluate its microbial safety. The microbial counts of potato flours stored up to 6 months under room and refrigerated temperature showed an increasing trend in total bacterial count with increase in storage time irrespective of cultivars and storage methods, but the increase was less than the ISI specifications for wheat flour. No coli forms could be detected in any of the potato flours during the 6 months of storage (Misra and Kulshrestha 2002).

Studies on seven potato cultivars (K.Chipsona-1, K.Chipsona-2, K. Chandramukhi, K. Badshah, K. Jyoti, K. Giriraj and K. Jawahar) revealed that the tubers of potato cultivars K. Chipsona-2, K. Chipsona-1, K. Chandramukhi had low content of reducing sugars and high content of dry matter, proteins and specific gravity were found more suitable for processing into flour with high yields. The potato flour of these cultivars resulted in lower non-enzymatic browning with better quality retention during storage period of 6 months (Raj *et al.* 2011).

Dehydrated Potato flour is highly versatile and inexpensive raw material that can be incorporated as an ingredient in various value added products such as soup mixes, bakery products, extruded or fabricated snacks (Singh *et al.* 2005, Raj *et al.* 2011). Potato flour can also be used as a thicker and color or flavor enhancer (Yadav *et al.* 2006).

Different products have been prepared by incorporating potato flour with other flours using different methods of cooking such as baking, roasting, steaming, boiling and deep fat frying (Gahlawat and Sehgal 1998). Chandra Shekhra and Shurpalekar (1984) and Misra and Kulshrestha (2003b) substituted wheat flour with potato flour in the preparation of biscuits. Biscuits prepared from potato flour were rated higher in terms of mouthfeel, color and texture. The effects of incorporating potato flour at different levels to wheat flour on textural properties of chapapti was studied (Singh *et al.* 2005). Addition of potato flour improved the extensibility, increased water absorption and lowered the peak force and energy to rupture chapatti.

Nanda and Khanna (1988) reported that potato flour incorporated food products such as dalia, tomato soup, vegetable stew, khichri, sev, parotha and upma were rated as very good and there occurred no deterioration in the appearance, color or taste of the product due to addition of potato flour. Kulkarni *et al.*(1997) suggested the incorporation of potato flour in various processed food products like gulabjamun and paranthas.

Recently Lakra and Sehgal (2011) prepared five products viz. sevian, cutlet, kofta, doughnuts and vadi incorporating potato flour, defatted soy flour and corn flour. Frying and fermentation were the major processing techniques employed for the development of these products. Significant differences in protein, ash and fat contents of all the products were observed. Processed products had significantly higher mineral availability and lower content of anti nutrients compared to raw products.

Aloo wari

Wari is a partially fermented indigenous traditional savory food. It is being prepared on cottage or home scale. For preparation of 'Aloo wari', split black gram (450 g) is washed thoroughly and soaked in about 550 ml of water overnight. The drained pulses are then ground in a grinder with small addition of water, till it became a paste. The paste is then whisked continuously with hand till it became light and fluffy due to incorporation of air. To the wet pulse paste, required amount of freshly prepared potato mash is added. The resultant paste is then mixed thoroughly with flavorings. The resultant fluffy batter is taken in hand and divided into small balls weighing 50-60 g. The prepared balls are spread on stainless steel trays smeared with oil, maintaining a distance of 1-2 inches between balls. The trays are then loaded in hot air cabinet drier and dried at a temperature of 60 5°C for 16 hours (Fig. 3.8).

Waris are used as an adjunct in curries. For preparation, the prepared waris areshallow-fried at 150°C for 30 sec and then cooked in a vegetable curry preparation using onion, garlic and tomato paste along with various spices (cumin, red pepper, coriander powder, salt). Shallow fried wari pieces are added to the above cooked paste along with 250 ml of water and are pressure cooked for 3 min.

Fresh potato mash/ potato flour

↓

Mix with pulse paste and flavourings

↓

Make round balls weighing 50-60 g

↓

Spread on steel trays smeared with oil

↓

Dry the waris in hot air cabinet drier (60±5°C /16 hours)

↓

Pack and store the waris in LDPE polybags

Fig. 3.8: Flow chart for the preparation of 'Aloo wari'

Kaur and Aggarwal (2016) developedwaris from potato and legume blends and analyzed them for organoleptic, physicochemical, phytochemical and shelf life quality. In this study, potato (boiled and dehydrated) was used to supplement black gram or urad dhal waris. Two processing cultivars (Kufri Chipsona-1, Kufri Chandramukhi) and one commonly grown cultivar (Kufri Pukhraj) were evaluated for processing into waris. Based on preliminary sensory trails, waris with potato (70%) and urad dhal (30%) level of supplementation (Table 3.7) were found to be most acceptable and these waris were subjected to nutritional evaluation. Storage stability of the waris was assessed by storing the product at room temperature for a period of 12 months. Results were compared with dhal waris (control). The data revealed that nutritional wariscontaining higher bioactive compounds including ascorbic acid, total phenolics and antioxidant activity and higher acceptability ratingscan be developed from both fresh potato mash as well as dehydrated potato flour compared to traditional dhal wari. Interestingly, this study also demonstrated that manufacturing of highly acceptable waris from varieties of potato generally not in demand is feasible. Storage studies showed that the potato wariscan be stored safely for 12 months with its nutrient constituents intact.

Table 3.7: Standardized Recipe for Aloowari

Ingredients	Quantity (g)
Potato mash	315
Pulse paste	135
Water	—
Dried fenugreek leaves	3.5
Coriander seeds	7.5
Cumin	7.5
Cinnamon	1.5
Black pepper	3.0
Red pepper	3.0
Cloves	3.0
Nutmeg	0.25
Asafetida	0.1

Source: Kaur and Aggarwal (2016)

Aloo papad

Papadalso known as *Appalam* is a popular snack item in India. A variety of *papads* are available in India, which are produced from a great diversity of ingredients. Usually, they are made either using only cereal flour or a combination of pulse flour with salt, spices and some additives (Garg and Dahiya 2003). The demand for *papad* is rising rapidly both in country and abroad. So, there is greater scope for introduction of varieties of *papads* prepared from cost effective raw ingredients. One such ingredient is potato.

For making *aloopapad,* freshly prepared potato mash/flour is blended thoroughly with gelatinized rice with simultaneous addition of papad khar, cumin, black pepper and salt (quantity as mentioned in Table 3.8) and kneaded uniformly to prepare soft dough. Dough is divided into small balls (20 g each). The dough balls are put on oil smeared polythene sheets and are pressed into thin (1 mm thick) *papad* sheets using a manual papad making machine. These papad sheets are then dried in hot air cabinet dryer at 40±5°C for 8 hours.

Prepared *papads* are sealed in 200 gauge low density polyethylene (LDPE) bags and stored at room temperature for further use. *Papads* are fried at 175°C for 30 sec for final consumption.The process flow chart for the manufacturing of *papad* is outlined in Fig. 3.9.

Fresh potato mash + gelatinized rice flour

↓

Mix with various spices

↓

Knead

↓

Soft dough

↓

Divide the dough into small balls (20 g)

↓

Prepare papad using papad machine

↓

Dry the papads in hot air cabinet dryer at 40±5°C for 8 hours

↓

Pack and store the dried papads in LDPE polybags

Fig. 3.9: Flow Chart for preparation of papads

Marwaha and Sandhu (2003a, b) developed a simple technique for preparation of potato-sago papadsutilizing commonly cultivated Indian potato varieties and some exotic cultivars. *Papads* were prepared from a mix containing 100g of mashed potato and 20g of partially cooked sabudana powder followed by sun-drying. Determination of quality characterstics revealed that *papads* from all the exotic cultivars showed higher sensory characteristics, yield recovery and lower oil uptake compared to Indian cultivars. Atlantic among exotic and K. Chandramukhi among Indian varieties were found to be most suitable for the preparation of *papads*. Among the commonly grown Indian cultivars, K. Pukhraj produced minimum yield of *papads* with poor quality having unacceptable dark color, bitter taste, hence unacceptable. However, in a study conducted by Kaur and Aggarwal (2015b), the authors successfully prepared nutritionally enriched potato rice *papads* from both medium (K. Chandramukhi) and high sugar potato cultivars (K. Pukhraj) which provide significantly more bioactive compounds including ascorbic acid, total phenolics and antioxidant activity and high acceptability ratings. Potato *papads* were found to be acceptable up to 6 months of storage in the scaled polythene bags at ambient temperature without any change in sensory characteristics.

Table 3.8: Recipe for Potato-rice Papad

Ingredients (g)	Quantity
Potato mash	60
Gelatinized rice flour	40
Salt	0.5
Black pepper	0.1
Cumin seeds	0.3
Carom seeds	0.2
Papad khar (sodium bicarbonate)	0.5

Source: Kaur and Aggarwal (2015b)

Dehydrated Potato Chips/slices

Dehydrated slices are prepared by peeling and cutting the potatoes into thin slices, blanching, followed by drying. These contain approximately half the fat content than that of fresh fried chips and are thus particularly important from health point of view. These slices can be consumed after frying or can be ground to make flour, which can be used as thickener - flavoring agent in soups and gravies (Marwaha and Pandey 2006). Upon rehydration, these chips can be cooked and form a component of several vegetarian and non-vegetarian dishes.

Raw potato tubers

↓

Peeling

↓

Slicing with rotary hand slicer (2-3 mm thick slices)

↓

Blanching to inhibit enzymatic browning (100°C/6 minutes)

↓

Dipping of blanched potato slices in 0.25% potassium metabisulphite to inhibit non-enzymatic browning

↓

Loading in trays

↓

Drying in hot air cabinet drier (60°C/5-6 hours)

↓

Packaging

Fig. 3.10: Flow chart for the preparation of dried potato chips

For making dehydrated slices, raw potato tubers are peeled and cut into 2-3 mm thick slices with a rotary hand slicer. The slices so obtained are blanched in hot water. The blanched slices are immediately dipped in water containing 0.25% potassium meta bisulphite (KMS) to prevent discoloration or the chips can also be blanched directly in water containing 0.25% KMS solution for 5 min. Immediately after cooking, potato slices are cooled under running tap water. The sulphited slices are drained, loaded in trays and dried at a temperature of 60°C in a hot air cabinet drier for 5 to 6 hours (Fig. 3.10).

Das *et al.* (2001) prepared dehydrated potato chips from freshly harvested and heap stored tuber of four potatoes varieties. Yield of dehydrated chips was higher in Kufri Chipsona-1 and Kufri Chipsona-2. There was no significant varietal difference in yield and quality of dehydrated chips produced from tubers after 30 and 60 days of storage in heaps. The authors also discovered that during the preparation of dehydrated chips, starch could be recovered as a by-product.

Suitability of potato cultivars grown in north Indian plains for processing into dehydrated chips was evaluated by Kaur and Aggarwal (2015g). Results revealed that the physicochemical parameters of dehydrated slices were almost similar to the raw tubers, indicating a non-significant effect of processing. However, processing of raw potato tubers into dried slices resulted in significant ($p<0.05$) reduction in the bioactive content and total antioxidant activity, regardless of the cultivars. Among the cultivars, Kufri Chipsona-1 and Kufri Chandramukhi were the best for processing into dehydrated slices due to lower reducing sugar, higher yield and lesser oil absorption.

Five commercial potato cultivars namely K. Badshah, K. Chandramukhi, K. Jyoti, K. Jawahar and K. Sindhuri were evaluated to find out their suitability for preparation ofdried potato cubes (Sandhu and Parhawk 2002). Different pre-treatments including blanching in different concentrations of boiling brine and dipping in different concentrations of potassium metabisulphite for different periods were used. K. Jawahar was found to have most desirable characteristics for preparation of dried cubes. The blanching of 1-cm^3 size potato cubes in boiling 2.0% brine solution for 3 min followed by dipping in 0.2% solution of KMS for 10min was the best pre-treatment. Among the drying methods (cabinet drying, sun-drying, combined microwave and cabinet drying and combined microwave and sun drying), the drying of 1 cm^3 size potato cubes by combined microwave for 17 min followed by cabinet drying at 90±5°C for 2 hr was found to be the best method.

FRIED POTATO PRODUCTS

Fresh potatoes can be processed into several low cost value added deep fat fried products other than already existing processed potato products (chips and French fries). Deep-fat fried snacks are listed for their crunchy texture and fried aroma (Kulkarni *et al.* 1994). The demand of such deep fried snacks is increasing continuously mainly due to convenience, improved living standards, urbanization growth, preference of new generation for fast foods and rise in per capita income. Further, to promote processing in the rural areas as a cottage industry, these products can be taken up by unemployed youth and rural women since these products are easy to prepare and require no investment on processing machinery.

Aloo Bhujia

Bhujia, a deep fat fried, salted and spiced snack item is popular throughout India. These are manufactured by organized sector as well as at smaller scale in cottage industries. The raw ingredients used for preparation of bhujia include legumes (such as chickpea), cereals (generally rice) or a combination of bothalong with spices (Kumari and Prakash 2009). Aloo *bhujia* is a crisp savory snack prepared by mixing potato with some legume flour along with various spices. Standardized recipe of aloo *bhujia* has the ingredients, boiled potato mash 70g, rice flour 35g, bengal gram flour 35g, cumin powder 0.5g, coriander powder 0.8g, red chilli powder 0.7g, salt 2g and oil 12 ml (Kaur and Aggarwal 2014d). The basic process of making aloo *bhujia* involves sieving of Bengal gram flour and rice flour, mixing well with mashed potato and spices and making very soft dough with requisite of oil. The dough is rounded off between the palms of the hands smeared with oil and fed to the hand operated vermicelli press. The dough (approx. 120 g) is extruded directly into 1 l refined oil, maintained at 175±5°C for 40-45 s with turning after 20 s to ensure even frying. The process flow chart is shown in Fig. 3.11.

Fresh potato mash/flour

↓

Mixing with gram flour, rice flour, spices and oil

↓

Kneading

↓

Preparation of soft dough

↓

Extrusion

↓

Frying (175±5°C/40-45 s)

↓

Cooling

↓

Packaging

Fig. 3.11: Flow chart for preparation of aloobhujia

Aloo *bhujia* is generally prepared by using low sugar potato varieties. Presence of high sugar in raw potato induce an unacceptable dark color in fried potato products because of their participation in the Millard browning reaction. Kaur and Aggarwal (2014d) developed *bhujia* from high medium under-utilized potato cultivars. Potatoes were incorporated at 50% to Bengal gram flour and rice flour which served as base flours using traditional recipe. Bhujia prepared from high sugar potato cultivars displayed excellent keeping quality during the entire storage period except its color was darker compared to those prepared from low sugar cultivars. The authors concluded that incorporation of such potato cultivars into low-cost value added products such as *bhujia* could serve as an excellent vehicle for enhancing the utilization of this resourceful food crop.

Aloo Chakli

Chakli is a popular rice based traditional deep-fat fried snack product, which is manufactured on cottage scale in rural areas of South India (Sebestian *et al.* 2005). It is prepared using different cereal (wheat, rice) and legume (Bengal, green and black gram) blends.

A highly nutritional snack food can be prepared by partial substitution of rice flour with potato either in fresh form or in dehydrated form (Kaur and Aggarwal 2015c).

Table 3.9: Standardized Recipe of Potato Incorporated Chakli

Ingredients	Quantity
Potato mash	80 g
Rice flour	80 g
Bengal gram flour	15 g
Cumin seeds	1.6 g
Corriander powder	1.6 g
Red chilli powder	1 g
Carom seeds	0.4 g
Salt	3.2 g
Oil	24 ml
Water	10 ml

Source: (Kaur and Aggarwal 2015c)

The basic process for making *aloo chakli* involves incorporating potato at 45% to a traditional Indian rice based deep-fat fried snackrecipe, mixing potato well with Bengal and rice flour and spices (Table 3.9) and making a very soft dough with requisite of oil. The dough is extruded through a die in the hot oil (175±5°C) in a circular manner in a thick strand with a diameter of 10 mm. After 3 minutes of frying, when the products turn golden brown, they are removed and drained (Fig. 3.12).

Fresh potato mash/flour

↓

Mixing with rice flour, Bengal gram flour and various spices

↓

Kneading

↓

Soft dough

↓

Extrusion through a die

↓

Frying (175±5°C/3 min)

↓

Cooling

↓

Packaging

Fig. 3.12: Flow Chart for preparation of aloo chakli

FROZEN READY TO FRY POTATO SNACKS

Convenient ready-to-eat snack foods including frozen foods are becoming popular both in developing and developed countries because they are easy to prepare, take less time for cooking, have a unique flavor and taste, and can be served to a large number of customers in a relatively short period of time (Bhat and Pathak 2011). Also most of the working women nowadays prefer easy to cook food. Many non-vegetable frozen snacks are available in the market but snacks containing animal fats have a negative reputation regarding increasing "bad" LDL cholesterol, which is a key dietary contributor to coronary heart disease (Zeb and Ali 2008). Also the cost of these products is high to be affordable to all the sections of society. Present trends in health awareness among consumers demand for nutritious, healthy and novel snack foods. Potato is a nutritionally rich and inexpensive raw material, which can be utilized for the production of ready to fry frozen potato vegetable snacks such as *shammi* kebabs and *hara bhara* kebab. Also, potato processing at the village level has considerable potential to reduce post-harvest losses and to generate income through the manufacture of these value-added food products.

Potato shammi kebab

Standardized recipe of potato shammi kebabs has the ingredients;potato flour (50g), defatted soy flour (25g), Bengal gram flour (25g), corn flour (8g), cumin powder (1g), coriander powder (1.2g), black pepper (0.3g), red chilli powder (0.8g), cardamom powder (0.8g), clove powder (0.15g), mace powder (0.15g) and salt (5g). Lukewarm water (200 ml) is added into the above mix and kneaded till the ingredients are uniformly mixed. Balls of 65g from the prepared dough are made and flattened with hand. To impart a crispy texture, outer coating is given with bread crumbs. The kebabs are then par-fried in deep fat fryer maintained at 175±5°C for 40 sec. After frying, the kebabs are drained and gently wiped with adsorbent paper to remove surface oil. After cooling, the snacks are packed and sealed in polyethylene pouches (Fig. 3.13). Subsequently the pre-cooled kebabs are stored in a deep freezer at –20°C until the final frying. Final frying is done at –180°C for 3 min.

Potato flour

↓

Mixing with legume flour and spices

↓

Addition of water

↓

Kneading

↓

Soft dough

↓

Division into balls (65 g)

↓

Flattening of balls with hand

↓

Coating with bread crumbs

↓

Par-frying
(175±5°C/40 sec)

↓

Cooling

↓

Packaging in polythene bags

↓

Frozen storage (–20°C)

Fig. 3.13: Flow-chart for the preparation of frozen potato legume shammi kebab

Quality of Frozen ready-to-fry potato legume based *shammi kebabs* prepared incorporating potato flour, defatted soy flour and Bengal gram flour was compared with a commercial chicken based *shammi kebab* (control) by Kaur and Aggarwal (2015d). It was observed that control and supplemented *kebabs* did not differ significantly ($p < 0.05$) in their protein content. Potato added *kebabs* had significantly ($p < 0.05$) lower oil uptake, free fatty acids (FFA) and peroxide value (PV) and higher total phenolic content and total antioxidant activity compared to control *kebabs*. Sensory evaluation indicated higher overall acceptability scores of potato enriched *kebabs* compared to control kebabs. Within the potato cultivars, *kebabs* prepared from K. Pukhraj flour showed the highest total phenolic content and total antioxidant activity. Under a storage temperature of –20°C, there was no significant difference in the total phenolic content and total antioxidant activity between fresh and stored *kebabs*. Non-significant ($p < 0.05$) changes were observed in FFA and PV of the kebabs with the progression of storage period. The developed frozen snack was found to be highly acceptable up to three months of storage.

Frozen potato *hara bhara kebab*

For preparation offrozenpotato *hara bhara kebab*, freshly boiled potato mash is blended with mashed peas, ginger, garlic and various spices (quantity as mentioned in Table 3.10) and kneaded into a soft dough. Balls of 25 g from the prepared dough are made and flattened with hand. To get crispy texture in the final fried snack, balls are given an outer coating of bread crumbs. The prepared kebabs are par-fried in a laboratory scale deep fat fryer maintained at 175±5°C for 40 sec. After frying, the kebabs are drained and gently wiped with adsorbent paper to remove surface oil. After cooling, the snacks are packed and sealed in polythene pouches. Various steps in the preparation of frozen snack are outlined in Fig. 3.14. The pre-cooled snacks are stored in a deep freezer at –20°C until final frying. Final frying is done at –180°C for 3 min.

Table 3.10: Standardized Recipe for Frozen Potato Hara Bhara Kebab

Ingredients	Quantity (g)
Fresh potato mash	100
Boiled mashed peas	30
Ginger paste	3
Garlic paste	3
Cumin	0.8
Green chilli powder	1.5
Garam masala	0.4
Salt	1.2
Corn flour	3.0

Source: Kaur and Aggarwal (2014e)

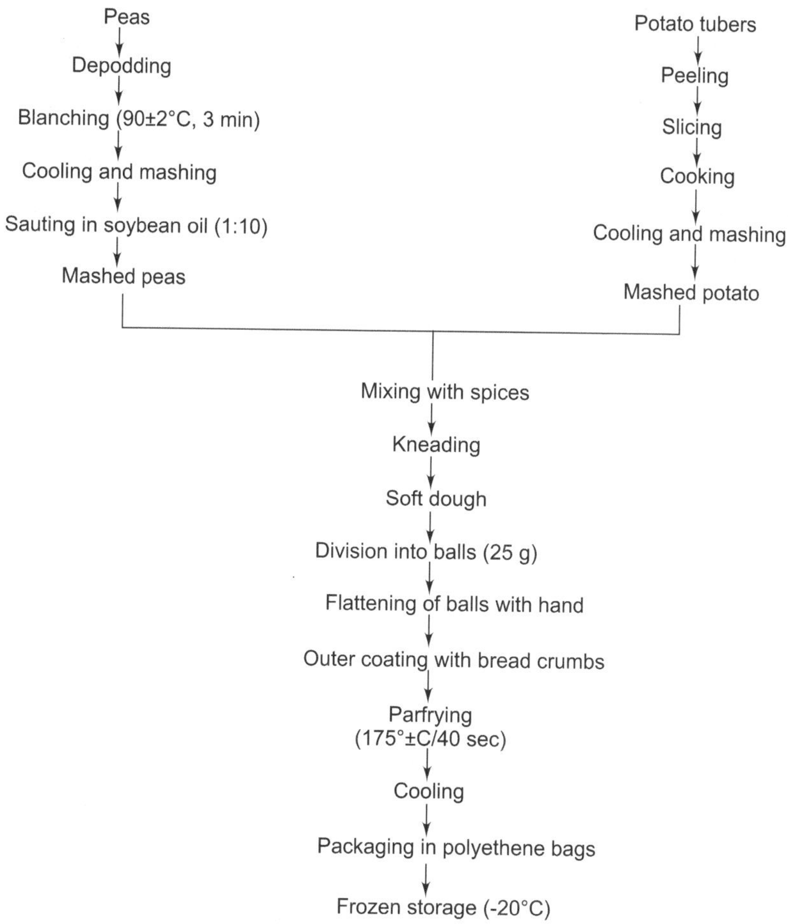

Fig. 3.14: Flow chart for the preparation of frozen potato hara bhara kebab

DEHYDRATED POTATO SNACK PREMIX

A premix is a mixture of ingredients designed to be mixed with other ingredients before use. The demand of such ready to fry premixes for the preparation of deep fried snacks is increasing continuously mainly due to convenience, improved living standards, preference of new generation for fast foods and rise in per capita income. Since production of potato is abundant in India, so there is greater scope for introduction of varieties of snack premixes prepared from these cost effective raw ingredients. Dehydrated potato flour is a highly versatile raw material that can be incorporated in dehydrated snack premixes, which have a long shelf life and diverse uses.

Standardized recipe ofdehydrated potato snack mixhas the ingredients; potato flour 60g, rice flour 20g, cassava flour 20g, ginger and garlic paste 1.5g, cumin 0.6g, coriander powder 1.6g, red chilli powder 1.0g, green chilli powder 2.0g, corn flour 7.0g (Kaur and Aggarwal 2015e). Dehydrated potato snack premix is packed in polythene bags and sealed in tight air containers (figure 3.15). This premix can be successfully stored at room temperature for a period of six months with its sensory properties intact.

To make ready to eat potato snack, add lukewarm water (240 ml) into the above mix and knead till the ingredients get uniformly mixed. Prepare balls of 65g from the prepared dough and flatten with hand. Bread crumbs are applied to provide crispy texture. The snacksare then deep fat fried in a laboratory scale deep fat fryer maintained at 175±5°C for 2 min.

Potato flour

↓

Mixing with rice and cassava flour

↓

Addition of dry spices

↓

Mixing well

↓

Packaging in polythene bags

↓

storage at ambient temperature

Fig. 3.15: Flow-chart for the preparation of dehydrated potato snack premix

Kaur and Aggarwal (2015e) prepared dehydrated potato snack premix utilizing potato flour, legume flours and various spices. The product was packed in LDPE bags and stored at room temperature for a period of 6 months to study its shelf-life and quality attributes. The physicochemical parameters including ash content, protein content, FFA and PVof dehydrated premix remained unaffected during storage upto six months with the exception of moisture which increased significantly ($p < 0.05$) during storage. Slight but significant ($p < 0.05$) reductions in bioactive components including total phenolicand total antioxidant activity of dehydrated snack premix occurred during storage.The ready to eat fried potato snack prepared from dehydrated premixwas found to be highly acceptable for up to 6 months of storage without any change in sensory quality.

CANNED POTATO PRODUCTS

Potatoes can be processed through canning which provide a longer shelf life and diversified uses. Generally, canned vegetables are prepared by hermetically sealing the blanched vegetables in pre-sterilized cans and then sterilizing them by heat for long storage. Canned potatoes (whole, cubes or curried) can be prepared when potatoes are cheap and used in the off season when potato prices are high. Canned potato products include canned whole potatoes, potato cubes and ready to eat potato curries. Canned whole potatoes and cubes can be further cooked and form a component of several vegetarian and non-vegetarian dishes. As far as canned curry is concerned, the demand of ready-to-eat foods is rising in both developing and developed countries mainly due to improved living standards, convenience, ease of preparation, unique taste and increase in the number of working women preferring ready-cooked food. Canned potatoes are shelf stable, easy to prepare and require no costly machinery for manufacture.

Canned potato cubes

Fresh potato tubers are washed, peeled, diced into small cubes (2.5 cm) and immersed in water containing 0.25% KMS to prevent enzymatic darkening (Marwaha and Pandey 2006). Potato cubes are blanched for 6 min in boiling water and then cooled to room temperature under running tap water. Potato cubes are then filled in pre-sterilized cans and hot brine solution (2%) is added to cover the cans. Cans containing potato cubes are exhausted till temperature in the centre of cans reach 85°C. After exhausting of cans for 10 mins, cans are sealed in a can seamer and are kept in retort for thermal processing. Canning of potato cubes is done at 121°C for 35 min (Lal and Siddapa 1986). The process flow chart for the manufacturing of canned potato curry is outlined in figure 3.16.

Washing
↓
Peeling
↓
Cutting
↓
Blanching
(100°C/6 min)
↓
Filling in pre-sterilized cans and pouring hot brine (2%) at 80°C
↓
Exhausting to remove air
↓
(90-100°C for 10 min until temperature in centre of can reach 85°C)
↓
Sealing by means of a can sealer
↓
Thermal processing (121°C/ 5 mins)
↓
Cooling
↓
Storage at room temperature

Fig. 3.16: Flowchart for the preparation of canned potato cubes

Canned Potato curry

Blanched potato cubes are prepared as above.For curry preparation, 40 ml of cooking oil is heated in a pan and seasoned with cumin seeds (1g). To this, paste containing ginger (5g), garlic (3g), onion (50g), tomato (66g) is added, along with salt (2g), turmeric (0.2g), coriander (1g) and red chilli powder (0.2g). Blanched potato cubes are added to the above cooked paste along with 250 ml of water and cooked for 5 min. Curried potato cubes are then filled in pre-sterilized cans. Cans containing curried potatoes are exhausted till temperature in the centre of cans reaches 85°C. After exhausting of cans for 10 mins, cans are sealed in a can seamer and are kept in retort for thermal processing. Canning of potato cubes is done at 121°C for 35 min (Lal and Siddapa 1986) (figure 3.17).

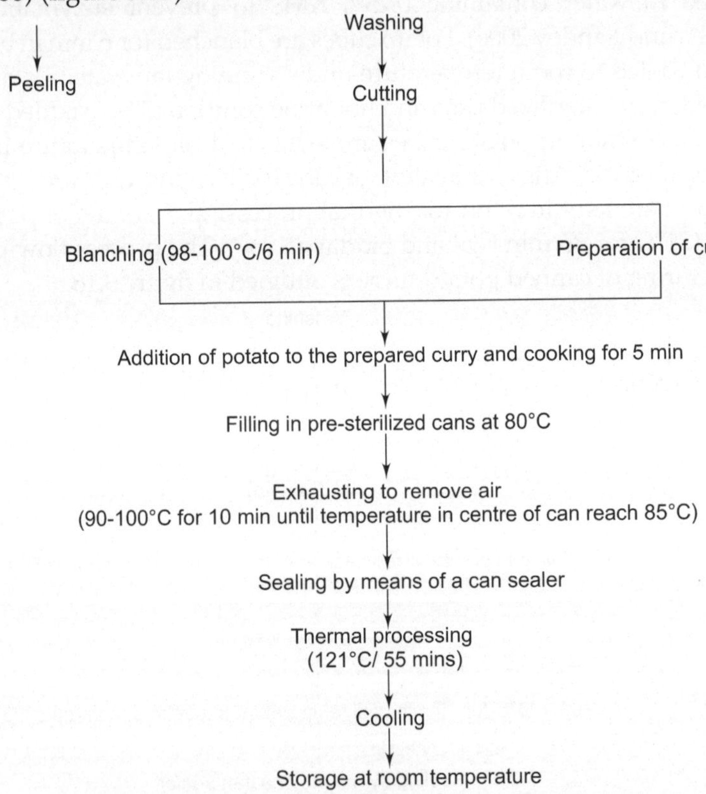

Fig. 3.17: Flowchart for the preparation of canned potato curry

Ready-to-eat canned potato curry made from three potato cultivars namely Kufri Chipsona-1, KufriChandramukhi and KufriPukhraj was evaluated for quality characteristics in order to determine their suitability for processing (Kaur and Aggarwal 2015f). Canned product was stored for a period of 6 months at room temperature to assess its shelf life properties. Incubation test on the product was carried at 55°C for 45 days. Significant differences in physico-chemical parameters were observed among the cultivars. During storage of canned potato curries, all the quality parameters remained almost stable with the exception of ascorbic acid which decreased during storage, irrespective of genotypes (Table 3.11). Physical conditions of cans were found to be satisfactory during storage. Storage study revealed that canned product can be safely stored for up to 6 months with high acceptability ratings. Also, product prepared from KufriPukhraj, a high sugar underutilized variety, displayed excellent keeping quality during the entire storage period.

Table 3.11: Cut Out Analysis of Canned Potato Curries from Different Potato Cultivars

Storage period (months)	Cultivars		
	K.Chipsona-1	K.Chandramukhi	K.Pukhraj
Total weight of can (g)			
0	530 2.5c	535 3.0a	530 2.5c
2	532 2.0b	535 2.5a	530 3.0c
4	530 2.5a	532 2.0b	535 2.0a
6	535 3.0a	530 2.0c	532 2.0b
Drained weight (g)			
0	460 3.0c	467 2.5a	461 2.2c
2	465 3.5a	462 2.0b	460 2.0d
4	463 2.8b	463 2.5c	463 2.5a
6	465 2.5a	460 2.5d	462 2.0b
Vacuum (Hg)			
0	11.00 0.40a	12.00 0.50a	11.00 0.50a
2	11.00 0.45a	11.00 0.45b	10.00 0.40b
4	10.05 0.30b	10.05 0.35c	10.00 0.45b
6	9.00 0.40c	10.00 0.30c	8.00 0.40c
Head space (cm)			
0	0.65 0.50a	0.60 0.04a	0.60 0.05a
2	0.60 0.04a	0.65 0.05a	0.65 0.05a
4	0.65 0.04a	0.70 0.08a	0.70 0.06a
6	0.70 0.08a	0.70 0.07a	0.70 0.05a
Ascorbic acid (mg/100 g)			
0	8.31 0.10a	9.42 0.25a	6.92 0.08a
2	8.10 0.10a	9.01 0.21b	6.41 0.09b
4	7.82 0.08b	8.84 0.15b	6.00 0.05c
6	7.41 0.10c	8.52 0.10c	5.89 0.05c

Acidity (%)			
0	0.064 0.001a	0.068 0.001a	0.065 0.001a
2	0.065 0.002a	0.065 0.00a	0.068 0.002a
4	0.060 0.003a	0.063 0.002a	0.064 0.001a
6	0.064 0.002a	0.067 0.003a	0.064 0.003a
External and internal condition of cans			
0	Satisfactory	Satisfactory	Satisfactory
2	Satisfactory	Satisfactory	Satisfactory
4	Satisfactory	Satisfactory	Satisfactory
6	Satisfactory	Satisfactory	Satisfactory

Values within a column with different letters are significantly ($p < 0.05$) different within the storage duration. Mean values SD (n=3)
Source: Kaur and Aggarwal (2015f)

KEY THRUST AREAS WHICH NEEDS TO BE ADDRESSED

Considering the importance of Potato in Indian agriculture and its ability to address the food security issue, following measures are required for sustainable potato production:

- Improving productivity through high quality seeds.
- Development of advanced varieties with high yielding capacities which can sustain weather conditions.
- Development of early maturing processing varieties.
- Breeding varieties resistant to cold sweetening.
- Increasing the storage capacities through energy-efficient cold storages.
- Development of improved infrastructure for facilities for frozen fried potato products.
- Development of inexpensive technologies for the production of diverse potato products.

REFERENCES

Abbas, G., Farooq, I. A., Hafiz, A., Hussain, A., Abbasi, N. A. and Shabbir, G. (2011): Assessment of Processing and Nutritional Quality of Potato Genotypes in Pakistan. Pakistan Journal of Agriculture Science, 48(3): 169-75.

Ah-Hen, K., Fuenzalida, C., Hess, S., Contreras, A., Vega-Galvez, A. and Lemus-Mondaca, R.(2012): Antioxidant Capacity and Total Phenolic Compounds of Twelve Selected Potato Landrace Clones Grown in Southern Chile. Chilean Journal of Agricultural Research, 72(1):3-9.

Al-Saikhan, M. S., Howard, L. R. and Miller, J. C. (1995): Antioxidant Activity and Total Phenolics in Different Genotypes of Potato (Solanumtuberosum L.). Journal of Food Science, 60: 341-43.

Amrein, T. M., Bachmann, S., Noti, A. *et al.* (2003): Potential of Acrylamide Formation, Sugars and Free Asparagine in Potatoes. Journal of Agricultural and Food Chemistry, 51:5556-5560.

Babbar, N., Oberoi, H. S., Uppal, D. S. and Patil, R. T. (2011): Total Phenolic Content and Antioxidant Capacity of Extracts Obtained from Six Important Fruit Residues. Food Research International, 44: 391-96.

Bhat, Z. F. and Pathak, V. (2011): Effect of Black Bean (Vignamungo) on the Quality Characteristics of Oven-roasted Chicken Seekh Kebabs. Journal of Stored Products and Postharvest Research, 2(1): 15-23.

Bons, H. K. and Kaur, A. (2009): Potato Potential Food Crop. Processing Food Industry, 12: 24-25.

Brown, C. R. (2005): Antioxidants in Potato. American Journal of Potato Research, 82: 163-72.

Camire, M. E., Kubow, S. and Donnelly, D. J. (2009): Potatoes and Human Health. Critical Review in Food Science and Nutrition, 49: 823-40.

Chandrashekara, S. and Shurpalekar, S. R. (1984): On the Use of Potato and Cassava Flours in Soft Dough Biscuits. Journal of Food Science and Technology, 21: 239-41.

Das, M., Ezekiel, R. and Shekhawat, G. S. (2001): Quality of Dehydrated Potato Chips Produced from Fresh and Heap Stored Tubers. Potato Journal, 28: 174-75.

Ezekiel, R., Singh, N., Sharma, S. and Kaur, A. (2013): Beneficial Phytochemicals in Potato—A Review. Food Research International, 50: 487-96.

FAO STAT (2015): Food and Drug Administration. Statistical Databases for Potato Production. www.fao.org

Gahlawat, P. and Sehgal, S. (1998): Protein and Starch Digestibilities and Mineral Availability of Products Developed from Potato, Soy and Gram Flour. Plant Foods for Human Nutrition, 52:151-60.

Ganga, H., Kulkarni, U. N., Yenegi, N. B., Basavaraj, N., Uppinal, N. and Ramachandra, K. N. (2013): Study on Physical Characteristics of Potato Genotypes. Pakistan Journal of Agriculture Science, 26(2): 281-84.

Garg, G. and Dahiya, S. (2003): Nutritional Evaluation and Shelf Life Studies of Papads Prepared from Wheat-legume Composite Flours. Plant Foods for Human Nutrition, 58: 299-307.

Gumul, D., Ziobro, R., Noga, M. and Sabat, R. (2011): Characterization of Five Potato Cultivars According to their Nutritional and Pro-health Components. Acta Scientiarum Polonorum Technologia Alimenteria, 10(1): 73-81.

Han, H., Sekikawa, M., Shimada, K. I. and Fukushima, M. (2007): Anthocyanin-rich Red Potato Flakes Affect Serum Lipid Peroxidation and Hepatic SOD mRNA Level in Rats. Bioscience Biotechnology Biochemistry, 71: 1356-1359.

Joshi, S. and Nath, N. (2002): Effect of Pre-treatments on Quality and Shelf Life of Fried Chips from Sprouted Tubers of Potato Variety Kufri Chandramukhi. Journal of Food Science and Technology, 39: 251-57.

Kasper, K. L., Park, J. S., Brown, C. R., Weller, K., Ross, C. F., Mathison, B. D. and Chew, B. P. (2013): Sensory Evaluation of Pigmented Flesh Potatoes (Solanum tuberosum L.). Food Nutrition Sciences, 4: 77-81.

Kaur, S. and Aggarwal, P. (2014b): Studies on Indian Potato Genotypes for their Processing and Nutritional Quality Attributes. International Journal of Current Microbiology and Applied Sciences, 3(8): 172-177.

Kaur, S. and Aggarwal, P. (2014a): Chipping and Nutritional Quality of Potato Cultivars Grown in North Indian Plains. Hortflora Research Spectrum, 3(3): 218-224.

Kaur, S. and Aggarwal, P. (2014c): Evaluation of Antioxidant Phytochemicals in Different Genotypes of Potato. International Journal of Engineering Research and Applications, 4(7): 167-172.

Kaur, S., Aggarwal, P., Vashisht, V. K. and Kaur, A. (2016): Suitability of Different Potato Cultivars for Processing into Value Added Products. Journal of Research PAU, 53(2): 260-263.

Kaur, S. and Aggarwal, P. (2015a): Influence of Drying Methods on Phytonutrients of Potato Flour. Progressive Research-An International Journal, 10(1): 76-79.

Kaur, S. and Aggarwal, P. (2016): Development and Quality Characteristics of Nutritionally Enhanced Potato Legume Based Wari-An Indian Traditional Savoury. Journal of Food Science and Technology, 53(4): 1899-1908.

Kaur, S. and Aggarwal, P. (2015b): Effect of Addition of Potato Flour on the Quality of Rice Papads. The Ecoscan, 9(1&2): 305-310.

Kaur, S. and Aggarwal, P. (2015c): Development and Quality Characteristics of Nutritionally Enhanced Potato Rice Based Chaklis—An Indigenous Snack Food. The Ecoscan, 9(1&2): 349-356.

Kaur, S. and Aggarwal, P. (2015f): Suitability of Indian Potato Genotypes for Preparation of Ready-to-serve Canned Curries. Food Science Research Journal, 6(1): 108-114.

Kaur, S. and Aggarwal, P. (2015d): Development and Evaluation of Ready-to-fry Frozen Potato Legume Based Shammi Kebab: A Vegetarian Substitute. Green Farming, 6(6): 1380-1384.

Kaur, S. and Aggarwal, P. (2014e): Development of Ready-to-Fry frozen Potato Snacks and Its Quality Evaluation during Storage. Hort Flora Research Spectrum, 3(4): 315-322.

Kaur, S. and Aggarwal, P. (2015e): Development and Shelf Life Studies of Ready-to-fry Dehydrated Potato Snack Premix. Hort Flora Research Spectrum, 4(3): 209-213.

Kaur, S. and Aggarwal, P. (2015g): Quality Characteristics of Dehydrated Potato Slices Prepared from Cultivars Grown in North Indian Plains. Progressive Research—An International Journal, 10(1): 16-19.

Kaur, S. (2014): Development of Indigenous Potato Products. Ph.D. Thesis, Punjab Agricultural University, Ludhiana, Punjab.

Kaur, C. and Kapoor, H. C. (2002): Antioxidant Activity and Total Phenolic Content of Some Asian Vegetables. International Journal of Food Science and Technology, 37: 153-61.

Kumari, R. K. R. and Prakash, J. (2009): Influence of Soy Protein Incorporation on Acceptability and Shelf-stability of Sorghum Based Seviya. Indian Journal of Science and Technology, 2(4): 53-58.

Khan, A., Chauhan, G. S. and Tomar, N. S. (1997): Physio-chemical Characteristics of Potatoes as a Function of Cultivars. Indian Food Packer, 51: 15-21.

Kaur, S., Sandhu, K. S. and Aggarwal, P. (2012): Chlorpropham Affects Processing Quality of Potato during Storage. International Journal of Vegetable Science, 18: 328-45.

Kulkari, K. D., Govind, N. and Kulkarni, D. (1997): Production and Use of Raw Potato Flour in Mauritian Traditional Foods. Food Nutrition Bulletin, 18(4): 328-45.

Lisinska and Leszczynski. (1989): Potato Science and Technology. Elsevier Publishing Co. Inc., USA. pp. 16-44, 205-12.

Lachman, L. and Hamouz, K. (2005): Red and Purple Colored Potatoes as a Significant Antioxidant Source in Human Nutrition—A Review. Plant Soil Environment, 51: 477-82.

Lakra, P. and Sehgal, S. (2011): Influence of Processing on Total and Extractable Mineral Content of Products Prepared from Potato Flour. Journal of Food Science and Technology, 48(6): 735-39.

Lokendrajit, N., Singh, C. B., Swapana, N. and Singh, M. S. (2013): Evaluation of Nutritional Value of Two Local Potato Cultivars (Aberchaibi and Amubi) of Manipur, North East India. The Bioscan, 8(2): 589-93.

Lamberti, M., Geiselmann, A., Conde-Petit, B. and Escher, F. (2004): Starch Transformation and Structure Development in Production and Reconstitution of Potato Flakes. Food Science and Technology-Lebensmittel-Wissenschaft Technology, 37: 417-427.

Lal, G. and Siddapa, G. S. (1986): Preservation of Fruits and Vegetables. ICAR, New Delhi. pp. 261.

Mahajan, B. V. C., Dhatt, A. S., Sandhu, K. S. and Garg, A (2008): Effect of CIPC (isopropyl-N (3-chlorophenyl carbamate) on Storage and Processing Quality of Potato. Journal of Food Agriculture and Environment 6: 34-38.

Marwaha, R. S. (1997): Processing of Potatoes: Current Status, Need, Future Potential and Suitability of Indian Varieties—A Critical Appraisal. Journal of Food Science and Technology, 34: 457-71.

Marwaha, R. S. and Sandhu, K. S. (2003a): Yield, Sensory and Nutritional Qualities of Potato Flours Prepared from Low and High Dry Matter Cultivars Stored at Different Temperatures. Journal of Food Science and Technology, 40: 638-45.

Marwaha, R. S. and Sandhu, K. S. (2003b): Potato-sabudana Papads—A New Dehydrated Product for Cottage Industry. Journal of Food Science and Technology, 40: 642-45.

Marwaha, R. S., Kumar, D., Singh, S. V. and Pandey, S. K. (2009): Chipping and Nutritional Qualities of Indian and Exotic Potato Processing Varieties Stored under Different Conditions. Journal of Food Science and Technology, 46: 354-58.

Marwaha, R. S., Pandey, S. K., Kumar, D., Singh, S. V. and Kumar, P. (2010): Potato Processing Scenario in India: Industrial Constraints, Future Projections, Challenges Ahead and Remedies—A Review. Journal of Food Science and Technology, 47: 137-56.

Marwaha, R. S., Pandey, S. K. and Kumar, D. (2004): Dehydrated Potato Chips. Technical Bulletin. Central Potato Research Institute, Shimla, India, 63:1-4.

Matsuura-Endo, C., Takada, A. O., Chuda, Y., Ono, H., Yada, H., Yoshida, M., Kobayashi, A., Tsuda, S., Takigawa, S., Noda, T., Yamauchi, H. and Mori, M. (2006): Effect of the Storage Temperature on the Contents of Sugars and Free Amino Acids in Tubers from Different Potato Cultivars and Acrylamide in Chips. Bioscience, Biotechnology and Biochemistry 70: 1173-80.

Misra, A. and Kulshrestha, A. (2003a): Effect of Storage on Nutritional Value of Potato Flour Made from Three Potato Varieties. Plant Foods for Human Nutrition, 58: 1-10.

Misra, A. and Kulshrestha, A. (2003b): Potato Flour Incorporation in Biscuit Manufacture. Plant Foods for Human Nutrition 58: 1-9.

Misra, A. and Kulshrestha, K. (2002): Effect of Storage on Microbial Safety of Potato Flour. Journal of Food Science and Technology, 39(5): 517-19.

Nanda, P. and Khanna, P. (1988): Nutritive Value and Shelf Life of Home Based Potato Flour. Indian Journal of Nutrition and Dietetics, 25: 288.

Pandey, S. K., Singh, S. V. and Sarkar, D. (2005): Potato (SolanumtuberosumL.) for Sustaining Food and Nutrition Security in Developing World. Indian Journal of Agricultural Sciences, 75: 3-18.

Pandey, S. K., Singh, S. V., Marwaha, R. S. and Pattanayak, D. (2009): Indian Potato Processing Varieties: Their Impact and Future Priorities. Potato Journal, 36: 95-114.

Pressey, R. (1970): Changes in Sucrose Synthetase and Sucrose Phosphate Synthetase Activities During Storage of Potatoes. American Potato Journal, 47: 245-51.

Raj, D., Joshi, V. K. and Lal, B. B. (2011): Yield, Quality and Storability of the Potato Flour of Different Indian Cultivars. International Journal of Food and Fermentation Technology, 1(1): 111-17.

Sandhu, K. S. and Parhawk, B. (2002): Studies on the Preparation of Dehydrated Potato Cubes. Journal of Food Science and Technology, 39: 594-602.

Saxena, R. and Mathur, P. (2013): Analysis of Potato Production Performance and Yield Variability in India. Potato Journal,40(1): 38-44.

Sebastian, L., Gowri, B. S. and Prakash, J. (2005): Quality Characteristics of Ragi (Eleusinecoracana) Incorporated Chakli—An Indian Deep-fried Product. Journal of Food Processing and Preservation, 29: 319-30.

Shekhar, V.C., W.R. Iritani, and J. Magnuson. (1979): Starch Sugar Interconversion in SolanumtuberosumL. American Potato Journal, 56: 225-235.

Singh, N., Kaur, S. P., Kaur, L. and Sodhi, N. S. (2005): Physico-chemical Rheological and Chapati Making Properties of Flours from Indian Potato Cultivars. Journal of Food Science and Technology, 42(2): 344-48.

Singh, S. V., Marwaha, R. S., Kaur, D., Kumar, P. and Pandey, S. K. (2009): Suitability of Potato Varieties Grown in North-Eastern Indian Plains for Processing. Potato Journal, 36: 25-34.

Willard, M. J. and Hix, V. M. (1987): Potato Flour In: Talburt, W. F. and Smith, O. (eds.) Potato Processing. Van Nostrand Reinhold, New York. pp. 665.

Yadav, A. R., Guha, M., Tharananthan, R. N. and Ramteke, R. M. (2006): Influence of Drying Conditions on Functional Properties of Potato Flour. European Food Research and Technology, 223: 553-60.

Zeb, A. and Ali, M. (2008): Thermal Stability of Animal Tallow used in Kebab Preparation. Journal of the Chemical Society of Pakistan, 30(5): 750-55.

Agriculture Crops and Food Security
Edited by: Dr. Pawan Kumar 'Bharti' and Alka Chauhan
ISBN: 978-93-5056-881-1
Edition: 2017
Published by: Discovery Publishing House Pvt. Ltd., New Delhi (India)

4

Soybean
An Overview

[1]Archana Rani, [2]Sanjeev Kumar, S.K. Pandey[1], Rajni Bisen[1], Stuti Mishra[1]

INTRODUCTION

The soybean (*Glycine max* (L.) Merrill) is one of the most important food crops worldwide due to its potential for large-scale production and it has excelled in the world agricultural economy as a major oilseed crop. Cultivated soybean, *G. max* (L.) Merr., is a diploidized tetraploid ($2n$=40), in the family *Leguminosae*, the subfamily *Papilionoideae*, the tribe *Phaseoleae*, the genus *Glycine* Willd. And the subgenus *Soja* (Moench). It is an erect, bushy herbaceous annual that can reach a height of 1.5 metres. Three types of growth habit can be found amongst soybean cultivars: determinate, semi-determinate and indeterminate (Bernard and Weiss, 1973;). Legends exist claiming use of domesticated soybeans as early as 2500–2300 B.C., though the first historical evidence places the emergence of soybean as a food crop in Northeastern China around 1700–1100 B.C. Whole beans were cooked or fermented into a paste and used in various dishes. By the 16th century A.D., soybeans were used in Thailand, Burma, Nepal, the Indonesia, Korea, Japan, Philippines, India, Malaysia, and Vietnam. There is some confusion regarding the origin of soyabean although North-eastern China is generally considered as the original home. In Chinese records it is considered to be the most important legume and also one of the five sacred grains-rice, soyabean, wheat, barley and millet essential for existence of Chinese civilization.

The area under soyabean cultivation in India is about one Ten million hectares. Although, presently Madhya Pradesh and Maharashtra are the major soyabean producers in the country. Other states like Rajasthan, Andhra Pradesh and Karnataka also provide bright prospects for soyabean production. The soybean is adapted primarily to the Temperate Zone. Each improved variety has an adaptation determined in large part by latitude.

[1] Department of Plant Breeding and Genetics, College of Agriculture, Jawaharlal Nehru Krishi Vishwa Vidyalaya, Jabalpur – 482 004, Madhya Pradesh (India)

[2] Department of Plant Pathology, College of Agriculture, Jawaharlal Nehru Krishi Vishwa Vidyalaya, Jabalpur – 482 004, Madhya Pradesh (India)

Soybean requires careful home processing to bring out its best qualities, and if not well prepared, it has an off-flavor that is seldom appreciated. Soybean seeds are important for both protein meal and vegetable oil. The crop is grown on an estimated 6% of the world's arable land and since the 1970s, the area in soybean production has the highest percentage increase compared to any other major crop. Recent increases in production coincide with increases in demand for meal and oil. Soybean production was 17 million metric tons (MMT) in 1960 and increased to 230 MMT in 2008. Future soybean production is expected to increase more than other crops, due to expanded production area and higher yields. There are a number of important abiotic and biotic constraints that threaten soybean production by directly reducing seed yields and/or seed quality (Hymowitz, T; 1970). Abiotic constraints include extremes in nutrients, temperatures and moisture. These may reduce production directly, but also indirectly through increases in pathogens and pests. Biotic constraints tend to be geographically and environmentally restricted. Some diseases like soybean rust may be explosive by producing copious amounts of air-borne spores. This disease, more so than most, caused great concern when first found invading soybean production areas in Brazil and the United States of America. In contrast, red leaf blotch is a disease restricted to a few countries in Africa, but deserving attention since it has not been intensely studied and adequate management strategies, such as the use of resistant varieties, are not available. Significant losses in soybean yield beyond current levels may have implications for food security because of our dependence on the soybean crop, directly and indirectly for food products (Johnson; 1987). In addition, because the crop is highly nutritious and versatile it offers resources to address world food issues through current and future utilization practices (Gandhi; 2009 and AOAC. 2004). Future soybean production is expected to increase in proportion to increased demand and with application of newer genomic technologies, the crop has enormous potential to improve dietary quality for people throughout the world whether consumed as a vegetable crop or processed into various soybean food products (Bernard and Weiss; 1973; Upfold and Olechowski, 1988).

SOPA today released its estimates for area under soybean cultivation, Production and Productivity for Kharif 2015. The Association has also revised its estimates of Kharif 2014 soybean crop to 90 lakh tonnes. The carryover of Soybean from last year is estimated at 9 lac tons. This year SOPA conducted Satellite based survey to ascertain the area under soybean cultivation in 58 major Soybean growing districts in Madhya Pradesh, Maharashtra and Rajasthan. For rest of the country, Government's area figures have been considered.

To access the estimates of Productivity and Production, an extensive survey of standing and under harvest Crop was conducted in Madhya Pradesh, Maharashtra and Rajasthan during 15th September, 2015 to 24th September,

2015. To calculate the realistic Productivity and Production of Soybean, all the major factors have been taken into account.

According to Satellite survey, the area under Soybean Cultivation is 110.656 lac hectares in the country, which is 5.629 lac hectares less than Government of India's figure of 116.285 lac hectares. According to SOPA's assessment, the production estimates of Soybean during kharif 2015 is 86.426 lac ton, which is 3.574 lac ton down (3.97 per cent) as compared to previous years revised estimates of 90 lac ton.

Botanical Characteristics: (Hymowitz and Newell; 1981).

Kingdom:	Plantae
Phylum:	Magnoliophyta
Class:	Magnoliopsida
Order:	Fabales
Family:	Fabaceae
Subfamily:	Faboideae
Genus:	*Glycine*
Species:	*G. max*

Soybean is an erect, bushy, rather leafy growth and annual plant. The plant varies from 0.5 to 2 metre in height. The branches may be spreading or ascending, short or elongated depending on growing conditions.

• The soybean cultivars are grouped into two types based on growth habit i.e. indeterminate and determinate.

1. **Indeterminate:** Flowering starts before stem elongation ceases and flowers are borne on axillary racemes. Flowering period is longer and extensive.
2. **Determinate:** Flowers are born on both axillary and terminal racemes. Stem elongation ceases with differentiation of terminal bud. The flowering period is shorter and more intense.

Seed: Soybean seeds vary in shape having spherical, spherical flattened, elongated, elongated flattened. Seed has small scar, the hilum, which mark the seed's former point of attachment to the legume (pod). The area surrounding the hilum may be of different shades of black, gray or yellow. Hilum varying in shape from linear to oval. The one end of the hilum a tiny hole formed by integument is called micropyle. The hypocotyl-radicle axis is found just below the micropyle. The other end of hilum there is a small groove extending to the chalaza known as raphe. The mature seed consists a large embryo and a seed coat (a leathery textured structure, the testa) which covers the embryo. The embryo has two large fleshy cotyledons, a plumule with two well developed primary leaves and a hypocotyl-radicle axis. The soybean seed is devoid of endosperm. The colour of seed coat may be yellow, yellow green, green, brown, black or variegated. The cotyledon colour may be yellow (more common), green yellow or green.

Root: The primary root appears from the seed coat grows as main root axis and penetrate soil more or less straight downward is called tap root. The secondary lateral rootlets branch from this tap root and multi branched adventitious roots also emerged. The bacterial root nodules appear after 8-10 days of planting and begin nitrogen fixation about two weeks later. The nodules have pink colour due to presence of leg haemoglobin similar to the haemoglobin of animals blood.

Stem: The stem is usually erect in cultivated types while prostrate/ trailing/ twining in wild types. The structure of the stem is solid and cylindrical with wider base to tapering towards tip. The part of stem between primary root to cotyledonary node known as hypocotyl elongates during germination and pulls the cotyledons and epicotyl above the soil. The Violet (anthocyanin) or green colour hypocotyls are found. The stem may be pubescent (hairy) or glabrous (smooth). The colour of hairs may be gray or tawn.

Leaves: Leaves may be of light green medium green or dark green colours. They may be pubescent or glabrous. There are four kinds of leaves in soybean:

1. **Cotyledons or Seed leaves:** With the growth of hypocotyl the two cotyledons emerged above the soil which separate, become green and take part in photosynthetic activity in addition to supply nutrition to the plant.
2. **Simple Primary leaves or Unifoliate leaves:** The first true leaves are unifoliate (single blade per petiole) appear on first node and both are formed at opposite sides.
3. **Trifoliate leaves or Compound leaves:** All the leaves above first node produced on main stem or branch are trifoliate (three blades per petiole) and arranged on alternate nodes one by one in opposite sides. In some varieties trifoliate to pentafoliate leaves have been found. These leaflets are generally triangular, pointed ovate and rounded ovate and lanceolate in shape.
4. **Prophylls:** At the base of each lateral branch and below the inflorescence a tiny pair of simple leaves lacking petioles and pulvini is called prophylls.

At the base of the petiole, two distinctive structures are present. One is the stipules, a pair of spear-or lance-shaped modified leaves formed on the petiole stem junction. At the very base of the petiole is a large cell group, the pulvinus which is an integral part of the junction.

Inflorescence: The receme type of inflorescence is found in soybean. The flowers are borne on axillary racemes with few on terminal receme in indeterminate soybeans, while in determinate soybean flowers borne on axillary and terminal racemes. The individual flowers are arranged on a stem like branch called a peduncle. The flowers may occur in cluster of 3-15 per node.

Flowers: Soybean flowers are 6-7 mm long, bisexual and self pollinated. Flowers are pedicellate, zygomorphic, pentamerous, bracteate and typical papilionaceous with a tubular calyx of five unequal lobes. Calyx are persistent and attached with pods. The corolla comprised of a posterior banner or standard petal, two lateral wings petals and two anterior keel petals. The keel petals are attached to each other but not fused. The petal colour is either violet (Violet) or white. The 10 stamens (androecium) are in diadelphous pattern. The nine stamens are fused and develop in a tube around the pistil. The tenth stamen remains free. Anthers are bilobed, dorsifixed and introse. The single pistil (gynoecium) is unicarpellary, superior, unilocular, curved style towards the free posterior stamens. The pistil has one to four campylotropous (curved) ovules with marginal placentation. Hairs are present on outer surface of ovary or calyx tube.

Fig. 4.1: Soybean during irrigation

The soybean is self pollinated crop. In prolonged cooler temperatures flowers do not open and behave as cleistogamous. In normal conditions flowers open but pollen shedding occurs before opening. The pollens are heavy and seldom wind borne. Insect may carry pollen from one plant to other. Generally flowers open in morning hours. Natural crossing may occur to the extent of 0.5 to 1% when plants grown in close spacing.

Pods: Pods are borne on main stem or branches in bunches. Pods may be flattened or cylindrical in shape. At maturity pods colour may be brown, tawn or black. Pods are found pubescent (grey or tawn hairs) or glabrous. Pods may bear 1-5 seeds per pod however 2-3 seeds per pod are common.

The Reproductive Biology of Soybean

The stigma is receptive to pollen approximately 24 hours before anthesis and remains receptive 48 hours after anthesis. The anthers mature in the bud and directly pollinate the stigma of the same flower. As a result, soybeans exhibit a high percentage of self-fertilization and cross pollination is usually less than one percent (Caviness, 1966). A soybean plant can produce as many as 400 pods, with two to twenty pods at a single node. Each pod contains one to five seeds. Neither the seed pod, nor the seed, have morphological characteristic that would encourage animal transportation (Biology Document. BIO.1996-10. 1996).

The impact of most of the nutritionally and physiologically functional components of soybean have been summarized in Table 4.1.

Functional Components of Soy and their Impact

Lecithins	Improve memory and learning abilities, improve lipid metabolism
α-Linolenic acid	Essential fatty acid, hypotriglyceridemic, improves cardiac problems
Lectins	Anti-carcinogenic, immunostimulator
Protein	Hypocholesterolemic, antiatherogenic, reduces body fat
Isoflavones	improve lipid metabolism, improves digestive tract function, Isoflavones Estrogenic, hypocholesterolemic, prevents breast, prostate, and colon cancer, bone health
Linoleic acid	Essential fatty acid, hypocholesterolemic
Phytosterols	Hypocholesterolemic, improves prostate cancer
Saponln	Regulates lipid metabolism, antioxidant
Peptides	Readily absorbed, reduce body fat, anticancer

Biochemical Properties:

Constituents of soybean(Liu, K.S.1997)

Proteins

Soybean contains 35–40% protein on a dry-weight basis, of which, 90% is comprised of two storage globulins, 11*S* glycinin and 7*S* β-conglycinin. These proteins include all amino acids necessary to human nutrition, which makes soy products almost equivalent to animal sources in protein quality but with less saturated fat and no cholesterol. Soybean also contains hemagglutinin, trypsin inhibitors, α-amylase and lipoxygenases. As per the FDA's 'Protein Digestibility Corrected Amino Acid' source method, soybean is not only high quality protein, but it is now thought to play preventive and therapeutic roles for several diseases.

Carbohydrates

Soybean contains ~35% carbohydrates, most of which is nonstarch polysaccharides. It also contains oligosaccharides such as, stachyose (4%), and raffinose (1.1%). Stachyose is a tetraose with a galactosegalactose-glucose-fructose structure, while raffinose is a triose with a structure of galactose-glucose-fructose. Polysaccharides are composed mainly of insoluble dietary fiber (Dixit et.al., 2011). Soybean curd refuse (Okara) contains soluble polysaccharides with galacturonic acid as its underlying structure. In addition to use as a dietary fiber supplement, soluble polysaccharides have been used to modify the physical properties of various foods

Oil

Soybean contains roughly approx 19% oil, of which the triglycerides are the main component. Soy oil is characterized by relatively huge amounts of the polyunsaturated fatty acids (PUFA), *i.e.*, ~55% linoleic acid and ~8% α-linolenic acid, of total fatty acids. Linoleic acid in soy oil is an essential fatty acid (EFA) belonging to the ω-6 family of PUFAs, which exerts main nutritional and physiological functions. Even the α-linolenic acid is also an EFA belonging to ω-3 fatty acid family, and plays an important role in the regulation of a number of metabolic pathways (Dixit *et.al.*, 2011. However, due to the presence of lipoxygenases in soybean, linoleic acid renders the soybean oil prone to rancidification .

Vitamins and Minerals

Soybean is a better source of B-vitamins compared to cereals, although it lacks B12 and vitamin C. Soybean oil also contains tocopherols which are excellent natural antioxidants. Soybean oil contains α-tocopherol, β-tocopherol, γ-tocopherol, and δ-tocopherol in trace amount (mg/kg). Soybean also contains ~5% minerals. It is relatively rich in K, P, Ca, Mg, and Fe. Soy ferritin can supplement reasonable quantities of iron.

Isoflavones

The soybean is most abundant source of isoflavones (up to 3 mg/g dry weight) in the nature. Soybean contain three types of isoflavone aglycone *viz.*, daidzein, genistein and glycitein; each of them present in three glycosidic forms in addition to their aglycone form. Daidzein, genistein and their glycosides contribute to >90% of total isoflavone; whereas glycetein and its glycoside are present as minor component (<10%), only.

Phytosterols

Soybean oil contains about 300 to 400 mg of plant sterols per 100 g. The major components of soy sterols are β-sitosterol (53 to 56%), campesterol (20 to 23%), and stigmasterol (17 to 21%). These sterols are proven to have cholesterol-lowering activity, though the mechanism is not completely understood.

Saponins

Soybean also contains ~2% soy saponins (triterpene glycosides) which are currently attracting lot of scientific attention. Soybean saponins have unique chemical structures and physiological functions. Soy saponins are oleonane type triterpene glycosides. Soy saponins are found to have several biological activities such as hepatoprotective, anti-hyperlipidemic, anti-cancer, anti-oxidative and anti-HIV *etc.*

Phospholipids

Soybean oil contains 1-3% phospholipids, of which ~35% phosphatidyl choline, ~25% phosphatidyl ethanolamine, ~15% phosphatidyl inositol, ~5-10% phosphatidic acid (Dixit et.al., 2011. The phospholipids are removed from the oil mainly during the 'degumming' process and are used as a natural food emulsifier. They are polar lipids and contribute to the structure of cell membrane.

Ferritins

Soybean contains ferritin, a multimeric iron storage protein. It is now well proven that the iron from soybean ferritin is as much absorbed and bio-available as much it is from the animal products. Therefore, soybean is recommended to be incorporated in the diet of people suffering from anemia.

Soybean Seed Type and Applications

1. Large seeded soybeans for tofu, soymilk

   Large seeded soybeans are mainly bred for tofu and soymilk production. They are moderately high in protein content . Tofu beans also have a high NSI or PDI, high water up take, low calcium and high germination rate.

2. Medium sized soybeans for bean sprouts, meal and oil

   Soybeans with medium seed size (10 to 12 g/100 g) and a high germination rate are preferred for bean sprouts. High protein, high isoflavone, high sugar and lipoxygenase free soybeans are desirable for bean sprouts.

Flour

Soy flour refers to defatted soybeans where special care was taken during desolventizing (not toasted) in order to minimize denaturation of the protein to retain a high Nitrogen Solubility Index (NSI), for uses such as extruder texturizing (TVP). It is the starting material for production of soy concentrate and soy protein isolate.

Nut Butter

Soybeans have been made into a spread called soynut butter, similar to peanut butter but with soybeans instead. Soy nut butter is made from fresh roasted whole soybeans. It is remarkably similar to peanut butter in taste and texture but has significantly less total and saturated fat than peanut butter and is cholesterol free. It is also suitable for those allergic to nuts or to butter. Open package of cream cheese with chives, a soy milk based cream cheese alternative.

Soy Protein Isolates

It is made wholly from defatted soy meal and is used as an ingredient in high protein foods including dairy foods, nutritional supplements, meat systems, infant formulas, nutritional beverages, cream soups, sauces and snacks. It is also a good source of protein in milk replacers. Due to high protein content, it is highly suited for those people who have high protein needs due to growth (children), famine (acute needs) and chronic diseases (HIV/AIDS/tuberculosis). ASA has prescribed the following requirements.

Texturised Soy Protein

It is made wholly from either defatted soy meal flakes or soy protein concentrates. It is widely used as ingredient in ground meat for patties, sausages, and meal loaf, and in vegetarian foods and stews.

Soy Biscuits

Soy biscuits are consumed directly at any time either with tea or alone. They are available in sealed polythene bags (HDPE 400 microns)/laminated packages/ hermetically sealed metal containers.

Soy Bread

Soy bread is consumed directly at any time either with tea or alone. It is available in sealed polythene bags (HDPE 400 microns)/laminated packages. It will be fresh for 6 day's at normal retail shelf temperatures.

Soy Milk

Soy milk (plain/flavored) is ready to drink and applicable to all sections of people suffering from lactose intolerance (Infants/youth/old/pregnant etc). The soymilk may consist of pure water, soybean extract, sugar and salt. It has 3-4% protein, 1.5-2.0% fat and 8-10% carbohydrates. Flavored soymilk may consist of pure water, soybean extract, sugar, salt, flavors and permitted food colors.

Soy Paneer (Tofu)

It is also known as soybean curd and is a good source of protein and isoflavones. It is made by adding calcium or magnesium salts to soy milk, which enables the soy protein to coagulate to form curd. A simple and low cost technology for making tofu was developed at domestic level. When the tofu is made with calcium, calcium becomes an essential component. The texture of tofu can vary from extra firm, firm, soft and silken, can be used in almost any culinary capacity. ((Gandhi; 2009; AOAC. 2004 and Shurtleff and Aoyagi; 2013)

Cultivation

Season

- Soybean cultivate well in warm and moist climate.
- A temperature of 26.5 to 30°C appears to be the optimum for most of the varieties.
- Soil temperatures of 15.5°C or above favor rapid germination and vigorous seedling growth. A lower temperature tends to delay the flowering.
- Day length is the key factor in most of the soybean varieties as they are short day plants.

Soil

- Soyabean can grow on all types of soils except deep) sands.
- The soil should be well drained and fertile. It grows best on sandy loams as well as clay loams.
- The soil pH ranging from 6.0 to 7.5 is the most suitable for its cultivation.
- The crop requires moist soil for germination.
- However, the field should have an efficient drainage during growing period.

Land Preparation

- It requires leveled field free from clods, weeds, stones, stubbles, etc.
- Well drained and fertile loam soils with a pH between 6.0 and 7.5 are most suitable for the cultivation of soybean.
- Sodic and saline soils inhibit germination of seeds. Water logging is also injurious to the crop.
- A well prepared seedbed will help the seeds to germinate quickly and uniformly. The field should be ploughed 30 to 35 cm deep with a soil turning plough, 3-4 ploughings with desi plough and followed by planking.
- The farmyard manure or compost is applied at the time of last ploughing.
- Apply BHC 10% or Aldrin 5% or Heptachlor @ 25 kg/ha before last ploughing in, furrows to avoid insects contact with the seed.

Sowing

There are two cropping seasons of soyabean namely kharif and spring. In case of kharif season the most common time of sowing is onset of monsoon or last week of June to first week of July. But in case of irrigated conditions sowing of crop by mid of June results in a better crop growth and less weed problem. The spring sowing is done between 15th of February and 15th of March.

1. Seed rate and spacing and sowing depth

- Seed rate is governed by numerous factors such as seed size, seed weight, spacing, cropping season, germination and purity percentage of the seed.
- Soyabean grown for grain purpose needs about 20-30 kg seed per hectare but the fodder crop needs about 70-75 kg/hectare during kharif season and 100-120 kg/hectare during spring or summer season which is because of closer spacing.
- The row to row distance should be kept 30 to 45 cm Iand plant to plant 4 to 5 cm.
- Sow the seeds about 4-5; cm deep. Spacing is maintained by thinning or gap filling which is done 5 to 10 days after germination.
- There should be about 5 lakh plants per hectare.

Fig. 4.2: Soybean plant spacing (plant after 20 days of sowing)

2. Seed treatment

- Treat the seeds with Thiram 75 % or 1 : 1 mixture of Captan and Thiram @ 3 g/kg of seed. This will protect the seed and seedlings from different diseases like rotting, etc.
- Soyabean is a leguminous crop which has Rhizobium bacteria in its roots which is responsible for nodulation.

- For better nodulation and good growth of the crop, it is important to treat the seed before sowing. There are two ways to treat the seed. The first way is to bring some soil from the field where it was grown earlier and mix the soil with seed before sowing. The second way is to use the Rhizobium culture and treat the seed with it.

Irrigation

- Dry spell adversely influence the crop, therefore irrigation, if offered, should be used as per requirement.
- For quicker coverage, sprinkler system can be used for good results. One life saving irrigation at the critical crop growth stage has been found to increase the yield by 50%.
- It is observed that maximum reduction in yield due to moisture stress occurs during the last week of pod development and filling stage.

  Further, water stress at the end of bean filling stage or at beginning of flowering has only small effects on soyabean yield but stress during flowering and pod development appears to be responsible for flower and pod abortion.

Fig. 4.3: Soybean at flowering stage

- Stress during bean filling reduces seed size. Therefore, it is essential to apply sufficient water to the field for better germination and then to irrigate the crop between pod development and pod filling stages for obtaining higher grain yield.

Fig. 4.4: Soybean at pod filling stage

- Soyabean requires about 60-65 cm annual rainfall.
- It needs irrigation if the rainfall is lower than 60 cm.
- However, higher rainfall is equally or more harmful than lower rainfall because higher moisture at germination causes rotting of seeds or seedlings.
- Water logging in soyabean field at later stages of growth causes anaerobic conditions, poor nodulation and poor yield of the crop.

Harvesting Soybean

The maturity period ranges from 90 to 120 days depending on the varieties. When the plants reach maturity, the leaves turn yellow and drop and soybean pods dry out quickly. There is a rapid loss of moisture from the seed. At harvest, the moisture content of the seeds should be 15%. Harvesting can be done by hand, breaking the stalks on the ground level or with sickle. Alternatively, the crop can be harvested when the seeds are at the hard-dough stage, when the seed moisture content is between 14 and 16%. Cut the mature plants at ground level. Stack them loosely on tarpaulin and allow them to dry in the open for 2 weeks before threshing. Do not harvest by hand pulling because this may remove the nutrient that the soybean has added to the soil.

Postharvest Operations

Threshing soybean

Thresh manually or mechanically when the plants are properly dry and as soon as possible. Manual threshing is mainly recommended for small-scale production. It involves piling soybean plants on tarpaulin or putting dry soybean pods in sacks and beating them with a stick. The material is then winnowed to remove the seeds from the debris. Use mechanical threshers in large-scale production. Such threshers are equipped.

Diseases and Pests

A. Diseases

In India soyabean is affected by many fungi and, bacteria resulting in heavy loss in yield. These are ordinary in the early growth stage and at maturity stage. Important diseases are given below.

1. *Pod blight:* This disease is caused by Colletotrichum spp and in this disease the pods at first become yellowish green and soon dry out. Consequently, the seed formation is severely affected. The seeds in diseased pods may be shrivelled and mouldy.

Control: Spray Zineb @ '2-5 kg/ha in 1000 litres of water.

2. *Mosaic:* It is a viral disease. In this disease mottling of leaves accompanied with a light crankling and reduction in size of pods occurs. Plants produce only a few pods and remain stunted in growth.

Control: Spray Metasystox 25 EC @ 1 kg per 1000 litres of water per hectare at 10 days interval till crop becomes 75 days old.

3. *Bacterial pustules:* Lesions appear on leaves as yellow and pustular outgrowth. Later on these spots turn reddish brown in colour with margins yellow. On the pods also small reddish brown spots appear.

Control

- Seed treatment with Ceresan (0.2%) effectively reduces the seed-borne inoculum of the pathogen .
- Spray Carboxin (1,500 ppm) i.e. 1.5 g in 1 litre of water
- Seed treatment with fungicides like Thiram (3 g per kg seed) or Carbendazin (2 g per kg seed) fairly reduces the seedborne inoculum. Spraying with Mancozeb (0.3%), Carbendazin (0.1%) or Benomyl (0.1%) minimises the disease severity.

4. *Dry root rot*

The disease is caused by *Macrophomina phaseolina*. Small irregular or round black spots appear below the epidermis on the affected roots and stems.

Control

- Seed dressing with Thiram, Quintozene or Captan.
- Adopt crop rotations.

5. *Late blight:* This disease is caused by *Phytophthora infestans* .Black, water soaked irregular spots are formed on the leaves and mottled like marble stone, rust brown patches are seen on the fruits. Low temperature (10-15 °C) with cloudy weather for 3-4 days favours the disease. The infected portion of the fruit shrinks.

Control

- Spray the crop with Bordeaux mixture 1.0 per cent.
- Spray zineb or Dithane Z- 78.
- Remove all the infested parts and burn them.

Weed Control

Because of more space between the rows, slow growth at early stage and warmer season, weeds grow profusely, competing with the crop for water, light and nutrients. This adversely affects the total yield. Inadequate weeding may reduce the yield by 55-65%. During rainy season the infestation of weeds is high. The timely control of weeds is necessary. One or two weedings are generally needed by the crop. Sometimes due to rains or water in the field or non-availability of labour, manual weeding may not be possible. In such a case application of herbicides will be more beneficial.Two types of weeds are found in soya bean field;

1. Narrow leaved weeds e.g. doob grass, banra, narku/ and makra.
2. Broad leaved weeds e.g. sated murgi, nunia, rasbhari.

Control

- Apply Basalin @ 1 kg per hectare in 800-1000 litres of water before the sowing of seeds after the final preparation of land.
- Never allow the weeds to grow in the first for weeks after sowing.
- Spray Tok-E-25 or Lasso @ 4 litres in 600 litres of water per hectare on soil surface.
- Two weedings at 15 days and 35 days after sowing are necessary.
- At the time of hoeing and interculture remove the weeds and destroy them.

1. *Thrips:* The dry weather favours in its production. The adults are tiny black insects and nymphs are yellowish in colour. They suck the sap of the plant which results in the fall of the leaves and form very small spots on the leaves.

Control: Spray Matasystox 25 EC/Rogur 30EC @ 600-700 ml per ha.

2. *White fly:* The adults of this fly transmit yellow mosaic virus. It is a very serious pest of Tarai region of U.P. and Delhi. The infected plants have reduced pod formation that results in low yield.

Control: Spray Metasystox @ 750 mg/ha at an interval of 10 days. Generally 3 to 4 sprays will be required.

3. *Jassids:* The small, greenish leaf hoppers, nymphs and adults are found on the underside of the leaves sucking the cell sap. The leaves of the infested plants turn yellow and start curling. In severe cases the infested leaves turn brown red in colour and crumple. The growth of the plants remains stunted.

Control: Spray 0.03 % Phosphamidon or Malathion (0.1%)

4. *Blue beetle:* The beetle is 4.5 to 6 mm long, metallic blue in colour, causes 30-55% seedling damage. The infected plants remain stunted and produce less grains. The pest can cause upto 27% reduction in yield.

Control

- Spray Thiodan 35 EC 1.5 litre in 1000 litres of water.
- Adopt crop rotation.

5. *Stem fly:* On opening the damaged steam, yellowish maggots or brown drum shaped pupae are found in the tunnelled stems. The infested plants dry up and leaves start to drop.

Control

- Use Phosphamidon 100-250 ml per hectare. Repeat the spray after 10 days.

6. *Storage:* Soybean should be stored at a moisture content of 10% or less. A soybean seed is sufficiently dry when it cannot be dented with the teethor fingernails. At harvest, the grains usually contain about 14% moisture. Dry to 13% moisture for storage of 6–12 months and to 10–11% for longer storage. Open-air drying is the most practical way to protect soybean in storage. Place 50-kg or 100-kg bags of clean soybean on a rack in the cold room or in shade. High moisture content in stored soybean encourages the development of various agents of deterioration, such as insects and microorganisms. Good storage management can greatly influence the storability of soybean and subsequent germination when planted in the field. Do not leave soybean exposed to high temperatures, as it will increase deterioration and reduce seed viability.

Varieties: The description of some of the important and suitable variety is given below.

- *JS 95-60:* It is suitable for growing in Punjab, Delhi, Haryana, Uttar Pradesh, Madhya Pradesh, Gujarat and Rajasthan. It matures in about 82-88 days and yields 18-20 quintals per hectare. It has Violet flowers, glabrous leaf, stem and pod, four seeded pods, lanceolate leaf, yellow testa, grey hilum, determinate.

- *JS 71-05:* This variety is moderately resistant to stem fly, BP, MLS and anthracnose. It matures in 90-95 days and yields about 20-25 quintals per hectare. The plant is early bold seeded, high oil content, low emergence.

7. *Ankur:* This variety is developed at Pantnagar Agriculture University and released in 1974 for general cultivation. The plants are tall (120-130) cm with white flowers. The seeds are small, a bit flat, and yellow in colour with light brown hilum. Due to smaller seed size, it has better germination. It is susceptible to yellow mosaic virus but resistant to rust and bacterial pustule. The crop matures in 125 days and yields about 20-25 quintals of grain per hectare.

8. *Shilajeet:* This variety was released in 1979 by Pantnagar Agricultural University. It is suitable for northen plains and hills. It matures in about 105 days and produces 20-25 quintal grains. It is suitable for mixed cropping system. It is moderately resistant to rust, bacterial pustules and yellow mosaic.

- *JS 335:* Resistant to bacterial pustule, bacterial blight and tolerant to green mosaic. Susceptible to YMV.This variety is with outstanding with wide adaptability. Early and with high germination rate. It matures in 95-100 days and yields about 25-30 quintals per hectare.
- *NRC 12(Ahilya2):* It is suitable for growing in Punjab, Delhi, Haryana, Uttar Pradesh, Madhya Pradesh, Gujarat and Rajasthan. It matures in about 96-99 days and yields 25-30 quintals per hectare. It is resistant to shattering, BP, MLS, BB, RAB, tolerant to defoliators, stem fly & girdle beetles.

9. *Lee:* It is an introduction from the USA. It is resistant to bacterial pustule and susceptible to yellow mosaic. It is good for all the soyabean growing states of the country. It matures in about 100 days and yields about 20 to 25 quintals per hectare. The plant has greenish stem and leaves. Pods are usually three-seeded, seeds are yellow in colour, 100 seeds weighing 17-18 grams.

- *Punjab-1:* It is suitable for growing in Punjab, Delhi, Haryana, Uttar Pradesh, Madhya Pradesh, Gujarat and Rajasthan. It matures in about 120-130 days and yields 20-25 quintals per hectare. It is resistant to root rot but susceptible to bacterial pustules and yellow mosaic. Pods are usually three-seeded, flowers are purple coloured, pods and leaves are covered with brownish hairs, stem green; 100 seeds weigh about 16-17 grams.
- *Clark-63:* It is an introduction from the USA. The leaves and pods are covered with brown hairs, flowers are white, seeds are yellow, shiny and with black hilum. It matures in about 105 days and yields 25-30 quintals per hectare. The variety is resistant to the bacterial pustules but susceptible to yellow mosaic and rots. It is suitable for all soyabean growing areas of the country, especially rainfed areas.

- *Bragg:* It has also been introduced from the USA. It is susceptible to rot and yellow mosaic but resistant to bacterial pustule. It is suitable for all the soya bean growing states of the country. It matures in about 120 days and yields 20-25 quintals pre hectare. The plant is green stemmed, leaves and pods covered with brown hairs, 2-3 seeds/pods; 100 seeds weigh 12-18 g, Flowers are white, seeds are yellow, shiny and with black hilum.
- *Kali Tur:* It has an excellent germination capacity in adverse climatic conditions. It yields about 15-20 quintals per hectare and matures in 120-125 days. It is a late maturing variety. In this variety the plant is tall; stem thin; leaves pointed, green in colour and flowers are blue.
- *PK-262:* This variety was released in 1982 for general cultivation in Tarai and Bhabar areas of Uttar Pradesh. It is resistant to lodging. It yields about 30 quintal grains per hectare.
- *JS 97-52:* This veriety is with wide adaptable culture of medium duration. Excellent regarding germinability, field emergence and longevity. It provides high yields in varied ecoadaphic situations and rated as a multiple resistant variety.
- *Durga(JS 72-280):* Tolerant to bacterial pustules. It contains white flowers, tawny pubescence, yellow seed coat, black hilum, tall and indeterminate, fast growing.
- *Pusa 22:* It contains purple flowers, tawny pubescene, creamy seed coat, brown hilum and tall plants. It is highly tolerant to yellow maosaic, resistant to bacterial pustule, rhizoctonia wilt and Alternaria blight and tolerant to bud blight.

Crossing Technique in Soybean

Soybean contains small floral parts due to which artificial cross-pollination becomes a difficult work. Therefore, special care should be taken for successful hybridization programme. Parental cultivars may be grown in pots or in fields (pair rows) with sufficient spacing at different intervals. This way crossing between early and late types of cultures become possible and sufficient number of crossed pods or seeds can be achieved. Rains, temperatures and humidity have great effect in the success of artificial hybridization. Flowers are prepared for crossing just as the floral bud is swollen and the corolla is visible through the calyx. The other buds should be removed gently with forceps with out making any injury to the desirable bud. In the process of emasculation the very first operation is to remove the sepals with the help of forceps by pulling down the lobes one by one. In this way, corolla is exposed then with the help of forceps by catching them and pulling upward all petals are removed. Simultaneously,

10 anthers are also removed generally. However, if some stamens are left, with the help of forceps gently keep them out. In this whole operation it must be taken care that pistil may not get any injury. This emasculated plant is treated as female parent.

Fresh open flowers are collected from the desirable male parent. Corolla is removed with the help of forceps and catching the base of flower, emasculated bud stigma (female parent) is brushed with the anthers (male parent). In event of successful pollination and fertilization a pod is visible after seven days. The cross should be marked by tagging with prize labels and write name of parents (name of female parent X name of male parent) and put date also. The removal of other pods of same axis should be done. The scar made by removal of the calyx helps in identifying the crossed pods. An efficient person may have 50% success. However, usually achievement rate varies from 10% to 20% depends upon several factors. The proper time for this important work is most suitable 8-10 a.m.

Problems in Cross Breeding

1. Small flowers size
2. High percentage of Selfing
3. Low seed setting

Health Risks

Phytoestrogen

Soybeans contain isoflavones called genistein and daidzein, which are one source of phytoestrogens in the human diet. Because most naturally occurring estrogenic substances show weak activity, normal consumption of foods that contain these phytoestrogens should not provide sufficient amounts to elicit a physiological response in humans. Plant lignans associated with high fiber foods such as cereal brans and beans are the principal precursor to mammalian lignans which have an ability to bind to human estrogen sites. Soybeans and processed soy foods do not contain the highest "total phytoestrogen" content of foods.

In Women

A 2001 literature review suggested that women with current or past breast cancer should be aware of the risks of potential tumor growth when taking soy products, based on the effect of phytoestrogens on breast cancer cell growth in animals.

A 2006 commentary reviewed the relationship with soy and breast cancer. They stated that soy may prevent breast cancer, but cautioned that the impact of isoflavones on breast tissue needs to be evaluated at the cellular level in women at high risk for breast cancer.

In Men

Because of the phytoestrogen content, some studies, but not all, have suggested that there is an inverse correlation between soybean ingestion and testosterone in men. For this reason, they may protect against the development of prostate cancer. A theoretical decrease in the risk of prostate cancer should, however, be weighed against the possible side-effects of decreased testosterone, which are still unclear.

Allergens

About 9% of children in the USA are allergic to soybean proteins. Common symptoms are urticaria, rash, itching and redness of the skin.

Brain

Estrogen helps protect and repair the brain during and after injury.The mimicry of estrogen by the phytoestrogens in soy has introduced a controversy over whether such a replacement is harmful or helpful to the brain.

Carcinogen

Raw soy flour is known to cause pancreatic cancer in rats. Whether this is also true in humans is unknown because no studies comparing cases of pancreatic cancer and soy intake in humans have yet been conducted, and the doses used to induce pancreatic cancer in rats are said to be larger than humans would normally consume. Heated soy flour may not be carcinogenic in rats.

REFERENCES

Singh RJ, Hymowitz T (1999) Soybean Genetic Resources and Crop Improvement. *Genome* 42:605-616.

Singh, Goriqpal. (2010). Soybean Botany Production and uses. Departmenrt of Plant Breeding and Genetics Punjab Agricultural University, Ludhiana. ISBN No. 13:9781845936440. Printed and Bound in The UK by CPI Antony Rowe.

Bhatnagar, P.S. (1984). Soybean in India: Potential and Research Direction. Paper Prepared for the Regional Soybean Meeting, 20–22 Jul 1984, AVRDC/IRRI, Jakarta, Indonesia.

Bhatnagar, P.S. (1985). Prospects of Soybean in India. Presented at the Workshop on Modern Trends in Oils and Allied Industries, 22 Nov to 2 Dec 1985, New Delhi, India.

Hymowitz, T. and Harlan, J.R. (1983). Introduction of Soybeans to North America by Samuel Bowen in 1765. Economic Botany 37:371–379.

Liu, K.S. (1997) Chemistry and Nurtitional Value of Soybean Components. *In Soybean: Chemistry, Technology, and Utilization*. Chapman & Hall, New York: 25-113.

Dixit, A. K., Antony J. I. X., Sharma N K.1 and Tiwari R K.(2011). Soybean Constituents and their Functional Benefits. *Opportunity, Challenge and Scope of Natural Products in Medicinal Chemistry*. ISBN: 978-81-308-0448-4: 367-383

Bernard, R.L. and M.G. Weiss (1973). Qualitative Genetics. Soybeans, Production and Uses. B.E. Caldwell (ed.). Agronomy Series, American Society of Agronomy, Madison, Wisconsin, USA.pp. 117-154.

Biology Document. BIO. 1996-10. (1996). The Biology of *Glycine max* (L.) Merr (Soybean):1-11

Upfold, R. A. and H. T. Olechowski (1988). Soybean Production. Publication 173. Ministry of Agriculture and Food.

Hymowitz, T. and C. A. Newell (1981). Taxonomy of the Genus Glycine, Domestication and Uses of Soybeans. Econ. Bot. 37: 371-379.

Duffy C, Perez K and A Partridge (2007). Implications of Phytoestrogen Intake for Breast Cancer. *CA Cancer Journal for Clinicians*. 57: 260-277.

Hadley, H.H. and T. Hymowitz (1973). Speciation and Cytogenetics. Soybeans, Production and Uses. B.E. Caldwell (ed.). *Agronomy Series, American Society of Agronomy, Madison, Wisconsin, USA*. 97-116.

Hymowitz, T. (1970). On Domestication of Soybean. Economic Botany 24:408–421.

Shurtleff, William; Aoyagi, Akiko.(2013). History of Whole Dry Soybeans, Used as Beans, or Ground, Mashed or Flaked (240 BCE to 2013). Lafayette, California, 950 pp.

Hymowitz, T., and C.A. Newell (1981). Taxonomy of the Genus Glycine, Domestication and Uses of Soybeans. Econ. Bot. 35:272-278.

Johnson, R.R. (1987). Crop Management, In Soybeans: Improvement, Production and Uses. P. 355-390. *In J.R. Wilcox, (ed). Amer. Soc. Agronomy, Madison, WI.*

Gandhi, A. P. (2009). Review Article Quality of Soybean and Its Food Products. *International Food Research Journal* 16: 11-19.

AOAC. (2004). Official Methods of Analysis of AOAC, International. *Association of Analytical Chemists International, Gaithersburg, Maryland.*

James, C. (2010). Global Status of Commercialized Biotech/GM crops: 2010. Ithaca, NY, US, ISAAA. ISAAA Brief No. 42. 279 p.

Bernard, R.L. and M.G. Weiss 1973 Qualitative Genetics. Soybeans, Production and Uses. B.E. Caldwell (ed.). Agronomy Series, American Society of Agronomy, Madison, Wisconsin, USA. pp. 117-154.

Upfold, R. A. and H. T. Olechowski 1988 Soybean Production. Publication 173. Ministry of Agriculture and Food.

Agriculture Crops and Food Security
Edited by: Dr. Pawan Kumar 'Bharti' and Alka Chauhan
ISBN: 978-93-5056-881-1
Edition: 2017
Published by: Discovery Publishing House Pvt. Ltd., New Delhi (India)

5

Functional Foods

[1]Priyanka Shukla and [2]Priyadarshini

The tenet "Let food be thy medicine and medicine be thy food," espoused by Hippocrates nearly 2,500 years ago, is receiving renewed interest. In particular, there has been an explosion of consumer interest in the health enhancing role of specific foods or physiologically-active food components, so-called functional foods (Hasler, 1998). Clearly, all foods are functional, as they provide taste, aroma, or nutritive value. Within the last decade, however, the term functional as it applies to food has adopted a different connotation—that of providing an additional physiological benefit beyond that of meeting basic nutritional needs. This Scientific Status Summary reviews the literature for the primary plant and animal foods that have been linked with physiological benefits. Although a plethora of biologically active compounds have been identified in this regard (Kuhn, 1998), this review focuses on foods, rather than specific compounds isolated from foods.

DEFINITION

The term functional foods was first introduced in Japan in the mid-1980s and refers to processed foods containing ingredients that aid specific bodily functions in addition to being nutritious. To date, Japan is the only country that has formulated a specific regulatory approval process for functional foods. Known as Foods for Specified Health Use (FOSHU), these foods are eligible to bear a seal of approval from the Japanese Ministry of Health and Welfare (Arai, 1996). Currently, 100 products are licensed as FOSHU foods in Japan. In the United States, the functional foods category is not recognized legally. Irrespective of this, many organizations have proposed definitions for this new and emerging area of the food and nutrition sciences. The Institute of Medicine's Food and Nutrition Board (IOM/FNB, 1994) defined functional

1 Junior Research Fellow, National Institute of Food Technology, Enterpreneurship and Management, Kundli, Haryana,131028
2 Guest Faculty, Department of Food and Agriculture Engg., Faculty of Engg. and Technology M.G.C.G.V Chitrakoot Satna (M.P) INDIA - 485780

foods as "any food or food ingredient that may provide a health benefit beyond the traditional nutrients it contains."

Health-conscious baby boomers have made functional foods the leading trend in the U.S. food industry (Meyer, 1998). Estimates, however, of the magnitude of this market vary significantly, as there is no consensus on what constitutes a functional food. Decision Resources, Inc. (Waltham, 1998) estimates the market value of functional foods at $28.9 billion. More significant, perhaps, is the potential of functional foods to mitigate disease, promote health and reduce health care costs.

FUNCTIONAL FOODS FROM PLANT SOURCES

Overwhelming evidence from epidemiological, in vivo, in vitro, and clinical trial data indicates that a plant-based diet can reduce the risk of chronic disease, particularly cancer. In 1992, a review of 200 epidemiological studies (Block *et al.*, 1992) showed that cancer risk in people consuming diets high in fruits and vegetables was only one-half that in those consuming few of these foods. It is now clear that there are components in a plant-based diet other than traditional nutrients that can reduce cancer risk. Steinmetz and Potter (1991a) identified more than a dozen classes of these biologically active plant chemicals, now known as "phytochemicals."

Health professionals are gradually recognizing the role of phytochemicals in health enhancement (ADA, 1995; Howard and Kritcheveky, 1997), aided in part by the Nutrition Labeling and Education Act of 1990 (NLEA). The NLEA required nutrition labeling for most foods and allowed disease- or health-related messages on food labels.

(a) Oats: Oat products are a widely studied dietary source of the cholesterol-lowering soluble fiber b-glucan. There is now significant scientific agreement that consumption of this particular plant food can reduce total and low density lipoprotein (LDL) cholesterol, thereby reducing the risk of coronary heart disease (CHD). For this, the Food and Drug Administration (FDA) awarded the first food-specific health claim in January 1997 (DHHS/FDA, 1997), in response to a petition submitted by the Quaker Oats Company (Chicago, Ill.).

In its health claim petition, the Quaker Oats Company summarized 37 human clinical intervention trials conducted between 1980 and 1995. The majority of these studies revealed statistically significant reductions in total and LDL-cholesterol in hypercholesterolemic subjects consuming either a typical American diet or a low fat diet. The daily amount of oat bran or oatmeal consumed in the above studies ranged from 34 g to 123 g. Quaker Oats determined that 3 g of b-glucan would be required to achieve a 5% reduction in serum cholesterol, an amount equivalent to approximately 60 g of oatmeal or 40 g of oat bran (dry weight). Thus, a food bearing the health claim must contain 13 g of oat bran or 20 g oatmeal, and provide, without fortification, at least 1.0 g of bglucan per serving. In February of 1998, the soluble fiber health claim was extended to include psyllium fiber.

Soy. Soy has been in the spotlight during the 1990s. Not only is soy a high quality protein, as assessed by the FDA's "Protein Digestibility Corrected Amino Acid Score" method, it is now thought to play preventive and therapeutic roles in cardiovascular disease (CVD), cancer, osteoporosis and the alleviation of menopausal symptoms.

The cholesterol-lowering effect of soy is the most well-documented physiological effect. A 1995 meta-analysis of 38 separate studies (involving 743 subjects) found that the consumption of soy protein resulted in significant reductions in total cholesterol (9.3%), LDL cholesterol (12.9%) and triglycerides (10.5%), with a small but insignificant increase (2.4%)in high density lipoprotein (HDL) cholesterol (Anderson *et al.*, 1995). Linear regression analysis indicated that the threshold level of soy intake at which the effects on blood lipids became significant was 25 g. Regarding the specific component responsible for the cholesterol-lowering effect of soy, recent attention has focused on the isoflavones (Potter, 1998). Isoflavones, however, were not effective in lowering cholesterol in two recent studies (Hodgson *et al.*, 1998; Nestle *et al.*, 1997). The exact mechanism by which soy exerts its hypocholesterolemic effect has not been fully elucidated.

On May 4, 1998, Protein Technologies International (PTI, St. Louis, Mo.) petitioned the FDA for a health claim on soy protein containing products pertaining to reduced risk of CHD. Based on an effective daily level of 25 g soy protein, PTI proposed that the amount of soy protein required to qualify an individual food to bear the health claim is 6.25 g with a minimum of 12.5 mg of total isoflavones (aglycone form) per reference amount customarily consumed. On August 12, the FDA accepted PTI's petition and is in the process of formulating a proposed rule.

Several classes of anticarcinogens have been identified in soybeans, including protease inhibitors, phytosterols, saponins, phenolic acids, phytic acid, and isoflavones (Messina and Barnes, 1991). Of these, isoflavones (genistein and daidzein) are particularly noteworthy because soybeans are the only significant dietary source of these compounds. Isoflavones are heterocyclic phenols structurally similar to the estrogenic steroids. Because they are weak estrogens, isoflavones may act as antiestrogens by competing with the more potent, naturally-occurring endogenous estrogens (e.g., 17b-estradiol) for binding to the estrogen receptor. This may explain why populations that consume significant amounts of soy (e.g., Southeast Asia) have reduced risk of estrogen-dependent cancer. However, the epidemiological data on soy intake and cancer risk are inconsistent at the present time (Messina *et al.*, 1997). To date, there are no published clinical intervention trials investigating the role of soy in reducing cancer risk.

Soy may also benefit bone health (Anderson and Garner, 1997). A recent clinical study involving 66 post-menopausal women conducted at the University of Illinois (Erdman and Potter, 1997) found that 40 g isolated soy protein (ISP) per day (containing 90 mg total isoflavones) significantly increased (approximately 2%) both bone mineral content and density in the lumbar spine after 6 months.

The theory that soy may alleviate menopausal symptoms was prompted by the observation that Asian women report significantly lower levels of hot flushes and night sweats compared to Western women. Most recently, 60 grams of ISP daily for 3 months reduced hot flashes by 45% in 104 postmenopausal women (Albertazzi *et al.*, 1998). Although these observations are exciting, there is a significant placebo effect in these studies, and it is too premature to suggest that soy may substitute for hormone replacement therapy.

(b) Flaxseed: Among the major seed oils, flaxseed oil contains the most (57%) of the omega-3 fatty acid, a-linolenic acid. Recent research, however, has focused more specifically on fiber-associated compounds known as lignans. The two primary mammalian lignans, enterodiol and its oxidation product, enterolactone, are formed in the intestinal tract by bacterial action on plant lignan precursors (Setchell *et al.*, 1981). Flaxseed is the richest source of mammalian lignan precursors (Thompson *et al.*, 1991). Because enterodiol and enterolactone are structurally similar to both naturally-occurring and synthetic estrogens, and have been shown to possess weakly estrogenic and antiestrogenic activities, they may play a role in the prevention of estrogendependent cancers. However, there are no epidemiological data and relatively few animal studies to support this hypothesis. In rodents, flaxseed has been shown to decrease tumors of the colon and mammary gland (Thompson, 1995) as well as of the lung (Yan *et al.*, 1998).

Fewer studies have evaluated the effects of flaxseed feeding on risk markers for cancer in humans. Phipps *et al.* (1993) demonstrated that the ingestion of 10 g of flaxseed per day elicited several hormonal changes associated with reduced breast cancer risk. Adlercreutz *et al.* (1982) found that the urinary lignan excretion was significantly lower in postmenopausal breast cancer patients compared to controls eating a normal mixed or a lactovegetarian diet.

Consumption of flaxseed has also been shown to reduce total and LDL cholesterol (Bierenbaum *et al.*, 1993; Cunnane *et al.*, 1993), as well as platelet aggregation (Allman *et al.*, 1995).

(c) Tomatoes: Selected by Eating Well magazine as the 1997 Vegetable of the Year, tomatoes have received significant attention within the last three years because of interest in lycopene, the primary carotenoid found in this fruit (Gerster, 1997) and its role in cancer risk reduction (Weisburger, 1998).

In a prospective cohort study of more than 47,000 men, those who consumed tomato products 10 or more times per week had less than one-half the risk of developing advanced prostate cancer (Giovannucci *et al.*, 1995). Interestingly, lycopene is the most abundant carotenoid in the prostate gland (Clinton *et al.*, 1996). Other cancers whose risk have been inversely associated with serum or tissue levels of lycopene include breast, digestive tract, cervix, bladder, and skin (Clinton, 1998) and possibly lung (Li *et al.*, 1997). Proposed mechanisms by which lycopene could influence cancer risk are related to its antioxidant function. Lycopene is the most efficient quencher of singlet oxygen in biological systems (Di Mascio *et al.*, 1989). The antioxidant function of lycopene may also explain the recent observation in a multi-center European study that adipose tissue levels of carotenoids were inversely associated with risk for myocardial infarction (Kohlmeier *et al.*, 1997b).

(d) Garlic: Garlic (*Allium sativum*) is likely the herb most widely quoted in the literature for medicinal properties (Nagourney, 1998). Thus, its not surprising that garlic has ranked as the second best selling herb in the United States for the past two years (Anon., 1998). The purported health benefits of garlic are numerous, including cancer chemopreventive, antibiotic, antihypertensive, and cholesterol-lowering properties (Srivastava *et al.*, 1995).

The characteristic flavor and pungency of garlic are due to an abundance of oiland water-soluble, sulfur-containing elements, which are also likely responsible for the various medicinal effects ascribed to this plant. However, intact, undisturbed bulbs of garlic contain only a few medicinally active components. The intact garlic bulb contains an odorless amino acid, alliin, which is converted enzymatically by allinase into allicin when the garlic cloves are crushed (Block, 1992). This latter compound is responsible for the characteristic odor of fresh garlic. Allicin then spontaneously decomposes to form numerous sulfur-containing compounds, some of which have been investigated for their chemopreventive activity.

Garlic components have been shown to inhibit tumorigenesis in several experimental models (Reuter *et al.*, 1996). However, additional reports have shown garlic to be ineffective. Inconclusive results are likely due to differences in the type of garlic compounds or preparations used by various investigators. Considerable variation in the quantity of organosulfur compounds available in fresh and commercially available garlic products has been demonstrated (Lawson *et al.*, 1991).

Several epidemiologic studies show that the garlic may be effective in reducing human cancer risk (Dorant *et al.*, 1993). A relatively large case-control investigation conducted in China showed a strong inverse relationship between stomach cancer risk and increasing allium intake (You *et al.*, 1988). More recently, in a study of more than 40,000 postmenopausal women, garlic consumption was associated with nearly a 50% reduction in colon cancer risk

(Steinmetz *et al.*, 1994). Not all epidemiological studies, however, have shown garlic to be protective against carcinogenesis. A 1991 review of 12 case-control studies (Steinmetz and Potter, 1991b), found that eight showed a negative association, one showed no association and three studies showed a positive association. A more recent review of 20 epidemiological studies (Ernst, 1997) suggests that allium vegetables, including onions, may confer a protective effect on cancers of the gastrointestinal tract.

Garlic has also been advocated for the prevention of CVD, possibly through antihypertensive properties. According to Silagy and Neil (1994a), however, there is still insufficient evidence to recommend it as a routine clinical therapy for the treatment of hypertensive subjects. The cardioprotective effects are more likely due to its cholesterol-lowering effect. In a metaanalysis, Warshafsky *et al.* (1993) summarized the results of five randomized, placebo-controlled clinical trials, involving 410 patients. They showed that an average of 900 mg garlic/day (as little as one half to one clove of garlic) could decrease total serum cholesterol levels by approximately 9%. In a second meta-analysis involving 16 trials, Silagy and Neil (1994b) reported that 800 mg garlic/day reduced total cholesterol levels by 12%. The validity of both of these reports, however, is reduced by methodological shortcomings, including the fact that dietary intake, weight, and/or exogenous garlic ingestion was not always well-controlled. In a recent multicenter, randomized, placebo-controlled trial in which dietary assessment and supervision were strictly controlled, 12 weeks of garlic treatment was ineffective in lowering cholesterol levels in subjects with hypercholesterolemia (Isaacsohn *et al.*, 1998). It is currently unclear which component in garlic is responsible for its cholesterol-lowering effect.

(e) Broccoli and other Cruciferous Vegetables: Epidemiological evidence has associated the frequent consumption of cruciferous vegetables with decreased cancer risk. In a recent review of 87 casecontrol studies, Verhoeven *et al.* (1996) demonstrated an inverse association between consumption of total brassica vegetables and cancer risk. The percentages of case-control studies showing an inverse association between consumption of cabbage, broccoli, cauliflower, and Brussels sprouts and cancer risk were 70, 56, 67 and 29%, respectively. Verhoeven *et al.* (1997) attributed the anticarcinogenic properties of cruciferous vegetables to their relatively high content of glucosinolates.

Glucosinolates are a group of glycosides stored within cell vacuoles of all cruciferous vegetables. Myrosinase, an enzyme found in plant cells, catalyzes these compounds to a variety of hydrolysis products, including isothiocyanates and indoles. Indole-3 carbinol (I3C) is currently under investigation for its cancer chemopreventive properties, particularly of the mammary gland. In addition to the induction of phase I and II detoxification reactions, I3C may reduce cancer risk by modulating estrogen metabolism. The C-16 and C-2 hydroxylations of estrogens involve competing cytochrome P-450-dependent pathways, each sharing a common estrogen substrate pool. Studies suggest that the increased formation of 2-hydroxylated (catechol) estrogen metabolites relative to 16-hydroxylated forms, may protect against cancer, as catechol estrogens can act as antiestrogens in cell culture. In contrast, 16-hydroxyestrone is estrogenic and can bind to the estrogen receptor. In humans, I3C administered at 500 mg daily (equivalent to 350-500 g cabbage/day) for 1 week significantly increased the extent of estradiol 2-hydroxylation in women (Michnovicz and Bradlow, 1991), suggesting that this compound may be a novel approach for reducing the risk of breast cancer. However, since I3C has also been shown to enhance carcinogenesis in vivo, caution has been urged before proceeding with extensive clinical trials (Dashwood, 1998), although such phase I trials are currently ongoing (Wong *et al.*, 1998).

Although a wide variety of naturally occurring and synthetic isothiocyanates have been shown to prevent cancer in animals (Hecht, 1995), attention has been focused on a particular isothiocyanate isolated from broccoli, known as sulforaphane. Sulforaphane has been shown to be the principal inducer of a particular type of Phase II enzyme, quinone reductase. Fahey *et al.*, (1997) recently demonstrated that 3-day-old broccoli sprouts contained 10-100 times higher levels of glucoraphanin (the glucosinolate of sulforaphane) than did corresponding mature plants. However, in view of the importance of an overall dietary pattern in cancer risk reduction, the clinical implications of a single phytochemical in isolation has been questioned (Nestle, 1998).

(f) Citrus Fruits: Several epidemiological studies have shown that citrus fruits are protective against a variety of human cancers. Although oranges, lemons, limes, and grapefruits are a principal source of such important nutrients as vitamin C, folate, and fiber, Elegbede *et al.* (1993) have suggested that another component is responsible for the anticancer activity. Citrus fruits are particularly high in a class of phytochemicals known as the limonoids (Hasegawa and Miyake, 1996).

Over the last decade, evidence has been accumulating in support of the cancer preventative effect of limonene (Gould, 1997). Crowell (1997) showed this compound to be effective against a variety of both spontaneous and chemically- induced rodent tumors. Based on these observations, and because it has little or no toxicity in humans, limonene has been suggested as a good candidate for human clinical chemoprevention trial evaluation. A metabolite of limonene, perrillyl alcohol, is currently undergoing Phase I clinical trials in patients with advanced malignancies (Ripple *et al.*, 1998).

(g) Cranberry: Cranberry juice has been recognized as efficacious in the treatment of urinary tract infections since 1914, when Blatherwick (1914) reported that this benzoic acid-rich fruit caused acidification of the urine. Recent investigations have focused on the ability of cranberry juice to inhibit

the adherence of Escherichia coli to uroepitheial cells (Schmidt and Sobota, 1988). This phenomenon has been attributed to two compounds: fructose and a nondialyzable polymeric compound. The latter compound, subsequently isolated from cranberry and blueberry juices (Ofek *et al.*, 1991), was found to inhibit adhesins present on the pili of the surface of certain pathogenic E. coli.

Avorn *et al.* (1994) published the results of the first randomized, doubleblind, placebo-controlled clinical trial designed to determine the effect of a commercial cranberry juice beverage on urinary tract infections. One hundred-fifty three elderly women consuming 300 mL cranberry beverage per day had significantly reduced (58%) incidence of bacteriuria with pyuria compared to the control group after six months. Based on the results of these studies, prevailing beliefs about the benefits of cranberry juice on the urinary tract appear to be justified.

(h) Tea: Tea is second only to water as the most widely consumed beverage in the world. A great deal of attention has been directed to the polyphenolic constituents of tea, particularly green tea (Harbowy and Balentine, 1997). Polyphenols comprise up to 30% of the total dry weight of fresh tea leaves. Catechins are the predominant and most significant of all tea polyphenols (Graham, 1992). The four major green tea catechins are epigallocatechin-3-gallate, epigallocatechin, epicatechin-3-gallate and epicatechin.

In recent years, there has been a great deal of interest in pharmacological effects of tea (AHF, 1992). By far, most research on health benefits of tea has focused on its cancer chemopreventive effects, although the epidemiological studies are inconclusive at the present time (Katiyar and Mukhtar, 1996). In a 1993 review of 100 epidemiological studies (Yang and Wang, 1993), approximately 2/3 of the studies found no relationship between tea consumption and cancer risk, while 20 found a positive relationship and only 14 studies found that tea consumption reduced cancer risk. A more recent review suggests that benefits from tea consumption are restricted to high intakes in high-risk populations (Kohlmeier *et al.*, 1997a). This hypothesis supports the recent finding that the consumption of five or more cups of green tea per day was associated with decreased recurrence of stage I and II breast cancer in Japanese women (Nakachi *et al.*, 1998).

In contrast to the inconclusive results from epidemiological studies, research findings in laboratory animals clearly support a cancer chemopreventive effect of tea components. In fact, Dreosti *et al.* (1997) stated that "no other agent tested for possible chemoprevention effects in animal models has elicited such strong activity as tea and its components at the concentrations usually consumed by humans."

There is some evidence that tea consumption may also reduce the risk of CVD. Hertog and coworkers (1993) reported that tea consumption was the major source of flavonoids in a population of elderly men in the Netherlands. Intake of five flavonoids (quercetin, kaempferol, myricetin, apigenin, and luteolin), the majority of which was derived from tea consumption, was significantly inversely associated with mortality from CHD in this population. Although several other prospective studies have demonstrated a substantial reduction in CVD risk with tea consumption, the evidence is not presently conclusive (Tijburg *et al.*, 1997).

(i) Wine and Grapes: There is growing evidence that wine, particularly red wine, can reduce the risk of CVD. The link between wine intake and CVD first became apparent in 1979 when St. Leger *et al.* (1979) found a strong negative correlation between wine intake and death from ischemic heart disease in both men and women from 18 countries. France in particular has a relatively low rate of CVD despite diets high in dairy fat (Renaud and de Lorgeril, 1992). Although this "French Paradox" can be partly explained by the ability of alcohol to increase HDL cholesterol, more recent investigations have focused on the non-alcohol components of wine, in particular, the flavonoids.

The high phenolic content of red wine, which is about 20-50 times higher than white wine, is due to the incorporation of the grape skins into the fermenting grape juice during production. Kanner *et al.* (1994) showed that the black seedless grapes and red wines (i.e., Cabernet Sauvignon and Petite Sirah) contain high concentrations of phenolics: 920, 1800, and 3200 mg/L, respectively, while green Thomson grapes contain only 260 mg/kg phenolics. Frankel and coworkers (1993) attributed the positive benefits of red wine to the ability of phenolic substances to prevent the oxidation of LDL, a critical event in the process of atherogenesis.

Although the benefits of wine consumption on CVD risk reduction seem promising, a recent prospective study of 128,934 adults in Northern California concluded that the benefits of alcohol consumption on coronary risk were not especially associated with red wine (Klatsky *et al.*, 1997). Moreover, a note of caution is in order, as alcoholic beverages of all kinds have been linked to increased risk of several types of cancer, including breast cancer (Bowlin *et al.*, 1997). Moderate wine consumption has also been associated with a decreased risk of age-related macular degeneration (Obisesan *et al.*, 1998).

Those who desire health benefits of wine without potential risk may wish to consider alcohol-free wine, which has been shown to increase total plasma antioxidant capacity (Serafini *et al.*, 1998). Furthermore, Day *et al.* (1998) showed that commercial grape juice is effective in inhibiting the oxidation of LDL isolated from human subjects. Red wine is also a significant source of trans-resveratrol, a phytoalexin found in grape skins (Creasy and Coffee, 1988). Resveratrol has also been shown to have estrogenic properties (Gehm *et al.*,

1997) which may explain in part the cardiovascular benefits of wine drinking, and it has been shown to inhibit carcinogenesis in vivo (Jang *et al.*, 1997).

Functional Foods from Animal Sources

Although the vast number of naturally occurring health-enhancing substances are of plant origin, there are a number of physiologically-active components in animal products that deserve attention for their potential role in optimal health.

(a) Fish: Omega-3 (n-3) fatty acids are an essential class of polyunsaturated fatty acids (PUFAs) derived primarily from fish oil. It has been suggested that the Western-type diet is currently deficient in n-3 fatty acids, which is reflected in the current estimated n-6 to n-3 dietary ratio of 20:25-1, compared to the 1:1 ratio on which humans evolved (Simopoulos, 1991). This has prompted researchers to examine the role of n-3 fatty acids in a number of diseases—particularly cancer and CVD—and more recently, in early human development.

That n-3 fatty acids may play an important role in CVD was first brought to light in the 1970s when Bang and Dyerberg (1972) reported that Eskimos had low rates of this disease despite consuming a diet which was high in fat. The cardioprotective effect of fish consumption has been observed in some prospective investigations (Krumhout *et al.*, 1985), but not in others (Ascherio *et al.*, 1995). Negative results could be explained by the fact that although n-3 fatty acids have been shown to lower triglycerides by 25-30%, they do not lower LDL cholesterol. In fact, a recent review of 72 placebo-controlled human trials, showed that n-3 fatty acids increased LDL cholesterol (Harris, 1996).

Although eating large amounts of fish has not unequivocally been shown to reduce CVD risk in healthy men, consumption of 35 g or more of fish daily has been shown to reduce the risk of death from non sudden myocardial infarction in the Chicago Western Electric Study (Daviglus *et al.*, 1997), and as little as one serving of fish per week was associated with a significantly reduced risk of total cardiovascular mortality after 11 years in more than 20,000 U.S. male physicians (Albert *et al.*, 1998).

(b) Dairy Products: There is no doubt that dairy products are functional foods. They are one of the best sources of calcium, an essential nutrient which can prevent osteoporosis and possibly colon cancer. In view of the former, the National Academy of Sciences recently increased recommendations for this nutrient for most age groups. In addition to calcium, however, recent research has focused specifically on other components in dairy products, particularly fermented dairy products known as probiotics. Probiotics are defined as "live microbial feed supplements which beneficially affect the host animal by improving its intestinal microbial balance" (Fuller, 1994).

It is estimated that over 400 species of bacteria, separated into two broad categories, inhabit the human gastrointestinal tract. The categories are: those considered to be beneficial (e.g., Bifidobacterium and Lactobacillus and those considered detrimental (e.g., Enterobacteriaceae and Clostridium spp.). Of the beneficial microorganisms traditionally used in food fermentation, lactic acid bacteria have attracted the most attention (Sanders, 1994). Although a variety of health benefits have been attributed to probiotics, their anticarcinogenic, hypocholesterolemic and antagonistic actions against enteric pathogens and other intestinal organisms have received the most attention (Mital and Garg, 1995).

The hypocholesterolemic effect of fermented milk was discovered more than 30 years ago during studies conducted in Maasai tribesmen in Africa (Mann *et al.*, 1964). The Maasai have low levels of serum cholesterol and clinical coronary heart disease despite a high meat diet. However, they consume daily 4 to 5 L of fermented whole milk. Although a number of human clinical studies have assessed the cholesterol lowering effects of fermented milk products (Sanders, 1994), results are equivocal. Study outcomes have been complicated by inadequate sample sizes, failure to control nutrient intake and energy expenditure, and variations in baseline blood lipids.

More evidence supports the role of probiotics in cancer risk reduction, particularly colon cancer (Mital and Garg, 1995). This observation may be due to the fact that lactic acid cultures can alter the activity of fecal enzymes (e.g., b-glucuronidase, azoreductase, nitroreductase) that are thought to play a role in the development of colon cancer. Relatively less attention has been focused on the consumption of fermented milk products and breast cancer risk, although an inverse relationship has been observed in some studies (Talamini *et al.*, 1984; van't Veer *et al.*,1989).

In addition to probiotics, there is growing interest in fermentable carbohydrates that feed the good microflora of the gut. These prebiotics, defined by Gibson and Roberfroid (1995) as "nondigestible food ingredients that beneficially affect the host by selectively stimulating the growth and/or activity of one or a limited number of bacteria in the colon and thus improves host health," may include starches, dietary fibers, other nonabsorbable sugars, sugar alcohols, and oligosaccharides (Gibson *et al.*, 1996). Of these, oligosaccharides have received the most attention, and numerous health benefits have been attributed to them (Tomomatsu, 1994). Oligosaccharides consist of short chain polysaccharides composed of three and 10 simple sugars linked together. They are found naturally in many fruits and vegetables (including banana, garlic, onions, milk, honey, artichokes). The prebiotic concept has been further extended to encompass the concept of synbiotics, a mixture of pro- and prebiotics (Gibson and Roberfroid, 1995). Many synbiotic products are currently on the market in Europe.

(c) Beef: An anticarcinogenic fatty acid known as conjugated linoleic acid (CLA) was first isolated from grilled beef in 1987 (Ha *et al.*, 1987). CLA refers to a mixture of positional and geometric isomers of linoleic acid (18:2 n-6) in which the double bonds are conjugated instead of existing in the typical methylene interrupted configuration. Nine different isomers of CLA have been reported as occurring naturally in food. CLA is unique in that it is found in highest concentrations in fat from ruminant animals (e.g., beef, dairy, and lamb). Beef fat contains 3.1 to 8.5 mg CLA/g fat with the 9-cis and 11-trans isomers contributing 57-85% of the total CLA (Decker, 1995). Interestingly, CLA increases in foods that are cooked and/or otherwise processed. This is significant in view of the fact that many mutagens and carcinogens have been identified in cooked meats.

Over the past decade, CLA has been shown to be effective in suppressing forestomach tumors in mice, aberrant colonic crypt foci in rats, and mammary carcinogenesis in rats (Ip and Scimeca, 1997). In the mammary tumor model, CLA is an effective anticarcinogen in the range of 0.1-1% in the diet, which is higher than the estimated consumption of approximately 1 g CLA/person/day in the United States. These results are not due to displacement of linoleic acid in cells, suggesting that there may be unique mechanism(s) by which CLA modulates tumor development. Thus, there has been research designed to increase the CLA content in dairy cow milk through dietary modification (Kelly *et al.*, 1998).

More recently, CLA has been investigated for its ability to change body composition, suggesting a role as a weight reduction agent. Mice fed CLA-supplemented diets (0.5%) exhibited 60% lower body fat and 14% increased lean body mass relative to controls (Park *et al.*, 1997), possibly by reducing fat deposition and increasing lipolysis in adipocytes.

SAFETY ISSUES

Although "increasing the availability of healthful foods, including functional foods, in the American diet is critical to ensuring a healthier population" (ADA, 1995), safety is a critical issue. The optimal levels of the majority of the biologically active components currently under investigation have yet to be determined. In addition, a number of animal studies show that some of the same phytochemicals (e.g., allyl isothiocyanate) highlighted in this review for their cancer-preventing properties have been shown to be carcinogenic at high concentrations (Ames *et al.*, 1990). Thus, Paracelsus' 15th century doctrine that "All substances are poisons . . . the right dose differentiates a poison from a remedy" is even more pertinent today given the proclivity for dietary supplements.

The benefits and risks to individuals and populations as a whole must be weighed carefully when considering the widespread use of physiologically-active functional foods. For example, what are the risks of recommending the increased intake of compounds (e.g., isoflavones) that may modulate estrogen metabolism? Soy phytoestrogens may represent a "double-edged sword" because of reports that genistein may actually promote certain types of tumors in animals (Rao *et al.*, 1997). Knowledge of toxicity of functional food components is crucial to decrease the risk:benefit ratio.

CONCLUSION

Mounting evidence supports the observation that functional foods containing physiologically-active components, either from plant or animal sources, may enhance health. It should be stressed, however, that functional foods are not a magic bullet or universal panacea for poor health habits. There are no "good" or "bad" foods, but there are good or bad diets. Emphasis must be placed on overall dietary pattern—one that follows the current U.S. Dietary Guidelines, and is plant-based, high in fiber, low in animal fat, and contains 5-9 servings of fruits and vegetables per day. Moreover, diet is only one component of an overall lifestyle that can have an impact on health; other components include smoking, physical activity, and stress.

Health-conscious consumers are increasingly seeking functional foods in an effort to control their own health and well-being. The field of functional foods, however, is in its infancy. Claims about health benefits of functional foods must be based on sound scientific criteria (Clydesdale, 1997). A number of factors complicate the establishment of a strong scientific foundation, however. These factors include the complexity of the food substance, effects on the food, compensatory metabolic changes that may occur with dietary changes, and, lack of surrogate markers of disease development. Additional research is necessary to substantiate the potential health benefits of those foods for which the diet-health relationships are not sufficiently scientifically validated.

Research into functional foods will not advance public health unless the benefits of the foods are effectively communicated to the consumer. The Harvard School of Public Health (Boston, Mass.) and the International Food Information Council Foundation (Washington, D.C.) recently released a set of communication guidelines, aimed at scientists, journal editors, journalists, interest groups, and others for improving public understanding of emerging science. The guidelines are intended to help ensure that research results about nutrition, food safety, and health are communicated in a clear, balanced and non-misleading manner (Fineberg and Rowe, 1998).

Finally, those foods whose health benefits are supported by sufficient scientific substantiation have the potential to be an increasingly important component of a healthy lifestyle and to be beneficial to the public and the food industry.

REFERENCES

ADA. 1995. Position of the American Dietetic Association: Phytochemicals and Functional Foods. J. Am. Diet. Assoc. 95: 493-496.

AHF.1992. Physiological and Pharmacological Effects of Camellia Snensis (Tea): Implications for Cardiovascular Disease, Cancer and Public Health. American Health Foundation, Valhalla, New York, Prevent. Med. 21: 329-391 and 503-553.

Adlercreutz, H., Fotsis, T., Heikkinen, R., Dwyer, J.T., Woods, M., Goldin, B.R. and Gorbach, S.L. 1982. Excretion of the Lignans Enterolactone and Enterodiol and of Equol in Omnivorous and Vegetarian Postmenopausal Women and in Women with Breast Cancer. Lancet ii: 1295-1299.

Albert, C.M., Hennekens, C.H., O'Donnell, C.J., Ajani, U.A., Carey, V.J., Willett, W.C., Ruskin, J.N., and Manson, J.E. 1998. Fish Consumption and Risk of Sudden Cardiac death. J. Am. Med. Assoc. 279: 23-28.

Albertazzi, P., Pansini, F., Bonaccorsi G., Zanotti, L., Forini, E., and De Aloysio, D. 1998. The Effect of Dietary Soy Supplementation on Hot Flushes. Obstet. Gynecol 91: 6-11.

Allman, M.A., Pena, M.M., and Pang, D. 1995. Supplementation with Flaxseed Oil versus Sunflowerseed Oil in Healthy Young Men Consuming a Low Fat Diet: Effects on Platelet Composition and Function. Eur. J. Clin. Nutr 49: 169-178.

Ames, B.N., Magaw, R. and Gold, L.W. 1990. Ranking Possible Carcinogenic Hazards. Science 236: 271- 280.

Anderson, J.W., Johnstone, B.M., and Cook-Newell, M.E. 1995. Meta-analysis of the Effects of Soy Protein Intake on Serum Lipids. New Engl. J. Med. 333: 276- 282.

Anderson, J.J.B. and Garner, S.C. 1997. The Effects of Phytoestrogens on Bone. Nutr. Res. 17: 1617-1632.

Anonymous. 1998. U.S. Topselling Herbs and Supplements. Nutraceuticals Intl. 3 (2): 9.

Arai, S. 1996. Studies on Functional Foods in Japan– State of the Art. Biosci. Biotech. Biochem. 60: 9-15.

Ascherio, A., Rimm, E.B., Stampfer, M.J., Giovannucci, E.L., and Willett, W.C. 1995. Dietary Intake of Marine n-3 Fatty Acids, Fish Intake and the Risk of Coronary Disease Among Men. New Eng. J. Med. 332: 977-982.

Avorn, J., Monane, M., Gurwitz, J.H., Glynn, R.J., Choodnovskiy, I., and Lipsitz, L.A. 1994. Reduction of Bacteriuria and Pyuria after Ingestion of Cranberry Juice—A Reply. J. Am. Med. Assoc. 272: 589-590.

Bang, H.O. and Dyerberg, J. 1972. Plasma Lipids and Lipoproteins in Greenlandic West-coast Eskimos. Acta. Med. Scand 192: 85-94.

Bierenbaum, M.L., Reichstein, R. and Watkins, T.R. 1993. Reducing Atherogenic Risk in Hyperlipemic Humans with Flax Seed Supplementation: A Preliminary Report. J. Am. Coll. Nutr. 12: 501-504.

Blatherwick, N.R. 1914. The Specific Role of Foods in Relation to the Composition of the Urine. Arch. Int. Med. 14: 409-450.

Block, E. 1992. The Organosulfur Chemistry of the Genus Allium—Implications for the Organic Chemistry of Sulfur. Angew. Chem. Int. Edn. Engl. 31: 1135-1178.

Block, G., Patterson, B. and Subar, A. 1992. Fruit, Vegetables and Cancer Prevention: A Review of the Epidemiological Evidence. Nutr. Cancer 18: 1-29.

Bowlin, S.J., Leske, M.C., Varma, A., Nasca, P., Weinstein, A. and Caplan, L. 1997. Breast Cancer Risk and Alcohol Consumption: Results from A Large Case-Control Study. Intl. J. Epidemiol. 26: 915-923.

Clinton, S.K. 1998. Lycopene: Chemistry, Biology and Implications for Human Health and Disease. Nutr. Rev. 56: 35-51.

Clinton, S.K., Emenhiser, C., Schwartz, S.J., Bostwick, D.G., Williams, A.W., Moore, B.J. and Erdman, Jr, J.W. 1996. Cis-trans lycopene Isomers, Carotenoids and Retinol in the Human Prostate. Cancer Epidemiol. Biomarkers Prev. 5: 823-833.

Clydesdale, F.M. 1997. A Proposal for the Establishment of Scientific Criteria for Health Claims for Functional Foods. Nutr. Rev. 55 (12): 413-422.

Creasy, L.L. and Coffee, M.1988. Phytoalexin Production of Grape Berries. J. Am. Soc. Hort. Sci. 113: 230-234.

Crowell, P.L. 1997. Monoterpenes in Breast Cancer Chemoprevention. Breast Cancer Res. Treatment 46: 191-197.

Cunnane, S.C., Ganguli, S., Menard, C., Liede, A.C., Hamadeh, M.J., Chen, Z-Y., Wolever, T.M.S. and Jenkins, D.J.A. 1993. High-linolenic Acid Flaxseed (Linum usitatissimum): Some Nutritional Properties in Humans. Br. J. Nutr. 69: 443-453.

DHHS/FDA. 1997. Food Labeling: Health Claims; Oats and Coronary Heart Disease. Dept. Health and Human Services/Food and Drug Administration. Fed. Reg. 62: 3584-3601.

Dashwood, R.H. 1998. Indol-3-carbinol–Anticarcinogen or Tumor Promoter in Brassica Vegetables. Chem.-Biol. Ineractions 110: 1-5.

Daviglus, M.L., Stamler, J., Orencia, A.J., Dyer, A.R., Liu, K., Greenland, P., Walsh, M., Morris, D., and Shekelle, R.B. 1997. Fish Consumption and the 30-year Risk of Fatal Myocardial Infarction. New Eng. J. Med. 336: 1046-1053.

Day, A. P., Kemp, H.J., Bolton, C., Hartog, M., Stansbie, D. 1998. Effects of Concentrated Red Grape Juice Consumption on Serum Antioxidant Capacity and Low-density Lipoprotein Oxidation. Ann. Nutr. Metab. 41: 353- 357.

Decker, E.A. 1995. The Role of Phenolics, Conjugated Linoleic Acid, Carnosine and Pyrroloquinoline Quinone as Nonessential Dietary Antioxidants. Nutr. Rev. 53: 49-58.

Di Mascio, P., Kaiser, S., and Sies, H. 1989. Lycopene as the Most Efficient Biological Carotenoid Singlet Oxygen Quencher. Arch. Biochem. Biophys. 274: 532-538.

Dorant, E., van den Brandt, P.A., Goldbohm, R.A., Hermus, R.J.J., and Sturmans, F. 1993. Garlic and Its Significance for the Prevention of Cancer in Humans: A Critical Review. Br. J. Cancer 67: 424-429.

Dreosti, I.E., Wargovich, M.J., and Yang, C.S. 1997. Inhibition of Carcinogenesis by Tea: The Evidence from Experimental Studies. Crit. Rev. Food Sci. Nutr. 37: 761- 770.

Elegbede, J.A., Maltzman, T.H., Elson, C.E., and Gould, M.N. 1993. Effects of Anticarcinogenic Monoterpenes on Phase II Hepatic Metabolizing Enzymes. Carcinogenesis 14: 1221-1223.

Erdman, J.W., Jr., and Potter, S.M. 1997. Soy and Bone Health. The Soy Connection 5 (2): 1, 4.

Ernst, E. 1997. Can Allium Vegetables Prevent Cancer? Phytomed. 4: 79-83.

Fahey, J.W., Zhang, Y., and Talalay, P. 1997. Broccoli Sprouts: An Exceptionally Rich Source of Inducers of Enzymes that Protect Against Chemical Carcinogens. Proc. Natl. Acad. Sci. 94: 10366-10372.

Fineberg, H.V. and Rowe, S. 1998. Improving Public Understanding: Guidelines for Communicating Emerging Science on Nutrition, Food Safety and Health. J. Natl. Cancer Inst. 90: 194-199.

Frankel, E.N., Kanner, J., German, J.B., Parks, E. and Kinsella, J.E. 1993. Inhibition of Oxidation of Human Lowdensity Lipoprotein by Phenolic Substances in Red Wine. The Lancet 341: 454-457.

Fuller, R. 1994. History and Development of Probiotics. In "Probiotics," ed. R. Fuller, pp. 1-8. Chapman & Hall, N.Y.

Gehm, B.D., McAndrews, J.M., Chien, P.-Y., and Jameson, J.L. 1997. Resveratrol, A Polyphenolic Compound Found in Grapes and Wine, Is an Agonist for the Estrogen Receptor. Proc. Natl. Acad. Sci. 94: 14138- 14143.

Gerster, H. 1997. The Potential Role of Lycopene for Human Health. J. Am. Coll. Nutr. 16: 109-126.

Gibson, G. and Roberfroid, M.B. 1995. Dietary Modulation of the Human Colonic Mibrobiota: Introducing the Concept of Prebiotics. J. Nutr. 125: 1401-1412.

Gibson, G.R., Williams, A., Reading, S., and Collins, M.D. 1996. Fermentation of Non-Digestible Oligosaccharides by Human Colonic Bacteria. Proc. Nutr. Soc. 55: 899-912.

Giovannucci, E., Ascherio, A., Rimm, E.B., Stampfer, M.J., Colditz, G.A., and Willett, W.C. 1995. Intake of Carotenoids and Retinol in Relation to Risk of Prostate Cancer. J. Natl. Cancer Inst. 87: 1767-1776.

Gould, M.N. 1997. Cancer Chemoprevention and Therapy By Monoterpenes. Environ. Health Perspec. 105: 977- 979.

Graham, H.N. 1992. Green Tea Composition, Consumption and Polyphenol Chemistry. Prev. Med. 21: 334- 350.

Ha, Y.L., Grimm, N.K., and Pariza, M.W. 1987. Anticarcinogens from Fried Ground Beef: Health-altered Derivatives of Linoleic Acid. Carcinogenesis 8: 1881-1887.

Harbowy, M.E. and Balentine, D.A. 1997. Tea Chemistry. Crit. Rev. Plant Sci. 16: 415-480.

Harris, W.s. 1996. N-3 Fatty Acids and Lipoproteins–Comparison of Results from Human and Animal Studies.

Hasegawa, S. and Miyake, M. 1996. Biochemistry and Biological Functions of Citrus Limonoids. Food Rev. Intl. 12: 413-435.

Hasler, C.M. 1998. A New Look at An Ancient Concept. Chem. Industry Feb. 2: 84-89.

Hecht, S.S. 1995. Chemoprevention by Isothiocyanates. J. Cell. Biochem. Suppl. 22: 195-209.

Hertog, M.G.L., Feskens, E.J.M., Hollman, P.C.H., Katan, M.B., and Krumhout, D. 1993. Dietary Antioxidant Flavonoids and Risk of Coronary Heart Disease: The Zutphen Elderly Study. The Lancet 342: 1007-1011.

Hodgson, J.M., Puddey, I.B., Beilin, L.J., Mori, T.A., and Croft, K.D. 1998. Supplementation with Isoflavonoid Phytoestrogens does not Alter Serum Lipid Concentrations: A Randomized Controlled Trial in Humans. J. Nutr. 128: 728-732.

Howard, B.V. and Kritchevsky, D. 1997. Phytochemicals and Cardiovascular Disease–A Statement for Healthcare Professionals from the American Heart Association. Circulation 95: 2591-2593.

IOM/NAS. 1994. "Opportunities in the Nutrition and Food Sciences", ed. P.R. Thomas and R. Earl, p. 109. Institute of Medicine/National Academy of Sciences, National Academy Press, Washington, D.C.

Ip, C. and Scimeca, J.A. 1997. Conjugated Linoleic Acid and Linoleic Acid are Distinctive Modulators of Mammary Carcinogenesis. Nutr. Cancer 27: 131-135.

Isaacsohn, J.L., Moser, M., Stein, E.A., Dudley, K., Davey, J.A., Liskov, E., and Black, H.R. 1998. Garlic Powder and Plasma Lipids and Lipoproteins: A Multicenter, Randomized, Placebo-controlled Trial. Arch. Int. Med. 158:1189–1194.

Jang, M., Cai, J., Udeani, G., Slowing, K.V., Thomas, C.F., Beecher, C.W.W., Fong, H.H.S., Farnsworth, N.R., Kinghorn, A.D., Mehta, R.G., Moon, R.C., and Pezzuto, J.M. 1997. Cancer Chemopreventive Activity of Resveratrol, A Natural Product Derived from Grapes. Science 275: 218-220.

Kanner, J., Frankel, E., Granit, R., German, B., and Kinsella, J.E. 1994. Natural Antioxidants in Grapes and Wines. J. Agric. Food Chem. 42: 64-69.

Katiyar, S.K. and Mukhtar, H. 1996. Tea in Chemoprevention of Cancer: Epidemiologic and Experimental Studies (review). Intl. J. Oncol. 8: 221-238.

Kelly, M. L., Berry, J.R., Dwyer, D.A., Griinari, J.M., Chounard, P.Y., Van Amburgh, M.E., and Bauman, D.E. 1998. Dietary Fatty Acid Sources Affect Conjugated Linoleic Acid Concentrations in Milk from Lactating Dairy Cows. J. Nutr. 128: 881-885.

Klatsky, A.L., Armstrong, M.A., and Friedman, G.D. 1997. Red Wine, White Wine, Liquor, Beer, and Risk for Coronary Artery Disease Hospitalization. Am. J. Cardiol. 80: 416- 420.

Kohlmeier, L., Weerings, K.G.C., Steck, S., and Kok, F.J. 1997. Tea and Cancer Prevention–An Evaluation of the Epidemiologic Literature. Nutr. Cancer 27: 1-13.

Kohlmeier, L., Kark, J.D., Gomez-Gracia, E., Martin, B.C., Steck, S.E., Kardinaal, A.F.M., Ringstad, J., Thamm, M., Masaev, V., Riemersma, R., Martin-Moreno, J.M., Huttunen, J.K., and Kok, F.J. 1997. Lycopene and Myocardial Infarction Risk in the EURAMIC Study. Am. J. Epidemiol.146: 618-626.

Kuhn, M.E. 1998. Functional Foods Overdose? Food Proc. 59 (5): 21-48.

Krumhout, D., Bosschieter, E.B., and de Lezenne Coulander, C. 1985. The Inverse Relation Between Fish Consumption and 20-Year Mortality from Coronary Heart Disease. New Eng. J. Med. 312: 1205-1209.

Lawson, L.D., Wang, Z-Y.J., and Hughes, B.G. 1991. Identification and HPLC Quantitation of the Sulfides and Dialk(en)ylthiosulfinates in Commercial Garlic Products. Planta Med. 57: 363-370.

Li, Y., Elie, M., Blaner, W.S., Brandt-Rauf, P., and Ford, J. 1997. Lycopene, Smoking and Lung Cancer. Proc. Am. Assoc. Cancer Res. 38: 113 (abstract #758).

Mann, G.V., Schaffer, R.D., Anderson, R.D., and Sandstead, H.H. 1964. Cardiovascular Disease in the Maasai. J. Atheroscler. Res. 4: 289-312.

Messina, M. and Barnes, S. 1991. The Role of Soy Products in Reducing Risk of Cancer. J. Natl. Cancer Inst. 83: 541-546.

Messina, M., Barnes, S., and Setchell, K.D.R. 1997. Phytooestrogens and Breast Cancer. Lancet 350: 971- 972.

Meyer, A. 1998. The 1998 top 100® R&D Survey. Food Processing 58(8): 32-40.

Michnovicz, J.J. and Bradlow, H.L. 1991. Altered Estrogen Metabolism and Excretion in Humans Following Consumption of Indole Carbinol. Nutr. Cancer 16: 59-66.

Mital, B.K. and Garg, S.K. 1995. Anticarcinogenic, Hypocholesterolemic and Antagonistic Activities of Lactobacillus Acidophilus. Crit. Rev. Micro. 21: 175-214.

Nakachi, K., Suemasu, K., Suga, K., Takeo, T., Imai, K., and Higashi, Y. 1998. Influence of Drinking Green Tea on Breast Cancer Malignancy Among Japanese Patients. Jap. J. Cancer Res. 89: 254-261.

Nagourney, R.A. 1998. Garlic: Medicinal Food or Nutritious Medicine? J. Medicinal Food 1: 13-28.

Nestle, P.J., Yamashita, T., Sasahara, T., Pomeroy, S., Dart, A., Komesaroff, P., Owen, A., and Abbey, M. 1997. Soy Isoflavones Improve Systemic Arterial Compliance but not Plasma

Lipids In Menopausal And Perimenopausal Women. Arterioscler. Thromb. Vasc. Biol. 17: 3392-3398.

Nestle, M. 1998. Broccoli Sprouts in Cancer Prevention. Nutr. Rev. 56: 127-130.

Obisesan, T.O., Hirsch, R., Kosoko, O., Carlson, L., and Parrott, M. 1998. Moderate Wine Consumption is Associated with Decreased Odds of Developing Age-Related Macular Degeneration in NHANES-1. J. Amer. Geriatrics Soc. 46: 1-7.

Ofek, I., Goldhar, J., Zafriri, D., Lis, H., Adar, R., and Sharon, N. 1991. Anti-Escherichia Coli Adhesin Activity of Cranberry and Blueberry Juices. New Eng. J. Med. 324: 1599.

Park, Y., Albrigh, K.J., Liu, W., Storkson, J.M., Cook, M.E., and Pariza, M.W. 1997. Effect of Conjugated Linoleic Acid on Body Composition in Mice. Lipids 32: 853-858.

Phipps, W.R., Martini, M.C., Lampe, J.W., Slavin, J.L., and Kurzer, M.S. 1993. Effect of Flax Seed Ingestion on the Menstrual Cycle. J. Clin. Endocrin. Metab. 77: 1215-1219.

Potter, S.M. 1998. Soy Protein and Cardiovascular Disease: The Impact of Bioactive Components in Soy. Nutr. Rev. 56(8):231-235.

Rao, C.V., Wang, C.X., Simi, B., Lubet, R., Kellogg, G., Steele, V., and Reddy, B.S. 1997. Enhancement of Experimental Colon Cancer by Genistein. Cancer Res. 57: 3717-3722.

Reuter H.D., Koch, H.P, and Lawson, L.D. 1996. Therapeutic Effects and Applications of Garlic and Its Preparations. In: Garlic. The Science and Therapeutic Application of Allium sativum L. and Related Species, 2nd Ed., ed., H.P. Koch and L.D. Lawson, Williams & Wilkins, Baltimore.

Renaud, W. and de Lorgeril, M. 1992. Wine, Alcohol, Platelets and the French Paradox for Coronary Heart Disease. The Lancet 339: 1523-1526.

Ripple, G.H., Gould, M.N., Stewart, J.A., Tutsch, K.D., Arzoomanian, R.Z., Alberti, D., Feierabend, C., Pomplun, M., Wilding, G., and Bailey, H.H. 1998. Phase I Clinical Trial of Peillyl Alcohol Administered Daily. Clin. Cancer Res. 4: 1159-1164.

Sanders, M.E. 1994. Lactic Acid Bacteria as Promoters of Human Health. In: "Functional Foods—Designer Foods, Pharmafoods, Nutraceuticals", ed. I. Goldberg, pp. 294-322. Chapman & Hall, N.Y.

Schmidt, D.R. and Sobota, A.E. 1988. An Examination of the Anti-adherence Activity of Cranberry Juice on Urinary and Nonurinary Bacterial Isolates. Microbios. 55: 173- 181.

Serafini, M., Maiani, G., and Ferro-Luzzi, A. 1998. Alcohol-free Red Wine Enhances Plasma Antioxidant Capacity in Humans. J. Nutr. 128: 1003-1007.

Setchell, K.D.R., Lawson, A.M., Borriello, S.P., Harkness, R., Gordon, H., Morgan, D.M.L, Kirk, D.N., Adlercreutz, H., Anderson, L.C., and Axelson, M. 1981. Lignan Formation in Man-microbial Involvement and Possible Roles in Relation to Cancer. The Lancet ii: 4-7.

Silagy, C.A. and Neil, H.A.W. 1994a. A Meta-analysis of the Effect of Garlic on Blood Pressure. J. Hyper. 12: 463-468.

Silagy, C. and Neil, A. 1994b. Garlic as a Lipid-lowering Agent—A Meta-analysis. J. Royal Coll. Physicians Lond. 28: 39-45.

Simopoulos, A.P. 1991. Omega-3 Fatty Acids in Health and Disease and in Growth and Development. Am. J. Clin. Nutr. 54: 438-463.

Srivastava, K.C., Bordia, A., and Verma, S.K. 1995. Garlic (Allium sativum) for Disease Prevention. S. Afr. J. Sci. 91: 68-77.

St. Leger, A.S., Cochrane, A.L., and Moore, F. 1979. Factors Associated with Cardiac Mortality in Developed Countries with Particular Reference to the Consumption of Wine. The Lancet i: 1017-1020.

Steinmetz, K.A. and Potter, J.D. 1991a. Vegetables, Fruit and Cancer II. Mechanisms. Cancer Causes Control 2: 427-442.

Steinmetz, K.A. and Potter, J.D. 1991b. Vegetables, Fruit and Cancer I. Cancer Causes Control 2: 325-357.

Steinmetz, K.A., Kushi, H., Bostick, R.M., Folsom, A.R., and Potter, J.D. 1994. Vegetables, Fruit and Colon Cancer in the Iowa Women's Health Study. Am. J. Epidemiol. 139: 1-15.

Talamini, R., La Vecchia, C., Decarli, A., *et al.*. 1984. Social Factors, Diet and Breast Cancer in a Northern Italian Population. Br. J. Cancer 49: 723-729.

Thompson, L.U., Robb, P., Serraino, M., and Cheung, F. 1991. Mammalian Lignan Production from Various Foods. Nutr. Cancer 16: 43-52.

Thompson, L.U. 1995. Flaxseed, Lignans and Cancer. In: "Flaxseed in Human Nutrition," ed. S. Cunnane and L.U. Thompson, pp. 219-236. AOCS Press, Champaign, IL.

Tijburg, L.B.M. Mattern, T., Folts, J.D., Weisgerber, U.M., and Katan, M.B. 1997. Tea Flavonoids and Cardiovascular Diseases: A Review. Crit. Rev. Food Sci. Nutr. 37: 771-785.

Tomomatsu, H. 1994. Health Effects of Oligosaccharides. Food Technol. 48: 61-65.

Van't Veer, P., Dekker, J.M., Lamers, J.W.J., Kok, F.J., Schouten E.G., Brants, H.A.M., Sturmans, F., and Hermus, R.J.J. 1989. Consumption of Fermented Milk Products and Breast Cancer: A Case-control Study in the Netherlands. Cancer Res. 49: 4020-4023.

Verhoeven, D.T.H., Goldbohm, R.A., van Poppel, G., Verhagen, H., and van den Brandt, P.A. 1996. Epidemiological Studies on Brassica Vegetables and Cancer Risk. Cancer Epidemiol. Biomarkers Prev. 5: 733-748.

Verhoeven, D.T.H., Verhagen, H., Goldbohm, R.A., van den Brandt, P.A., and van Poppel, G. 1997. A Review of Mechanisms Underlying Anticarcinogenicity by Brassica Vegetables. Chem. Bio. Interactions 103: 79-129.

Waltham, M.S. 1998. Roadmaps to Market: Commercializing Functional Foods and Nutraceuticals, Decision Resources, Inc., p. 5.

Warshafsky, S., Kamer R.S., and Sivak, S.L. 1993. Effect of Garlic on Total Serum Cholesterol. A Meta-analysis. Ann. Int. Med. 119: 599-605.

Weisburger, J.H. (ed.). 1998. International Symposium on Lycopene and Tomato Products in Disease Prevention. Proc. Soc. Exp. Biol. Med. 218: 93-143.

Wong, G.Y.C., Bradlow, L., Sepkovic, D., Mehl, S., Mailman, J., and Osborne, M.P. 1998. Dose-ranging Study of Indole-3-carbinol for Breast Cancer Prevention. J. Cell. Biochem. 22 (Suppl. 28-29): 111-116.

Yan, L., Yee, J.A., Li, D., McGuire, M.H., and Thompson, L.U. 1998. Dietary Flaxseed Supplementation and Experimental Metastasis of Melanoma Cells in Mice. Cancer Lett. 124: 181-186.

Yang, C.S. and Wang, Z-Y. 1993. Tea and Cancer. J. Natl. Cancer Inst. 85: 1038-1049.

You, W-C., Blot, W.J., Chang, Y-S., Ershow, A.G., Yang, Z.-T., An, Q. Henderson, B., Xu, G.-W., Fraumeni, J.F., and Wang, T.-G. 1988. Diet and High Risk of Stomach Cancer in Shandong, China. Cancer Res. 48: 3518- 3523

Agriculture Crops and Food Security
Edited by: Dr. Pawan Kumar 'Bharti' and Alka Chauhan
ISBN: 978-93-5056-881-1
Edition: 2017
Published by: Discovery Publishing House Pvt. Ltd., New Delhi (India)

6 Biochemical Changes in Tomato Fruits

[1]Srinivasan, V.M. and [2]Daniel Jebaraj, M.

INTRODUCTION

Vegetable constitute an important item of our daily diet and they can play a momentous role in human food through the supply of vitamins and minerals. The recommended quantity of vegetables to be consumed by normal healthy adult is 300 g per day, while the present percapita consumption of vegetables was reported to be below 120 g per day (Veeraragavathatham *et al.*, 1994). Over last three four decades, the production of vegetable has increased rapidly .The area under the vegetable production in India was estimated to be 4.54 lakh ha with a total production of 6.88 m. tones. The contribution to the total world vegetable production by India is 11.30 per cent (Anjali Mehta and Som, 2002).

Tomato is one of the most important economically grown vegetables in Asia. It ranks tops in the list of industrial crops because of its exceptional processing qualities. Tomatoes are being used as an imperative food ingredient. The fruits are being consumed as raw, cooked or processed juice, ketchup, sauce and paste. It is a good resource for vitamin C, A and B.

In India, tomato ranks second among vegetables, in area and production and ranks first for processing of vegetable is concerned .The fruits are available in the market through out the year. The incredible increase in the attentiveness of tomato in the recent years, the crop is estimated to occupy an area of 4.54 lakh ha with a total production of 6.88 m. tonnes (Kaloo, 1997). In Tamil Nadu the area under tomato was estimated to be about 13,834 ha with a production of 3, 63,238 tones (Anon, 1995). However, utilization of tomatoes for processing is low in India compared to other countries. Only 1.30 per cent of total fruits and vegetables produced in India are being processed against 40 per cent in some developing countries and 70 per cent in the developed countries (Anjali

[1] Assistant Professor, Plant Pathology, Thanthai Roever Institute of Agriculture and Rural Development, Perambalur-621115. Tamil Nadu, India.

[2] Research Scholar, Department of Plant Pathology, Tamil Nadu Agricultural University, Coimbatore-3, Tamil Nadu, India.

Mehta *et al.*, 2002). In fact, about 40 per cent of fruits and vegetables worth of Rs. 230 crores are being wasted every year in India (Anon, 1996).

Even though India is having fabulous potential in vegetable production, a high proportion of harvested vegetables are being shattered before they reach the consumer echelon. In India, the loss of vegetables including those during storage and transit was estimated to be around Rs. 230 crores annually. Postharvest losses are due to many factors of which post harvest disease loss is considered as a principal origin. Das gupta and Mandal (1989) described more than 300 post harvest parasitic diseases of vegetables and fruits.

A substantial quantity of vegetable loss occurs every year due to microbial infection resultant in decay during in field, harvest, transit, storage and marketing (Srivastava *et al.*, 1965 Chenulu and Thakur, 1968). The market pathology of this fruit has not been studied well in our country. A systematic survey in Delhi market during 1964-1965 showed that the percentage loss in vegetables and fruits due to post harvest disease was 14.26 to 86.00 per cent (Thakur and Chenulu, 1988).

The estimated post harvest losses during 1993-1994 varied from 4.1-5.2 percent in tomato (Annon, 1996). Studies on post harvest loses of tomato were limited and fragmentary. The reports from areas showed that pre and post harvest spoilage of tomato is mainly due to *Alternaria* sp, *Colletotrichum* sp, *Fusarium* sp, *Phytophthora* sp, *Penicillium* sp, *Rhizopus* sp, *Erwina* sp *Clavibactor michiganense* subsp *michignense*. Tomato fruit is rich in organic acids, sugars, dietary fibre, pectic substances, proteins, fats, minerals (potassium, phosphorus, sulphur, magnesium, calcium, iron, copper, and sodium), vitamins (B1, B2, B3, PP, C, provitamin A, I, and H), and carotenoids possessing antioxidant qualities (lycopene, β-carotene, etc.). the infection tomato fruits with fungi and bacteria cause changes in biochemical components which drastically influence the quality of fruits used for consumption and postharvest processing. With this background the present investigation was carried out to work out the biochemical changes in tomato fruits upon inoculation with tomato fruit rot pathogens.

Material and Methods

The biochemical changes in the inoculated fruits were closely observed at one, two, three, four and five days after inoculation of *Alternaria solani*, *Fusarium solani*, *Colletotrichum capsici* and *Phytophthora capsici*. Fruits without inoculation were kept as control.

Estimation of Starch

Starch was estimated by the method described by Hedge and Hofrieter (1962). One hundred mg of sample was homogenized in hot 80 per cent ethanol to remove sugars. The homogenate was centrifuged and the residue was retained. The residue was repeatedly washed with hot 80 percent ethanol till the washings did not give color with anthrone reagent. The residue was well dried over the water bath and five ml of 52 percent chloric acid was added and extracted at 0°C for 20 min, centrifuged and the supernatant was saved. The extraction was repeated using perchloric acid, centrifuged and supernatant were pooled and the volume was made up to 100 ml with 52 per cent chloric acid .

To 0.1 ml of supernatant, 0.9 ml of distilled water and four ml of anthrone reagent were added and the reaction mixture was heated for eight min in a boiling water bath and cooled rapidly. The colour of the solution turned green to dark brown that was measured at 630 nm using spectrophotometer. D- Glucose was used as a standard. Starch content was expressed in terms of percentage on fresh weight basis.

Estimation of Sugars

One hundred mg of representative fruit sample was homogenized in five ml of 80 per cent ethanol. The homogenate was centrifuged at 1000 rpm for 10 min and used for the estimation of total sugar and reducing sugar.

Estimation of Total Sugars

Total sugar content was estimated by anthrone method (Hedge and Hofrieter, 1962). Two hundred micro litre of ethanol extract was evaporated using water bath at 80°C and one ml of water was added to dissolve the sugars. Four ml of anthrone reagent was added and the reaction mixture was heated for eight min. in a boiling water bath and cooled rapidly. The absorbance of the green colored solution was estimated at 630 nm using spectrophotometer. Anthrone reagent was prepared by dissolving 200 mg of anthrone in 100 ml ice cold 95 per cent sulphuric acid and was prepared fresh before use. D-Glucose was used as standard. The total sugar content was expressed in terms of percentage of fresh weight basis.

Reducing Sugar

The method of Somogyi (1952) was followed to estimate the reducing sugar. Two hundred micro litre of ethanol extract was evaporated by using water bath .The residues were dissolved in two ml of distilled water, to this one ml of alkaline copper tartarate was added and the reaction mixture was heated for ten min. in boiling water bath and cooled rapidly. One ml of alkaline copper tartarate was added and the volume was made upto ten ml with distilled water. Alkaline copper tartarate was prepared by dissolving 2.5 g anhydrous sodium carbonate, 2.0 g sodium bicarbonate, 2.5 g sodium potassium tartarate and 20 g anhydrous sodium sulphate in 80 ml of water and finally made up to 100 ml. The reaction mixture was incubated for 10 min at room temperature. The intensity of blue colour was measured at 620 nm using spectrophotometer.

D-glucose was used as standard. The reducing sugar content was expressed in terms of percentage on fresh weight basis.

Non-reducing Sugar

The difference between total sugar and reducing sugar corresponds to the non-reducing sugar. The non-reducing sugar content was expressed in terms of percentage on fresh weight basis.

Estimation of Vitamin C (Ascorbic acid)

Ascorbic acid content was estimated by 2, 6-dichloro phenol indophenol titration method described by Sadasivam and Balasubramanium (1987). One g of sample was extracted with four percent oxalic acid and filtered. The filtrate was made up to 100 ml with four percent oxalic acid. To ten ml of supernatant, ten ml of four percent oxalic acid was added and the content was titrated against 0.02 percent 2,6-dichlorophenol indophenol dye solution. The end point was the appearance of a light pink colour. Standardization was done with pure ascorbic acid solution. From the value of dye solution required to react with ascorbic acid present in the extract, the amount of ascorbic acid was calculated and expressed as mg/100 g of sample.

Estimation of Total Phenols

The total phenol content was estimated following the procedure given by Malik and Singh, (1980). One gram of sample was ground in two 5 ml portions of 80 percent ethanol and centrifuged. The supernatant was pooled and the volume was made up to 25 ml exactly 0.1 ml of ethanol extract was evaporated on a water bath. Six ml of distilled water was added and shaken well. To this 0.5 ml of Folinsciocalteau reagent was added. After five minutes, 2 ml of 20 percent sodium carbonate was added. The absorbance was read at 600 nm in a spectrophotometer after 30 minutes Pyrocatechol was used as standard and the amount of total phenol expressed as milligram equivalent to pyrocatechol was used as standared and the amount of total phenol was expressed as milligram pyrocatechol gm^{-1} fresh weight of the sample.

Estimation of Lycopene

Lycopene was estimated by following the procedure given by the Rodriguez Dimond, (1976). Exactly 2.5 g of tomato sample was repeatedly extracted with acetic acid using a pestle and mortar until the residue was colorless. The acetone extract was transformed to a separating funnel containing 20 ml of petroleum ether and mixed thoroughly and twenty ml of 5 percent sodium sulphate solution was added and shaken well gently. The upper petroleum ether layer was removed and lower aqueous phase was reextracted with 20 ml of petroleum ether .The petroleum ether extracts were pooled and washed once with little distilled water. Ten gram of anhydrous sodium sulphate was added in to the petroleum ether and kept aside for 30 min. The petroleum ether extract was decanted into 100 ml volumetric flask and the volume was made up with petroleum ether. The absorbance in spectrophotometer was measured at 453 nm for Lycopene using petroleum ether as blank. The content of Lycopene was estimated as 100 gm^{-1} of the sample.

Estimation of Protein

Protein content was estimated by following the procedure given by Lowry and Mansfield. (1951). Five hundred mg of sample was crushed thoroughly in the pestle and mortar using 10 ml of phosphate buffer. The extract was centrifuged at 2000 rpm for 10 min. and supernatant was taken for protein estimation. Exactly 0.2 ml of the extract was taken in a test tube and the volume was made up to 4.5 ml using distilled water. To this, 5 ml of alkaline copper tartarate solution was added. The contents were mixed well and allowed to stand for 10 minutes. Then 0.5 ml of Folinsciocalteu reagent was added and mixed well. The blank with out protein extract was maintained. The intensity of the blue colour developed was read after 30 minutes at 660 nm using a spectrophotometer. Bovine serum albumin was used as standard. The protein content was expressed as percentage.

Poly Galacturonase Activity

The activity of poly galacturonase was assayed as per the method described by Mahadevan and Sridhar (1982). One g of tissue was transferred to a warring blender and five ml of 0.1 M chilled phosphate buffer of pH 6.6 was added. The material was blended for five minutes and filtered through two layers of cheese cloth and centrifuged at 2000 rpm for 30 min at 4°C. The supernatant was decanted and the clear extract was taken as enzyme source.

Four ml of the substrate, one ml of acetate buffer of pH 5.2 and two ml of enzyme source were taken in a viscometer and the contents were mixed gently by drawing air rapidly through the large arm of viscometer by suction. The efflux time of the mixture was determined by suction through small arm (zero time).

$$V = \frac{T_o - T}{T_o - TH_2 0} \times 100$$

Where

V = Loss in viscosity

T_o = Flow time in seconds at zero time

T = Flow time of reaction mixture at time T

TH_20 = Flow time of distilled water

Pectin Methyl Esterase Activity

The enzyme was assayed as per the procedure given by Mahadevan and Sridhar (1982). Twenty ml of pectin solution was pipetted in 50 ml of beaker and the pH was adjusted to 7.0. Ten ml of enzyme solution was added and the pH was immediately adjusted to 7.0 by adding 1N NaOH. This was kept as zero time. At every 15 minutes, the pH was checked and alkali was added from the burette when the pH falls below the reference point, while stirring. To adjust the pH, 0.02 N NaOH was used and the volume of alkali was noticed at each interval. The enzyme activity was expressed as micromoles of hydrogen ion per min /ml of the enzyme preparation.

$$PME = \frac{(Vs - Vb)}{Vt} \times 100$$

Where,

PME = μ mol of hydrogen ion per min / ml

Vs = Titre value

Vb = Volume of 1N sodium hydroxide consumed to adjust the pH to 7.0

NaOH = Normality of sodium hydroxide

V = Volume of incubation mixture (ml)

t = Time period (min)

Statistical Analysis

The data gathered were subjected to statistical analysis adopting the standard procedure as laid down by Panes and Sukhatme (1967).

Results

Biochemical constituents changes in healthy, inoculated and *P. fluorescens* treated fruits were studied for all the four major pathogens in respect of starch, sugars, protein, vitamins, phenols and enzymes.

Changes in Starch Content

Starch is the major carbohydrate of tomato. The change in quantity was estimated in inoculated, healthy and *P.f3* treated fruits. The estimated result indicated that reduction of starch was observed from first day after inoculation. The reduction was more in *A. solani* inoculated fruits compared to other pathogens inoculation. The starch content was attained to the extent of 3.31 per cent in the *Alternaria solani and Phytophthora capsici* inoculated fruits. The reduction of starch was 3.51 per cent in *Colletotrichum capsici* and 4.61 per cent in *Fusarium solani* inoculated fruits. In uninoculated healthy fruits it was 5.03 percent where as in *P f3* treated fruits it attained significantly 6.47 per cent.

Changes in Sugar Content

Sugars play a major role in deciding the quality of the fruits. The decrease in sugar content affects market quality and consumer preference. An *in vitro* study was conducted to judge the quantity of change in sugars in inoculated, healthy and *P.f3* treated fruits.

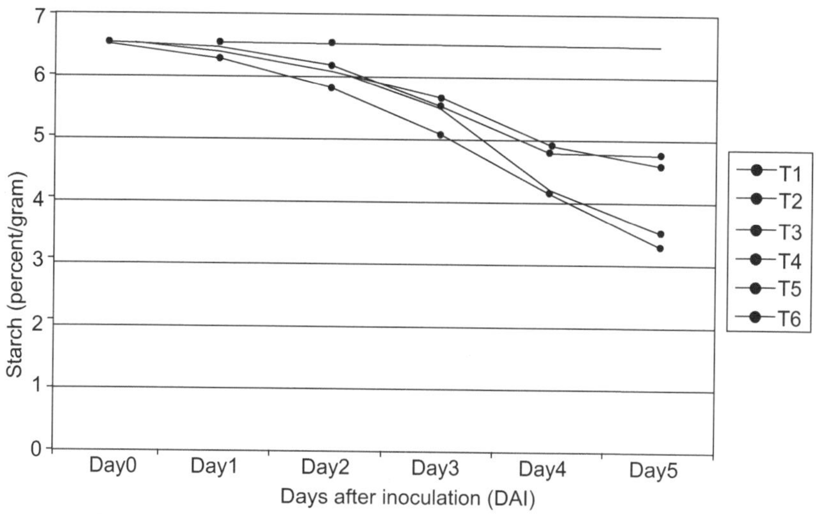

Fig. 6.1: Changes in Starch Content

Total Sugars

The total sugar content was decreased in inoculated fruits when compared to healthy and *P.f3* treated fruits. The analytical result showed that the reduction was observed since first day after inoculation and the rate of decrease was more in fruits inoculated with *F. solani* 1.97 per cent when compared to rest of them. The reduction of total sugars in *Colletotrichum capsici* was 1.99 per cent, in *A. solani* inoculated fruit was 2.06 per cent, and in *Phytophthora capsici* was 2.07 percent where as in uninoculated healthy fruits recorded 2.36 percent. But in *P.f 3* treated fruits significantly recorded 2.96 percent total sugar content.

Reducing Sugar Contents

A decreasing trend was noticed in reducing sugar content due to the invasion of pathogens. The rate of decrease on fifth day after inoculation was found to be highest in the fruits inoculated with *Alternaria solani* which recorded 1.49 percent followed by *Colletotrichum capsici* 1.50 percent, *Fusarium solani* 1.56 and *Phytopthora capsici* 1.57 percent. The reducing sugar content in uninoculated healthy fruits showed 1.67 percent and *P.f3* treated fruits significantly recorded 1.93 percent.

Non-reducing Sugar Contents

The results confirmed the reduction of non reducing sugar content from the first day after inoculation. The rate of decrease over control on fifth day was 0.14 percent in *Fusarium solani,* 0.27 percent in *Colletotrichum capsici,* 0.33 percent in *Alternaria solani* and 0.34 percent in *Phytophthora capsici.* The healthy uninoculated fruit showed 0.88 and the *Pseudomonas fluorescens* treated fruits significantly showed 1.03 percent of non reducing sugar.

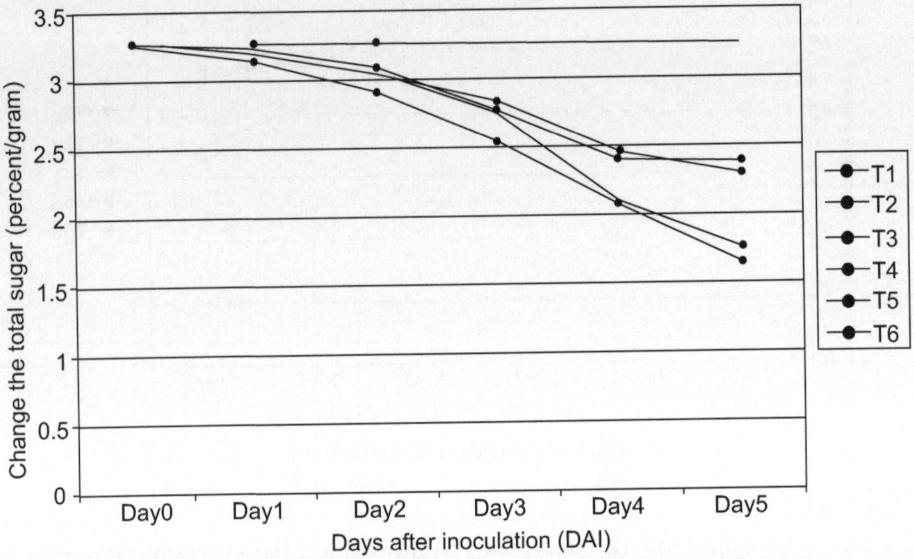

T1=-Alternaria solani, T2-Colletotrichum capsici, T3-Fusarium solani, T4-Phytophthora capsici, T5-Pseudomonas fluorescens, T6-Control

Fig. 6.2: Changes in Total Sugar Content

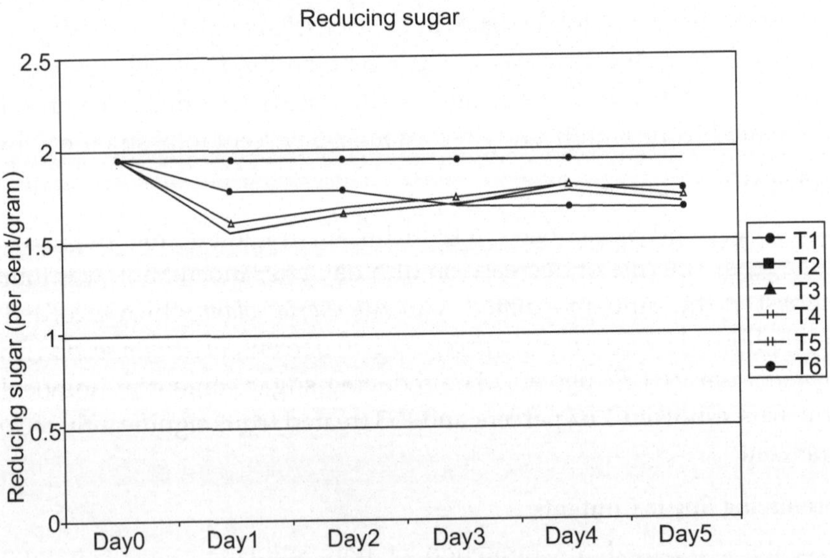

AYS After Inoculation (DAI)

T1=-Alternaria solani, T2-Colletotrichum capsici, T3-Fusarium solani, T4-Phytophthora capsici, T5-Pseudomonas fluorescens, T6-Control

Fig. 6.3: Reducing Sugar

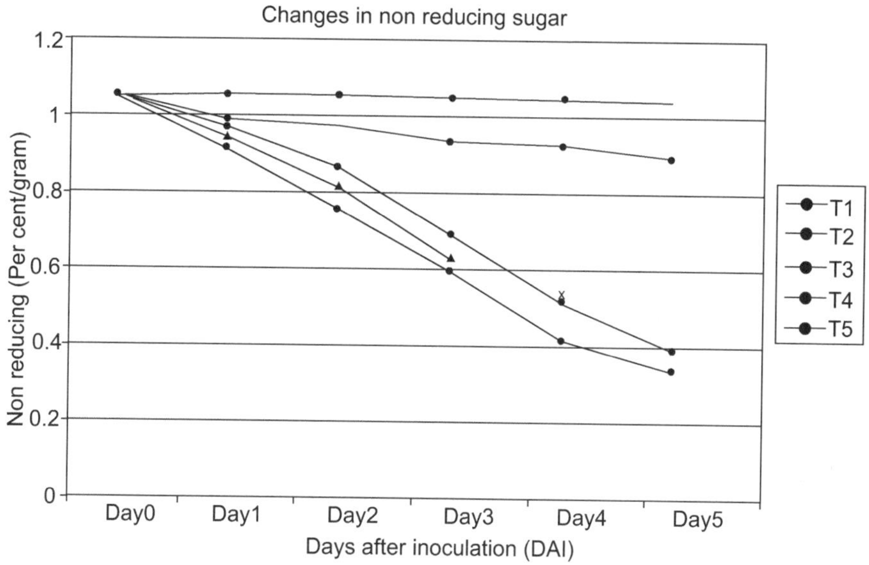

T1=-Alternaria solani, T2-Colletotrichum capsici, T3-Fusarium solani, T4-Phytophthora capsici, T5-Pseudomonas fluorescens, T6-Control

Fig. 6.4: Changes in Non-reducing sugar

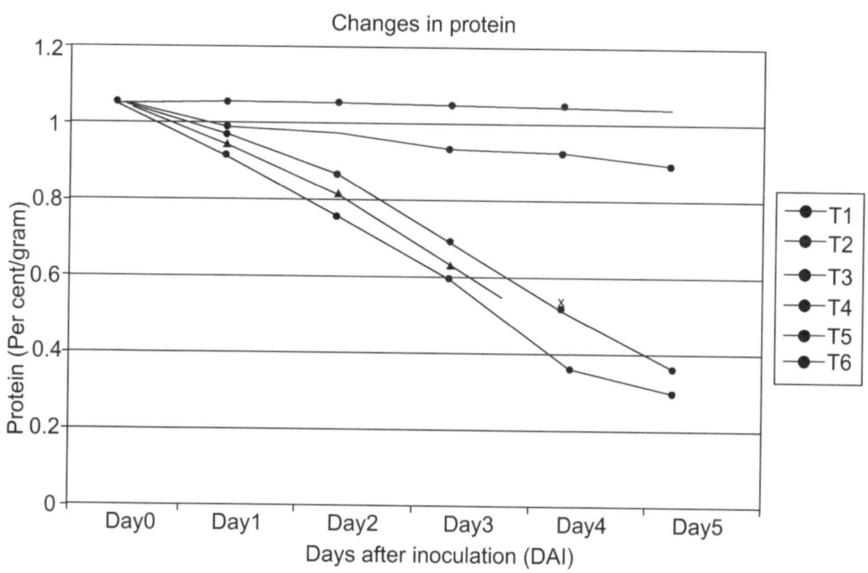

T1=-Alternaria solani, T2-Colletotrichum capsici, T3-Fusarium solani, T4-Phytophthora capsici, T5-Pseudomonas fluorescens, T6-Control

Fig. 6.5: Changes in Protein

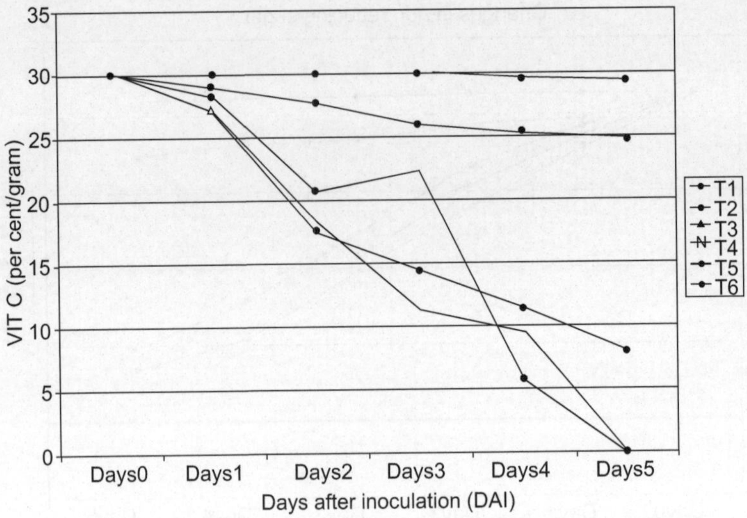

T1=-Alternaria solani, T2-Colletotrichum capsici, T3-Fusarium solani, T4-Phytophthora capsici, T5-Pseudomonas fluorescens, T6-Control

Fig. 6.6: Changes in Vitamin C

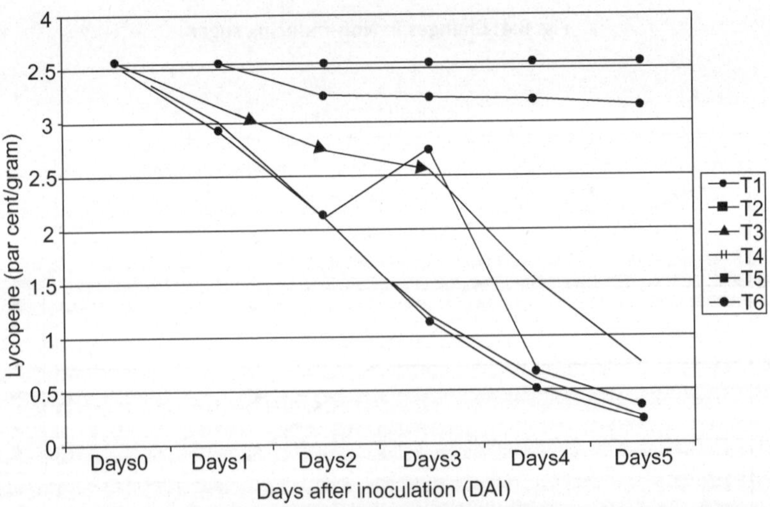

T1=-Alternaria solani, T2-Colletotrichum capsici, T3-Fusarium solani, T4-Phytophthora capsici, T5-Pseudomonas fluorescens, T6-Control

Fig. 6.7: Changes in Lycopene

Changes in Protein

The protein content in inoculated fruits, showed a decreasing trend. There was a significant reduction in protein content in the inoculated fruits from the first day onwards. The maximum reduction of 0.29 percent protein content was noticed in *Fusarium solani* inoculated fruits on the fifth day after inoculation followed by *Phytophthora capsici* 0.34 percent *Colletotrichum capsici* .0.36 percent and *Alternaria solani* 0.37 percent. But in uninoculated healthy fruits showed 0.89 percent protein and *P.f3* treated fruits significantly recorded maximum content of Protein 0.99 percent.

Estimation of Vitamins

Tomato fruits are being preferred by people from all walks of life because of its exceptional quantity of vitamins. The change in vitamin may affect consumer preference and its processing quality. An experiment was conducted to assess the change in vitamin content in inoculated, healthy and *P.f3* treated fruits.

Changes in vit. C

The vitamin C content decreased significantly as a result of invasion of pathogens. Complete reduction was noticed in fruits inoculated with *Alternaria solani* and *Phytophthora capsici* as these pathogens caused losses up to 100 percent (0.00 mg) on fifth day after inoculation. The fruits inoculated with *Colletotrichum capsici* showed 7.99 mg and *Fusarium solani* showed 0.20 mg on fifth day after inoculation. The uninoculated healthy fruit showed 24.63 mg and the fruits treated with *P.f3* significantly illustrated 29.35 mg.

Changes in Lycopene

Lycopene content decreased from first day after inoculation till fifth day and maximum decrease was noticed in fruits inoculated with *Alternaria solani* 0.24 mg followed by *Colletotrichum capsici,* 0.36 mg, *Fusarium solani* ,0.78 mg and *Phytophthora capsici* with 0.26 mg. The uninoculated healthy fruits showed 3.15 mg where as the *P.f3*treated fruits illustrated 3.50 mg .

Changes in Total Phenols

In the present study an increase in phenol content was noticed on first day after inoculation then on subsequent days reduction trend was noticed. The rate of decrease was higher in *Fusarium solani* 0.99 mg followed by *Alternaria solani* 1.06 mg, *Phytophthora capsici* 1.13 mg and *Colletotrichum capsici* 1.14 mg , the in uninoculated healthy fruits recorded 1.25 mg and the *P.f3* treated fruit illustrated 1.89 mg on fifth day after inoculation.

Enzyme Activities

Changes in Polygalacturonase Activity

In general, post harvest rot involves maceration of tissues due to the accumulation of pectolytic enzymes. It was clear that the fruits inoculated with *Colletotrichum capsici* exhibited highest accumulation of polygalacturonase compared to the fruits inoculated with other pathogens. The increase in enzymes activity observed from the first day after inoculation and the rate of increase in enzymes activity on fifth day after inoculation was found to be more which recorded 32.66 percent in *Colletotrichum capsici* followed by *Phytophthora capsici* 30.85, *Alternaria solani* 30.62 percent, and Fusarium *solani* 30.42 per cent. The uninoculated healthy fruits recorded 29.62 per cent and *P.f* 3 treated fruit illustrated minimum accumulation of 17.09 percent.

Changes in Pectin Methyl Esterase Activity

Pectin methyl esterase activity was found to be higher in fruits inoculated with *Fusarium solani* from first day of inoculation. The content in fruits inoculated with *Fusarium solani* was 0.12 per cent increase in enzyme activity on fifth day after inoculation over control, while the increase was 0.10 per cent in *Phytophthora capsici* followed by *Alternaria solani* 0.08 per cent and *Colletotrichum capsici* 0.07 per cent, un inoculated healthy fruits showed 0.08 percent *P.f* 3 treated fruit showed 0.07 per cent.

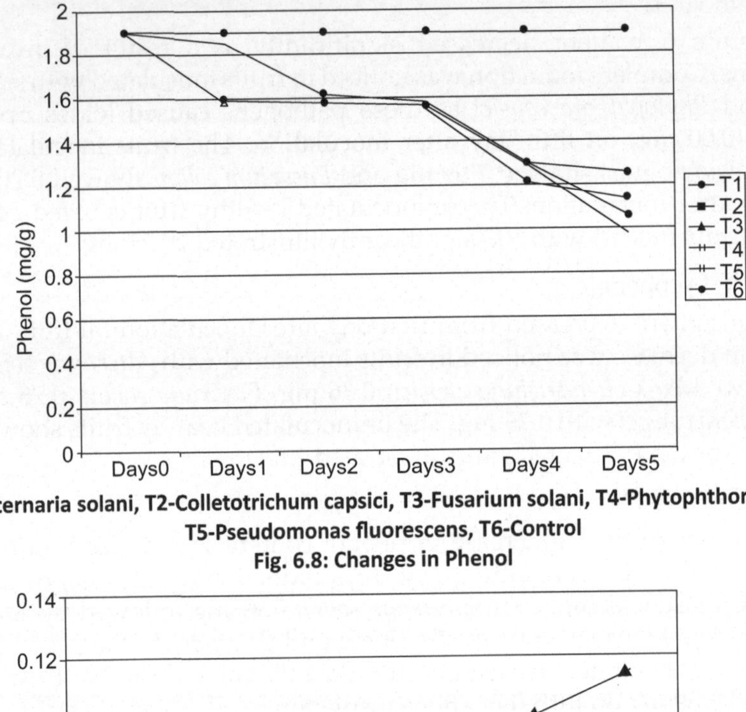

T1=-Alternaria solani, T2-Colletotrichum capsici, T3-Fusarium solani, T4-Phytophthora capsici, T5-Pseudomonas fluorescens, T6-Control

Fig. 6.8: Changes in Phenol

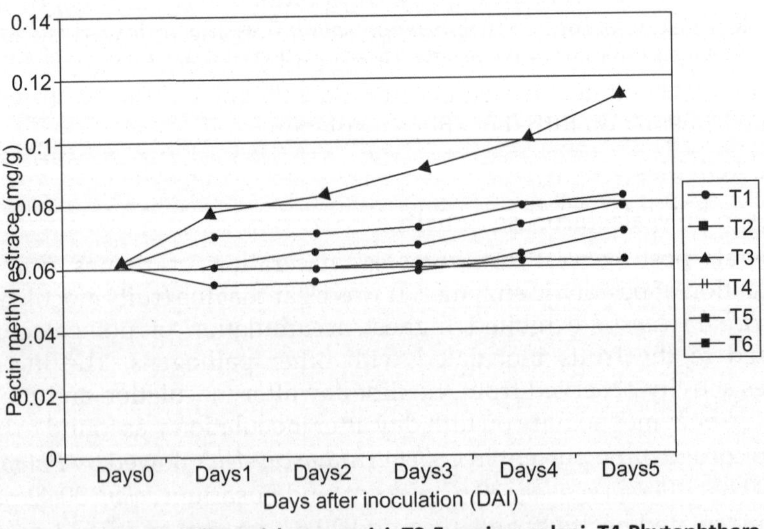

T1=-Alternaria solani, T2-Colletotrichum capsici, T3-Fusarium solani, T4-Phytophthora capsici, T5-Pseudomonas fluorescens, T6-Control

Fig. 6.9: Changes in Poly Galacturonase

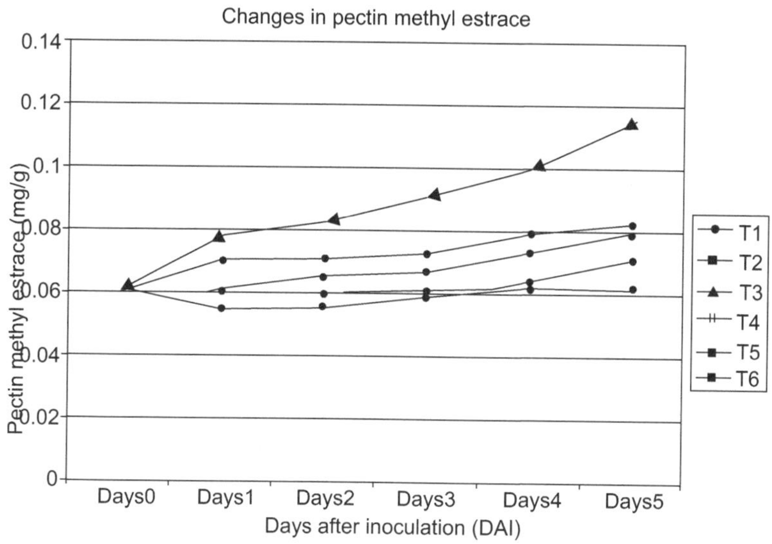

Fig. 6.10: Changes in Pectin Methyl Estrace

Discussion

During pathogenesis many fruit rot pathogens make severe alterations in the nutrient content of tomato either by utilization or decomposition. Hence changes in biochemical constituents namely, starch, sugars, ascorbic acid, Lycopene, Phenolics and enzyme activity *viz.*, polygalacturonase, and pectin methyl estrase were studied and compared with that of healthy and *Pseudomonas fluorescens* (*P.f* 3) treated fruits.

Starch content of healthy fruits showed minimum change during storage. But the starch content in fruits inoculated with pathogens was found to decrease significantly with in a period of five days. The content was very meager in *A.solani* and *Phytophthora capsici* (3.31 per cent) *inoculated* fruits, after fifth day, when compared to other pathogens inoculation. The variation in starch content per gram of tissue were analyzed every day after inoculation for other pathogens also and recorded as follows *Colletotrichum capsici* 3.51 per cent and *Fusarium solani 4.61* per cent. In healthy uninoculated fruits the content of starch was 5.03 percent where as in *Pseudomonas fluorescens* treated fruits the starch content was not reduced drastically and remain same even after five days 6.47 per cent. Such a trend was earlier reported in *Fusarium moniliforme* in jack fruit (Taneja, 1980). Das gupta and Mandal (1988) found that ability of reducing starch content by *Alternaria* sp, *Colletotrichum* sp. Taneja *et al.*, (1983) reported that starch content was decreased due to the infection of *Fusarium moniliforme* in Kathal fruits. The amount of reduction was more in *Fusarium solani* (31.46) infected fruits than other other pathoigens percent.

The total, reducing and non reducing sugars showed a decreasing trend through out experiment. It clearly indicated that the pathogens preferred total, reducing and non reducing sugars for its further invasion and establishment. It is also evident that the decreasing trend was not in healthy and *Pseudomonas fluorescens* treated fruits. Rate of decrease in total sugar was more in fruits inoculated with *Alternaria solani* 1.97 per cent when compare to rest of them. where as in healthy fruits recorded 2.36 percent. The *Pseudomonas fluorescens (P.f 3)* treated fruits the content was not reduced and recorded 2.96 per cent even after five days storage. The same trend was prevailed in reducing sugar also, the fruits inoculated with *Alternaria solani* recorded 1.49 per cent. The reducing sugar content in healthy fruits 1.67 per cent and in *Pseudomonas fluorescens* (*P.f3*) treated fruits the content was 1.93 percent. The non reducing sugar also showed reducing trend. But here the fruits inoculated with *Fusarium solani* recorded maximum reduction in non reducing sugar content (0.14 per cent) on fifth day after inoculation. In healthy uninoculated fruit showed 0.88 and the *Pseudomonas fluorescens* treated fruits showed 1.03 percent of non reducing sugar. Such a trend was already reported by Taneja *et al.,* (1983) also reported that decrease in reducing sugar content in kathal fruits which was affected by *Fusarium moniliforme*. Bhathagar and Kalpana (1995) reported that decrease in contents of soluble and reducing sugars in diseased plant tissue. Chandrasekhar and Rajappan, (2001) reported that content of protein and sugars in the plants were induced to increase when it was treated with plant extract, antagonist and chemicals.

The protein content of tomato fruit was decreased with increase in storage period in all the pathogens inoculated fruits. In storage, five days after inoculation, the content was very minimum in *Fusarium solani* inoculated fruits (0.29 percent) when compared to other pathogens inoculated fruits. In healthy uninoculated fruits and *Pseudomonas fluorescens* a treated fruit showed the protein content was not reduced as in the case of inoculated fruits which recorded 0.89, 0.99 percent respectively.

The study was clearly indicated that due to pathogen invasion the protein content in tomato fruit is being varied but the content was not varied in healthy un inoculated fruits. The protein content in *Pseudomonas fluorescens* treated fruits remain as such even after five days. This may be due to the systemic action of *Pseudomonas fluorescens (P.f3)* in preventing the degradation of protein .This findings is in accordance with the result given by Cooper *et al.,* (1981) in late blight infected potato tubers and Williams and Fernandez (1987) in *Aspergillus* and *Penicillium* infected onion bulbs. A slight reduction in the protein content of strawberry infected by *Mucor piriformis* was reported by Thompson and Eribo (1984). Tandon (1970) observed changes in free aminoacids content after the infection of *Botrytis cineria Colletotrichum coccodes, R. stolanifer* and *Penicillium expansum*. He reported that *Botrytis cineria* in tomato fruits caused drastic reduction in glutamic acid, increase in leucine and phenyl alanine, decrease in arginine, while aspartic acid, serine glycine aspergine, α-alanine and α-amino butyric acid remain unchanged. As a result of *Colletotrichum coccodes* infection the contents of glutemic acid declined, arginine increased, valine was newly formed, while others remained same. There was an increase in glycine and serine in *R. stolanifer* infected fruit, while there was no change in the contents of other amino acids.

Tomato fruit is act as a substitute for orange and considered as *"poor mans orange"* because of its exceptional quantity of vitamins and minerals. The reduction in vitamins and mineral content may indulge consumer preference. With this background an *in vitro* study was conducted to asses the variation in vitamin content due to pathogen invasion. A drastic reduction of Vitamin C content was noticed five days after inoculation of *Alternaria solani,* and *Phytophthora capsici* which recorded 0.00 mg. The fruits inoculated with *Colletotrichum capsici* showed 7.99 mg and *Fusarium solani* illustrated 0.20 mg on fifth day after inoculation. The uninoculated healthy fruit demonstrated 34.63 mg and the fruits treated with *Pseudomonas fluorescens* recorded 35.85 mg. This type of tendency was already reported by Prasad (1983) *Helminthosporium speciferum* infection in tomato caused 92.07 reductions in ascorbic acid content after 15 days of incubation. Some contrary results were also reported in the case of Ber. The ascorbic acid content increased due to Ethephon treatment (Cheema, 1982) and also treatment with naphthalene acetic acid and β-napthoxy acetic acid increased the ascorbic acid content (Johnson and coats, 1993).

Decreasing trend was noticed in Lycopene content also from the first day after inoculation till fifth day. The maximum amount of reduction was noticed in fruits inoculated with *Alternaria solani* (0.24 mg) followed by *Phytophthora capsici* (0.26 mg), *Colletotrichum capsici* (0.36 mg) and *Fusarium solani* (0.78 mg). The uninoculated healthy fruits recorded 3.15 mg where as the *Pseudomonas fluorescens* treated fruits showed 3.50 mg. The same trend was reported by Gangopadhyay and chattopadyay (1976) correlated the content of lycopene with brown spot of rice caused by *Helminthosporium oryzae*. They stated that the lycopene play a major role in reactions involving oxidation, reduction and production of sensitive enzymes in cells.

Phenols content is directly related with the defense mechanism of the tomato fruits against pathogen attack. After inoculation, total phenols content of tomato fruit was found to increase till 48 hours and then it was decreased. The rate of decline was higher in *Fusarium solani* (0.99 mg) followed by *Alternaria solani* (1.06 mg) *Phytophthora capsici* (1.13) mg and *Colletotrichum capsici* (1.14 mg). The phenol content in uninoculated healthy fruits was 1.25 mg but in *Pseudomonas fluorescens* treated fruit the phenol content was not varied even five days after inoculation which recorded 1.89 mg and confirmed it defence mechanism . This is in accordance with the results of Ray and Hammer Schmidt

(1998). A greater increase in the phenolic content in the resistant variety than the susceptible varieties. The phenolics are antibacterial to *Erwinia* sp. and are more effective together in properties in which they occur in wound periderm than individually. Poly phenol diffuses from natural periderm to wound periderm and inhibit the activity of quinones (Tripathi *et al.*, 1983). Agarwal and Agarwal (1982) qoted that phenolic content in tomato fruits was reduced at later stages of infection by *Colletotrichum phomoides* and *C. verticilloides*. De Boer *et al.*, (2003) reported that increase Phenolic content was observed in *P. fluorescens* treated banana fruit. Ramamoorthy and Samiyappan (2001) reported that increase in phenol, PO, PPO, in Chilli plants treated with *P. fluorescens* followed by the challenge inoculation of *Colletotrichum capsici*.

The degradation of complex organic substances to simple one is brought about by pathogens by means of producing different enzymes. Attempts were made to study the potentiality of pathogens to produce major pectic enzymes under *in vitro* conditions. Pectic enzymes are implicated almost routinely as a feature of the host pathogens interaction and it is more or less accepted that pectic enzymes are responsible for maceration of the tissues during the disease development. Polygalacturonase (PG) and pectin methyl esterase (PME) are the tow major components of pectic enzyme family. In the present study, an increasing trend of polygalcturonase activity was found to be significantly high in the case of *Colletotrichum capsici* 32.66 per cent followed by *Phytophthora capsici* 30.85, *Alternaria solani* 30.62 percent, *Fusarium solani* 30.42 percent. The uninoculated healthy fruits showed 29.62 per cent and *Pseudomonas fluorescens* treated fruit showed 17.09 percent. Agarwal (1979) reported the association of polygalacturonase, poly methylgalacturonase, pectin methyl esterase and pectin trans eliminase with rotting of tomato fruits by *Colletotrichum phomoides* and the enzyme activity was found to be influenced by metallic and metallic salts. The virulence and in vivo production of enzymes, *viz.*, poly galacturonase, poly methyl galacturonase, pectin methyl esterase and corboxy methyl cellulose by *C.phomoides* and *A. alternata* has been found to be correlated in tomato fruit rots (Gupta, 1978).

These pectic enzymes have been shown to be important virulent determinants of the soft rot Erwinia sp (Collmer and Keen, 1986). Webner and Wegener (1986) reported the close relationship of polygalacturonase activity and tissue maceration and also reported the Polygalacturonase activity was reported at 10 hours after inoculation of fruits. Cooper *et al.*, (1981) reported production of pectic enzymes by *Fusarium* sp and *Erwinia* carotovora fsp. *pisi*. In the present study PME activity was increased by all the pathogens. The activity was more in fruits inoculated with *Fusarium solani* was 0.11 percent increase in enzyme activity on fifth day after inoculation, while the increase was 0.10 percent in *Phytophthora capsici* followed by *Alternaria solani* 0.08 percent and *Colletotrichum capsici* 0.07 percent. The non inoculated healthy fruits showed 0.08 percent and *Pseudomonas fluorescens* treated fruit showed

0.07 percent. Dorel *et al.*, (1992) reported that PME had a major role in the infection process, due to presence of PME the potato tubers showed resistant to soft rot. Kloepper *et al.*, (2004) reported that chitinase, peroxidase activity and increased production of chitinase and β-1,3 glucanase was seen in *P. fluorescens* treated sugar beet.

Table 6.1: Analysis of Starch

S.No.	Pathogens	Starch (Percent)*					
		DAI					Percent decrease Over control at 5th day
		1	2	3	4	5	
1	*A. solani*	6.27	5.82	5.08	4.14	3.31	30.46
2	*C. capcici*	6.41	6.04	5.47	4.21	3.51	26.26
3	*F. solani*	6.38	6.08	5.66	4.93	4.61	3.15
4	*P. capcici*	6.37	5.80	5.18	4.44	3.31	31.46
5	Control	6.46	6.15	5.54	4.80	4.76	

CD(.05) = 0.13
*** = Mean of three replications**

Table 6.2: Analysis of Total Sugar

S.No.	Pathogens	Total Sugar (Percent)*					
		DAI					Percent decrease Over control at 5th day
		1	2	3	4	5	
1	*A. solani*	2.54	2.47	2.42	2.25	2.06	12.71
2	*C. capcici*	2.51	2.45	2.27	2.08	1.99	15.68
3	*F. solani*	2.45	2.37	2.28	2.15	1.97	16.53
4	*P. capcici*	2.55	2.48	2.44	2.24	2.07	12.29
5	Control	2.74	2.53	2.47	2.45	2.36	

CD (.05) = 0.0591
*** = Mean of three replications**

Table 6.3: Analysis of Reducing Sugars

S.No.	Pathogens	Reducing Sugar (Percent)*					
		DAI					Percent decrease Over control at 5th day
		1	2	3	4	5	
1	*A.solani*	1.61	1.63	1.70	1.80	1.77	18.79
2	*C.capcici*	1.56	1.65	1.73	1.81	1.73	16.77
3	*F.solani*	1.59	1.66	1.74	1.80	1.74	16.10
4	*P.capcici*	1.78	1.57	1.55	1.56	1.67	12.67
5	Control	1.78	1.56	1.55	1.57	1.49	

CD(.05) = 0.04
*** = Mean of three replications**

Table 6.4: Analysis of Non-reducing Sugar

S.No.	Pathogens	Non-reducing Sugar (Percent)*					
		DAI					Percent decrease Over control at 5th day
		1	2	3	4	5	
1	*A. solani*	0.96	0.85	0.66	0.47	0.33	62.5
2	*C. capcici*	0.90	0.73	0.55	0.36	0.27	69.32
3	*F. solani*	0.93	0.79	0.59	0.34	0.14	84.09
4	*P. capcici*	0.95	0.85	0.67	0.49	0.34	61.36
5	Control	0.98	0.96	0.92	0.91	0.88	

CD(.05)= 0.02
*** = Mean of three replications**

Table 6.5: Analysis of Protein

S.No.	Pathogens	Protein (Percent)*					
		DAI					Percent decrease Over control at 5th day
		1	2	3	4	5	
1	*A.solani*	0.77	0.59	0.58	0.45	0.35	35.19
2	*C.capcici*	0.81	0.69	0.55	0.47	0.34	37.03
3	*F.solani*	0.88	0.68	0.51	0.36	0.29	46.29
4	*P.capcici*	0.77	0.64	0.57	0.47	0.36	33.33
5	Control	0.87	0.73	0.58	0.56	0.54	

CD(.05)= 0.02
*** = Mean of three replications**

Table 6.6: Analysis of vit C

S.No.	Pathogens	Starch (Percent)*					
		DAI					Percent decrease Over control at 5th day
		1	2	3	4	5	
1	*A. solani*	47.26	23.68	22.20	5.82	0.00	100
2	*C. capcici*	46.87	37.50	14.35	11.37	7.99	76. 93
3	*F. solani*	47.17	38.48	20.92	9.84	0.20	99.42
4	*P. capcici*	47.36	38.58	19.34	9.47	0.00	100
5	Control	46.91	44.60	38.88	36.31	34.63	

CD(.05)= 0.74
*** = Mean of three replications**

Table 6.7: Analysis of β-carotene

S.No.	Pathogens	β-carotene (mg/100 g)*					
		DAI					Percent decrease Over control at 5th day
		1	2	3	4	5	
1	*A. solani*	2.78	2.12	1.15	0.53	0.24	94.01
2	*C. capcici*	2.49	2.13	2.74	0.67	0.36	91.02
3	*F. solani*	2.92	2.75	2.57	1.48	0.78	80.55
4	*P. capcici*	2.80	2.02	1.20	0.60	0.26	93.52
5	Control	3.14	3.24	3.49	3.91	4.01	

CD(.05)= 0.06

*** = Mean of three replications**

Table 6.8: Analysis of Phenol

S.No.	Pathogens	Phenol (mg/g)*					
		DAI					Percent decrease Over control at 5th day
		1	2	3	4	5	
1	*A. solani*	1.60	1.62	1.58	1.30	1.06	15.20
2	*C. capcici*	1.60	1.59	1.56	1.22	1.14	8.80
3	*F. solani*	1.59	1.58	1.57	1.29	0.99	20.80
4	*P. capcici*	1.86	1.62	1.59	1.31	1.13	9.60
5	Control	1.60	1.58	1.56	1.30	1.25	

CD(.05)= 0.04

*** = Mean of three replications**

Table 6.9: Analysis of Poly Galacto Uronase

S.No.	Pathogens	Poly Galacto Uronase (Percent reduction in viscosity after 30 min)					
		DAI					Percent decrease Over control at 5th day
		1	2	3	4	5	
1	*A. solani*	14.21	16.97	22.40	29.60	35.62	76.24
2	*C. capcici*	14.11	18.85	25.36	30.79	32.66	61.60
3	*F. solani*	14.60	17.39	24.33	29.60	35.42	75.26
4	*P. capcici*	15.95	20.09	29.75	33.37	35.85	77.39
5	Control	10.58	12.78	14.66	16.46	20.21	

CD (.05)= 0.61

*** = Mean of three replications**

Table 6.10: Analysis of Peroxidase

S.No.	Pathogens	Peroxidase (Change in absorbance/min/g)					
		DAI					Percent decrease Over control at 5th day
		1	2	3	4	5	
1	*A. solani*	2.66	2.54	2.49	2.31	2.24	9.27
2	*C. capcici*	2.48	2.39	2.34	2.22	2.12	3.41
3	*F. solani*	2.50	2.48	2.42	2.18	2.16	5.37
4	*P. capcici*	2.64	2.50	2.46	2.35	2.19	6.83
5	Control	2.38	2.34	2.27	2.16	2.05	

CD(.05) = 0.06
*** = Mean of three replications**

Table 6.11: Analysis of Pectin Methyl Estrase

S.No.	Pathogens	µ mole of hydrogen/min/ml					
		DAI					Percent decrease Over control at 5th day
		1	2	3	4	5	
1	*A. solani*	0.070	0.071	0.073	0.079	0.082	15.49
2	*C. apcici*	0.061	0.065	0.067	0.073	0.079	11.27
3	*F. solani*	0.078	0.083	0.091	0.100	0.115	61.97
4	*P. capcici*	0.069	0.077	0.086	0.091	0.101	42.25
5	Control	0.055	0.056	0.059	0.064	0.071	

CD = 0.007
*** = Mean of three replications**

CONCLUSION

Through this study it is evident that, maximum reduction in starch, sugars, protein, and vitamins were observed in pathogen inoculated fruits than in uninoculated healthy fruits but in *P.f3* treated fruits the reduction was very negligible. Drastic reduction in phenol content and increasing in enzyme activity like polygalacturonase and pectinmethylestrace were noticed in pathogen inoculated fruits five days after inoculation. But in uninoculated healthy and in *P.f 3* treated fruits slight reduction in phenol and slight increase in enzyme activity was observed five days after incubation.

REFERENCES

Agarwal, F.T.1979. Histopathological Changes Induced in Tomato Plants by Single and Combined Ability of Tobacco Mosaic Virus and *Alternaria solani*. *Indian phytopath,* 39:346-350

Agarwal, W.A. and Agarwal, F.T. 1982. Integrated Control of Foliar Disease of Tomato. *Phytopathology,* 84:1104

Anonymous 1995. Proc. III. Workshop, Indo-US – Project on Post Harvest Pathology of Fruits and Vegetables, New Delhi. 112-117.

Anonymous 1996. Tomatoes: *Indian Agriculture*. Vikas Singhal Production, New Delhi, p. 213-217.

Anjali Mehta and Som, A.w. 2002. Tomato-perishables Diet in India. *Indian Food Industry* 21: 37-40.

Bhathagar, A. and Kalpana, S. 1995. Effect of Certain Carbohydrates on the Pathogenesis of *Colletotrichum Capsici* Causing Anthracnose of Chillies., *Indian phytopath,* 24: 658-666.

Chandrashekar, A. and Rajappan, K. 2001 Alteration in Protein and Sugar Content of Soy Bean Plants as Induced by Plant Extract, Antagonist and Chemicals *J.Mycol.Pl.Pathol.,* 31(350-352)

Chenulu, V.V. and Thakur, D.P. 1968. Survey for Storage and Market Disease of Certain Fruits and Vegetables in Delhi and Control of Soft Rot Due to *Rhizopus, Indian phytopath,* 4:65-70.

Cheema, A. 1982. Effect on Inoculum Concentration on the Resistance of Tomato to *Alternaria solani. Fotipathologia Brasileira.* 24:463-465.

Collmer, P. and Keen, M.S 1986. An Easy Method of Preparing Inoculam of Alternaria Solani for Inoculation Experiments. *Indian phytopath,* 33 :359-365.

Cooper, R. M., Wardman, P.A. and Slelton, J.E. 1981. The Influence of Cell Walls from Host and Non-host Plants on the Production and Activity of Polygalactouronide-Degrading Enzymes From Fungal Pathogens. *phisiol.plant path* 10:239-255.

Das gupta, M.K. and Mandal, N.C. 1988. Post Harvest Pathology of Perishables. *Oxford and IBH publishing Co.Pvt. Ltd.,* New Delhi, Bombay, Calcutta.

Das gupta, P. and Mandal, R.1989. Tomatoes in Storage. *J.Agric. Res.*2:1624

De Boer. M., Bom. P., Kindt. F. Keurentjes. J. J. B., Vandersluis. I., Vanloon. L.C. and P. A. H. M. Bakker. 2003. Control of *Fusarium* Wilt of Radish by Combining *Pseudomonas putida* Strains that Different Disease Suppressive Mechanisms. Phytopathology; 93 : 626-632.

Dorel, C., Deceara, A. and Miller, S. 1992. Assesment of Losses in Tomato Yield Due to Early Blight. *Indian phytopath,* 34: 191-195.

Gangopadhyay, P. and Chattopadyay, A. 1976. Methods of Gram Staining. N.Y. State. *Agr.Expt.Sta.Tech.Bull.*129.

Gupta, M. 1978. Fundamentals of Plant Pathology, Acadeemic Press, Inc. Harcourt, Brace Jovanovich Publishers, Tokyo, 342.

Hammerschmidt, R., Nuckles, E.M and Kuc, J. 1998. Association of Enhanced Peroxidase Activity with Induced Systemic Resistance of Cucumber to *Colletotrichum lagenarium. Physiol.Pl. Pathol.* 20 : 73-82.

Hedge, A. and Hofrieter, M. 1962. Metabolites of Pseudomonas Involved in the Bio-control of Plant Disease. TIBTECH.,12: 133-141.

Johnson, G.I and Coats, L.M. 1993. Postharvest Disease of Vegetable Crops. *Postharvest News Information.*4: 27N-37N.

Kaloo, G.1997. Solanaceous Vegetables. In 50 years of Crop Science Research in India, New Delhi, p.109.

Kloepper. J. W., Ryu. C. M. and S. Zhang. 2004. Induced Systemic Resistance and Promotion of Plant Growth by *Bacillus spp.* Phytopathology; 94: 1259-1266.

Lowry, A. and Mansfield, J.W. 1951. Antimicrobial Compounds. In Biochemicals Plant Pathology (Callow. J. Ed.) John Wiley and Sons Ltd., U.K., pp. 237-265.

Mahadevan, S. and Sridhar. R. 1982. *Introduction to Research on Plant Disease*. John.S. Swift Co., New York, p. 177.

Malik and Singh, 1980. Systemic Resistance Induced by Phenol. Annu. Rev. Phytopathol., 36: 453-483.

Panes, K.N. and Sukhatme, B.L.1967. Analysis of Enzyme Activity. p. 176.

Prasad, 1983. Ecology of the Soft Rot *Erwinias. Ann.Rev. Phytopathol.*18: 361-387.

Ramamoorthy, V., Raguchander, T. and Samiyappan, R. 2001. Enhancing Resistance of Tomato and Hot Pepper to *Pythium* Diseases by Seed Treatment with Fluorescent Pseudomonads. European J. Plant Pathol., 108: 429-441.

Rodriguez, S. and Dimond, A.E. 1976. Interaction of Tissue Sugar, Growth Substances and Disease Susceptibility. *Z. pflanzenkrankh. Pflanzenschutz.*, 64: 415-421.

Sadasivam, R. and Balasubramanian. P. 1987. Biochemical Methods. 156-163.

Somogyi, N.F. 1952. Posyharvest Handling Practices and Postharvest Diseases of Fruit. *Plant. Dis.*, 36: 357-364.

Srivastava, Ward, K. 1965. Relative Resistance of Tomatoes at Various Stages of Ruipeness to Bacterial Soft Rot. Annual Meeting Abstracts of Tomato, 1315-1318

Tandon, 1970. Post Infection Changes in Sugar Contents of Tomato Fruits Caused by *Drecheslera Australiense. Indian phytopath.* 23:133-135.

Taneja, D.T., Rafter. G. and Dustur, H. 1983. Effect of Plant Extracts Against the Bacterial Soft Rot of Potatoes: *Erwinia carotovora. Agrarforschung*, 6:17-20.

Taneja, 1983. Antagonism Testing of Fungal Antagonist against the Causal Agents of A Disease on Onion. *Agricola*, 16:61-64.

Thakur, S. and Chenulu, S.S. 1988. Survey on Tomatoes—New Delhi Markets. *J.Pl.Pathol*, 10:241-244.

Thompson, V and Eribo, E. 1984. Accumulation of Phenols in Soybean after Inoculation with Fungi Non-pathogenic to Soybean. *Phytopathology*, 57:804.

Triapathi, R.K., Varma, N and Gupta, V.K., 1983. Peroxidase Activity and Isozyme in Relation to Resistance Potatoes against Rotting. *Indian.J. Exp. Biol.* 12: 591-592.

Veerargavathatham, D. and Muthuvel, I.1994. Analysis on Tomato Variability in PKM1 Variety. *South. Ind. Hort.* 89: 608-613.

Webner, M. and Wegner, B. 1986. Bacterials of Tort of Potatoes. *Phytopathology*. 49 : 290-292.

Williums, T. ans Fernandus, C. 1987. Studies on Post Harvest Disease of Potato. *Plant. Dis.*, 34:57-64.

Agriculture Crops and Food Security
Edited by: Dr. Pawan Kumar 'Bharti' and Alka Chauhan
ISBN: 978-93-5056-881-1
Edition: 2017
Published by: Discovery Publishing House Pvt. Ltd., New Delhi (India)

7

Sorghum Shoot fly (*Atherigona soccata*) its Control and Management

[1]Pamirelli Ranjith

INTRODUCTION

Sorghum (*Sorghum bicolor* Moench (L.)] is one of the most important cereal crops in the semi-arid tropics (SAT). Grain yields on peasant farms are generally low (500-800 kg ha-1), insect pests being one of the major factors limiting sorghum production. In India, nearly 32.1% of the actual produce is lost due to insect pests (Borad and Mittal 1983). The losses due to panicle-feeding insects alone have been estimated to be over $ 100 million annually (Leuschner and Sharma 1983). There are over 150 insect species which damage sorghum pianis from sowing to crop harvest (Seshu Reddy and Davies 1979a). In most of the sorghum-growing areas, the important pests found are the sorghum midge (*Contarinia sorghicola* Coq.), stem borers (*Chilo partellus* Swinhoe and *Busseola fusca* Fuller), head bugs (*Calocoris angustatus* Leth., *Eufystylus immaculatus Odh., Creontiades pallidus Ramb.* and *Campylomma* spp.), green bug (*Schizaphis graminum* Rondani), and shoot fly (*Atherigona soccata* Rondani). Others like the spider mite (*Oligonychus* spp.), shoot bug (*Peregrinus maidis Ashm.*), corn leaf aphid (*Rhopalosiphom maidis* Fitch.), and head caterpillars (*Helicoverpa armigera* Hb; *Eublemma* spp., *Cryptoblabes* spp., and *Pyroderces simplex* Wsm.) can be regarded as occasional pests. The locusts (*Schistocerca gregaria* Forsk. and *Locusta migratoria migratorioides* Linn.) and armyworms (*Mythimna separata* Walker, *Spodoptera exempta* Walker, and *Spodoptera frugiperda* J.E. Smith) also cause sporadic defoliation of the crop (Sharma 1985a).

Scientific Information

Crop: Sorghum

Scientific name: *Sorghum Bicolor*

Order: Cyperales

Family: Poaceae

---

[1] Pamirelli Ranjith (Ph.D Research scholar), Genetics and Plant Breeding Department, OUAT, Bhubaneswar, Odhisa-751003, India.

The major components of pest management in agroecosystems are cultural practices, natural enemies, insecticides, and host-plant resistance. Cultural practices are effective against certain pests, some having become an integral component of crop husbandry and farming systems. However, some of the cultural practices are only partially effective and are difficult to implement under rainfed conditions. It is difficult for all farmers to plant at times when pest incidence can be avoided so that population buildup of insects can be minimized. Chemical control is expensive and numerous applications may be required. This is often beyond the reach of most farmers in the SAT. In many areas, insecticides and spraying equipment are e ither not available or farmers lack the proper knowledge of their use. Under such circumstances, use of resistant or less-susceptible cultivars is one of the most important methods of keeping insect populations below economic threshold levels. Host-plant resistance does not involve any extra costs or application skills in pest control techniques. However, host-plant resistance is not a panacea for all pest problems. It is most useful when carefully utilized with other components of pest management (Painter 1951).

Pest information/status

Taxonomic Position

Class: Insecta;

Order: Diptera;

Family: Muscidae;

Genus: *Atherigona;*

Species: soccata.

PEST DETAILS

Atherigona soccata (Rondani, 1871). Common names: Sorghum shoot fly, sorghum stem fly, millet stem fly. Atherigona soccata is recognised as the major species of shoot fly infesting sorghum. Larvae of this genus live as primary pests in the stems/shoot of grasses. *Atherigona soccata* is almost certainly present in all the sorghum-growing areas in Africa, Asia and Mediterranean Europe. This species has not yet been reported in India, however damage by *A. soccata* has been observed in sorghum. Damage by *A. soccata* at the seedling stage (5 to 30 days after seedling emergence) leads to typical dead heart symptoms, whereby the maggot attacks cuts the growing point, and as a result the central leaf dries up forming a dead heart. If shoot infestation occurs under conditions of high humidity infested plants may not produce the typical dead heart symptoms and the damaged leaf becomes thin and papery and wraps around the other leaves. As a result, the plants may fail to grow normally.

Losses due to sorghum shoot fly vary between seasons and locations. The late sown crops generally suffer greater shoot fly damage because increase of shoot fly populations on the early sown crops. The losses are aggravated with uneven rainfall resulting in staggered plantings.

Fig. 7.1: Shoot Fly, Dead Heart, Eggs

Life Cycle

Sorghum shoot fly populations are usually abundant during the rainy season under moderate temperatures and high humidity with an increase in populations generally recorded 20 to 30 days after the onset of monsoon rains. Population density is generally low during the hot dry summer in southern India and during the winter season in northern India. Shoot-fly infestations are normally high in the post-rainy season crop planted in September-October. Temperatures above 35°C and below 18°C and continuous rainfall reduce shoot fly abundance (Taneja *et al.*, 1986). During the off-season, the insect survives on alternative hosts (*Sorghum* spp., *Echinochloa colonum, E. procera, Cymbopogon* sp., *Paspalum scrobiculatum* and *Pennisetum glaucum*), tillers of ratooned crops and volunteer/fodder sorghum.

Shoot fly females are attracted to the host plant for oviposition by the odours emitted from the host plant. Females of *A. soccata* are attracted both to the volatiles emitted by susceptible seedlings and to phototactic (optical) stimuli that facilitate orientation to the host for oviposition (Nwanze *et al.*, 1998).

Females of *A. soccata* lay cigar-shaped eggs singly on the lower surface of the leaves, at the 1- to 7- leaf stage. Eggs are laid generally singly parallel to the midrib on the under surface of the 3rd to 5th leaf. Under high shoot-fly pressure, there may be several eggs on the same leaf. Sometimes, as many as 25 eggs may be laid on the same seedling. Most often, these eggs are laid by different females. Eggs are deposited parallel to the midrib and hatch in the early morning hours 2 to 5 days later (Sharma 1996). Three larval instars develop over a period of about one week at an average temperature of 27°C (Swaine and Wyatt 1954).

The larva migrates to the upper side of the leaf, moves along the leaf whorl reac hing the growing point through the leaf sheath. The larva cuts the growing point, resulting in wilting and drying of the central leaf, known as dead heart. The larva feeds on the decaying plant tissue. The dead heart can be pulled out easily, and it produces an offensive smell. Normally, the damage occurs 1 to 4 weeks after seedling emergence. The damaged plants produce side tillers, which may also be attacked. Larval development is completed in 8-10 days, and pupation takes place mostly at the base of the stem, and sometimes in the soil. The pupal period lasts for 8 days in south India, and up to 14 days in north India (Sharma 1996). The pupae stage lasts for 7 to 10 days. Under favourable temperature (20-30°C) and relative humidity (>60%), the life cycle is completed in 15 to 18 days (Srivastava 1985).

The adults are dark brown and similar to domestic housefly, but nearly half the size with the males smaller than the females. The adults usually live for 10 to 20 days. Adult longevity is quite variable and depends on environmental conditions and the availability of host plants (Sharma 1996).

Sorghum shoot fly populations may be recorded throughout the year, and there may be 15 to 16 g enerations in a year. In more temperate areas (e.g. Italy) there may be 5 to 6 generations (Bene 1986). Priyavratha Rao and Narasimha Rao (1956) indicated that there is no diapause during the off-season and the adults hide in the stubble of the ratooned sorghum. In Italy, overwintering takes place as a mature larva or pupa (Bene 1986).

Dispersal

- Even though adult sorghum shoot flies have functional wings capable of flight that can allow dispersal into new areas and new fields, adults have been recorded to disperse only short distances. However, if strong winds are present adult flies can be displaced hundreds of kilometres in a day.
- In areas of intensive cultivation or areas with a continuous presence (gaps of no more than 10 km) of suitable hosts, adult insects may successfully disperse to adjacent grain fields.
- Sorghum shoot fly eggs, larvae and pupae can be readily transported with agricultural products in infested seedlings, soil, shipping containers or vehicles carrying agricultural produce.
- The pupal stage of this pest can survive for long periods without a host in dry soil and can therefore be spread in seed, machinery or equipment with soil contamination.

Symptoms

Damage by *A. soccata* at the seedling stage (5 to 30 days after seedling emergence) will lead to the typical dead heart symptoms. The larva migrates to the upper side of the leaf, and moves along the leaf whorl until it reaches the growing point where the larvae cut the growing point. As a result the central leaf dries up forming a dead heart, which can be pulled out easily and produces a rotting smell. Normally the damage occurs 1 to 4 weeks after seedling emergence. Seedlings of 5 to 30 days old are generally susceptible to shoot fly damage. Older plants (>30 days after seedling emergence) are not usually damaged by *A. soccata* however, under conditions of high humidity during the rainy season, infestation may occur. Under these conditions the infested plants do not produce the typical dead heart symptoms. In this instance, the damaged leaf becomes thin and papery, wrapping around the other leaves. The plants may fail to grow normally. Late infestations may also damage the panicle in the formative stage, resulting in rotting or drying up of a portion of the panicle affected by shoot fly damage.

As a result of damage to the growing point, the damaged plant produces side tillers, which often serve as a means of recovery for the plant unless the tillers are exposed to another infestation of *A. soccata* in the susceptible stage (0 days after initiation of tiller production)

Some seedlings may not have typical symptoms, but still produce side tillers in response to temperature or moisture stress. Some genotypes have an inherent capacity to produce more tillers.

Fig. 7.2: Symptoms of Shoot fly

Entry, Establishment and Spread

There is little scope for the movement of this insect from one region to another, except through live sorghum seedlings. There may be some short-distance movement through adult migration/dispersal. It is probably for this reason that this insect has not spread to areas where sorghum is grown. The invasive pest may enter Australia via imported plant material containing leaves, seedlings or material for propagation. Where the eggs and larvae are born internaly.

DIAGNOSTIC INFORMATION

Diagnostic Protocol

Shoot flies are identified by microscopic examination of adult flies. Pont (1973) and Pont and Magpayo (1995) give a comprehensive description of *A. soccata* males and females. The most important diagnostic characters are the male hypopygial prominence and trifoliate process.

The adult fly is about 4 mm long, looks like a small house fly, head and thorax of female are pale grey, the abdomen is yellowish with paired brown patches, and the male is more blackish. The larvae are 8-10 mm long, have white or yellowish colour. The eggs are white, elongate in shape and measure 0.8 × 0.2 mm.

A. soccata can be distinguished by the presence of yellow pulpy in the males, and dark brown interfrontalia. The male has the fore femur entirely yellow, fore tarsus without erect hairs, and the wings with a dark smudge around the tip of sub-costa (Pont, 1973). The stripes on the scutum are poorly developed, fore tibia is usually only darkened at the tip, fore tarsus mainly yellow, and tergites 1 + 2 and 5 have no dark spots. The hypopygial prominence has a pair of lateral branches, which are usually truncated. Species of *Atherigona* are most easily and reliably identified by the male genetalia. Because of the close similarity between species in external features, and the tendency for certain characters, colour and pattern to vary, the male genitalia need to be dissected for identification. The trifoliate process is dark brown, and with distinctly sloping shoulders. There is some variation in the width of the median piece and in the outline of its tip.

In females, the fore-legs are mainly dark brown, femur yellow, and tibia yellow on basal third. The shape of the tergite 8 is of importance, and can be used for a reliable separation from *A. oryzae*, as is the shape of the sternite 7; tergite 8 is brown, darker on the anterior margin, and divided into the usual three lobes, and with a pair of small, separated, anterioir sclerites, the lateral lobes narrow, median broad and shorter, and apically concave and almost straight (Pont (1973); Pont and Magpayo (1995)).

No diagnostic protocol is available.

Response Checklist

Checklist

Guidelines for Response Checklists are still to be endorsed. The following checklist provides a summary of generic requirements to be identified and implemented within a Response Plan:

Destruction methods for plant material, soil and disposable items:

- Disposal procedures
- Quarantine restrictions and movement controls
- Decontamination and farm cleanup procedures
- Diagnostic protocols and laboratories
- Trace back and trace forward procedures
- Protocols for delimiting, intensive and ongoing surveillance
- Zoning
- Reporting and communication strategy
- Delimiting survey and epidemiology study

Delimiting surveys should comprise local surveys around the area of initial detection concentrating on areas of poor growth, particularly where the seedlings have died. The extent of the survey beyond the initial infected crop should be guided by the test results from the surrounding crops. As sorghum shootfly can survive on wild grass hosts it may be necessary to include the adjoining grasslands and pastures in the survey.

Sampling Method

Adults of sorghum shoot fly *A. soccata* can be observed resting on the under surface of leaves, and can be caught in a fishmeal baited square pan or plastic jar trap (Taneja *et al.*, 1986). The presence of white cigar-shaped eggs on the under surface of the leaves, and dead hearts at the seedling stage (1 to 4 weeks after seedling emergence), can be used to detect shoot fly infestation. The presence of maggots in the damaged shoots can be used to confirm the shoot fly damage, but note that other species of Diptera (e.g. Chloropidae) also infest stems and may cause primary damage or secondary damage alongside *A. soccata*.

Sampling method can be taken from the Grains Industry Biosecurity Plan, Diagnostic protocol for the detection of leafminers prepared by Malipatil & Wainer (2006). Any personnel collecting insect or leaf samples for assessment should notify the diagnostic laboratory prior to submitting samples to ensure expertise is available to undertake the diagnosis.

Number of Specimens to be Collected

A large sample of specimens would be preferable. The aim is to obtain an adult male. Adult females are identifiable with certainty only to genus level;

therefore males are needed to examine genitalia details to confirm species identification.

Preferred Stage to be Collected

Of the four life stages (egg, larva, pupa and adult) only adults are identifiable to species using morphological features.

How to Collect

Adult sorghum shoot flies are found resting on the under surface of leaves and can be caught in a fishmeal baited square pan or plastic jar trap. Adult flies can be hand collected into glass vials or vacuum collected either with vacuum sampler, or swept from foliage with a hand net.

The leaves and seedlings containing pupae or mature larvae could also be collected in a large jar for rearing in the laboratory for obtaining adult shoot flies. They need to be kept in a constant temperature room and checked regularly for emergence of adult flies.

How to Preserve Sorghum Shoot Flies

Adults and larvae can be placed in 70% ethanol and stored indefinitely, although their colour fades gradually with time. Specimens required for molecular diagnostic work should be killed and preserved in absolute ethanol or frozen (–80°C).

How to Transport Sorghum Shoot Flies

Vials of ethanol should be sealed to avoid leakage and packed with cushioning material in a strong box.

Epidemiological Study

The degree of spread would depend on the amount of time the pest was present prior to detection. Due to its short life cycles (possibly 16-18 generations per year) the rate of increase could be high. It is unknown how far adults will travel to find a food source.

Models of Spread Potential

No modelling data are available for spread of sorghum shoot fly in broadacre cropping.

Pest Free Area (PFA) Guidelines

Pest free guidelines relevant to this pest. Points to consider are:

- Design of a statistical delimiting field survey for symptoms on host plants and for the presence or absence of Sorghum shoot fly adults or larvae.
- Plant and soil sampling using appropriate diagnostic tests.
- Survey around irrigation systems or waterways that may have transported the pest.

Additional information is provided by the IPPC (1995) in Requirements for the Establishment of Pest Free Areas. This standard describes the requirements for the establishment and use of pest free areas as a risk management option for phytosanitary certification of plants and plant products. Establishment and maintenance of a PFA can vary according to the biology of the pest, pest survival potential, means of dispersal, availability of host plants, restrictions on movement of produce, as well as PFA characteristics (size, degree of isolation and ecological conditions).

Availability of Control Methods

The cryptic nature of the pest hidden on the underside of the leaf and below thedeadheart near growing point in leaf whorl makes treatment difficult and therefore a combination of control measures are needed for successful eradication. Good hygiene methods are encouraged, including isolation of newly imported material to prevent any pest associated with a consignment spreading to other crops.

General Procedures for Control

- Keep traffic out of affected areas and minimize it in adjacent areas. For irrigated crops, stop irrigating affected areas. Use bunding to divert overland flood flows in both irrigated and dryland crops.
- Adopt best-practice farm hygiene procedures to retard the spread of the insect between paddocks and adjacent farms. Do not move soil from infested paddocks to non-infested paddocks.
- To minimise the build up of shoot fly populations, paddocks should be ploughed after crop harvest and shortly before sowing, and crop residues should be collected and destroyed before the onset of rains to reduce carry over from one season to the next.

Early and uniform sowing reduces the damage by sorghum shoot fly.

- Cultural pest control operations such as high seeding rates, balanced fertilizer application, field sanitation, weeding and intercropping with legumes reduce the damage by shoot fly but will not necessarily eradicate the pest.
- Sowing with shoot fly-resistant cultivars such as M 35-1, Swati, CSV-15R and Phule Yashoda during the post-rainy season will aid pest management.
- Overseas researchers have shown insecticide and seed treatment methods are also effective at reducing sorghum shoot fly populations.

Control if Small Areas are Affected

- Adopting best practice hygiene.

- Spraying/removing hosts (indication of area that would need to be managed around initial infection).
- Soil may contain pupae so should not be moved around, and hay/stubble should be destroyed by burning.
- Shoot flies are abundant during rainy season under moderate temperatures and high humidity.

Control if Large Areas are Affected

If large areas were affected control methods would be similar to the control of small areas. There may also be some scope for area wide management through cultural practices (see below).

Cultural Control

Crop husbandry practices to suppress shoot fly populations are best suited for sorghum growing countries of Africa and Asia. Some of the cultural practices that can be used to minimise shoot fly infestation are found in CABI (2007) and are:

Sowing date

Infestation can be reduced by early sowing, 7-10 days before the onset of monsoon rains, to avoid the active period of shoot fly emergence. If early sowing is not possible then use high seed rate to compensate for later thinning out of the dead hearts from infested fields.

Nutrient management

Shoot fly damage can be influenced by factors that affect plant growth. The application of nitrogen fertiliser and the biofertiliser *Azospirillum* together with the physical characteristics of the soil and moisture content can affect plant growth and influence shoot fly incidence.

Plant density

Plant stand has a significant effect on shoot fly infestation. High seeding rate helps reduce shoot fly damage. Seedlings under high planting density have narrow leaves, which are less attractive for egg laying.

Intercultivation/weeding

Intercultivation can reduce pest populations by exposing the pupae to parasite predators and other adverse environmental factors.

Pull out infested seedlings and alternate hosts such as fodder sorghums and grasses and their residues, and then destroy by burning.

Crop Rotation

Crop rotation can minimise pest damage by confusing the insects with chemical aromas emitting from non host plants and using crop combinations that encourage the activity and abundance of natural enemies.

It has been shown that shoot fly damage is reduced when sorghum is intercropped with leguminous crops.

Fallowing and a closed season will reduce the carryover and build-up of the shoot fly from one season to the next.

Field sanitation

Fallowing removes insects from their natural hosts reduces the carry over and build up of pests from one season to another.

Host plant resistance

Host plant resistance is an important component for the management of this pest in all areas where the sorghum shoot fly is a pest. Trials in southern Africa and Asia have shown significant differences in resistance to this pest damage among varieties tested. Some varieties in southern and eastern Africa have been identified as being medium to high level resistant to attack by sorghum shoot fly.

Resistance screening techniques

Various techniques to screen for resistance to shoot fly have been discussed by Pradhan (1971), Jotwani (1978) and Taneja and Leuschner (1985a).

Field Screening

Sowing Date. Adjust the sowing date so that the test material is exposed to optimum insect pressure. Use fishmeal-baited trap (figure 7.2) (Plate 2) to study the population dynamics of the shoot fly (Taneja and Leuschner 1986) to determine periods of greatest insect density (figure 7.3). In India, to screen for resistance to shoot fly, the best time to sow the test material is the second fortnight of July for the rainy season and October for the postrainy season (Taneja *et al.* 1986).

Inter lard-Fishmeal Technique. To ensure high and uniform

Cage Screening

To confirm resistance observed under field conditions, and to study various resistance mechanisms, a cage-screening method can be used. The cage-screening technique described by Soto (1972) has been modified at ICRISAT Center to closely simulate field conditions.

- Catch shoot flies in the fishmeal-baited trap , and collect them from the trap in the mornings and/or evenings.
- Separate A *soccata* from other species.
- Confine the flies wi th the sorghum seedlings for 1-2 days in a 30 × 30 × 30-cm cage.
- For every 100 plants, release 40 flies for 1 day or 20 flies for 2 days. shoot fly pressure under field conditions, use the interlard-fishmeal technique:

- Sow four rows of interlards of a susceptible cultivar (usually CSH 1) after every 24 rows, 20 days before sowing the test material.
- One week after seedling emergence, spread moistened fishmeal uniformly or keep it in plastic bags (Plate 3) in the interlards to attract the shoot flies. One generation of the shoot fly is completed on the interlards and the emerging flies infest the test material. Fishmeal can also be spread or kept in plastic bags in the test material. This method provides adequate and uniform shoot fly pressure for resistance screening (Taneja and Leuschner 1985a). The cage-screening technique can also be used for multiple- as well as no-choice conditions. For a multiple-choice test, several genotypes can be sown in the field in 3.4 × 2-m beds with a row spacing of 15 cm. Ten days after seedling emergence, cover the plants wi th a 3.4 × 2 × 1-m screened cage (Plate 5a), and introduce flies in the cage. After 1 week, count the eggs and deadhearts after removing the cage. For a no-choice test, sow only one genotype in 1 * 1-m beds and cover six beds with a 2 × 3 × 0.5-m cage having six compartments (Plate 5b). Ten days after seedling emergence, release 20 flies in each compartment and record observations as described earlier.

Fig. 7.3: Cage Screening

Rapid screening can also be carried out using plastic tray cages (Plate 5c). This system consists of two plastic trays (40 × 30 × 14 cm), one for sowing test material and the other (fitted with fine wire-mesh as shown in Plate 5c) clamped over the first tray thus serving as a cage. Ten days after seedling emergence, the second tray is placed over the first one upside down using clamps and 20 flies are released in each cage and observations recorded as described earlier.

Chemical Control

- ETL: 1 egg/plant in 10% of plants in the first two weeks of sowing or 10% dead hearts.
- Take up early sowing of sorghum immediately after the receipt of South West or North East monsoon to minimise the shoot fly incidence.
- Use seeds pelleted with insecticides.
- Seed treatment with imidacloprid 70 WS @ 10 g/kg of seeds.
- In case of direct sowing , use increased seed rate upto 12.5 kg/per hectare and remove the shoot fly damage seedling at the time of thinning or raise nursery and transplant only healthy seedlings.
- Plough soon after harvest, remove and destroy the stubbles.
- Set up the low cost fish meal trap @ 12/ha till the crop is 30 days old.

Spray one of the following for an area of 120 m2 nursery :

- Methyl demeton 25 EC 12 ml/ha.
- Dimethoate 30 EC 12 ml/ha.
- Methyl demeton 25 EC 500 ml/ha.
- Dimethoate 30 EC 500 ml/ha.
- Neem Seed Kernel extract 5%.

Soil application of phorate 10 G 18 kg/ha or carbofuran @ 33.3 kg /ha at the time of sowing.

- Early sowing – Low incidence.
- Late sowing – High incidence.
- Remove dead hearts.
- High seed rate 8 – 12 kg/ha.
- Seed treatment 60 % carbofuran 50% SP (100 gm/kg).
- Application of carbofuran 3 G, Phorate 10 G.
- Disulfoton 5G @ 2g/m.row.
- Spraying Carbaryl 0.2%,Dimethoate 0.03%.
- Tall variety with yellow glossy stem less attacked.
- Use resistant variety IS-2205,IS- 3962,I-5469,IS-1054,s-386,SPV-102

Mechanical Control

Mechanical cultivation can reduce pest populations by exposing the pupae to parasites and predators and other adverse environmental factors.

Biological Control

There is very little information available on the role of natural enemies in population dynamics of *A. soccota* and the extent of parasitism/predation. A range of natural enemies attack the sorghum shoot fly in other countries– parasitic wasps attack eggs and larvae, and predators cause high mortality of eggs. Some spiders are important predators on eggs. Some important parasitoids are *Trichogramma simmondsi* and *T. chilonis* (on eggs), *Neotrichoporoides nyemitawus, Aprostocerus* sp., *Opius* sp. and *Spalangia endius* (on larvae). Mass rearing techniques are available only for *T. chilonis* (Singh and Sharma 2002).

Course of Action–Eradication Methods

Additional information is provided by the IPPC (1998) in Guidelines for Pest Eradication Programmes. This standard describes the components of a pest eradication programme which can lead to the establishment or re-establishment of pest absence in an area. A pest eradication programme may be developed as an emergency measure to prevent establishment and/or spread of a pest following its recent entry (re-establish a pest free area) or a measure to eliminate an established pest (establish a pest free area). The eradication process involves three main activities: surveillance, containment, and treatment and/or control measures.

Destruction Strategy

Destruction Protocols

- Di sposable equipment, infected plant material or soil should be disposed of by autoclaving, high temperature incineration or destroyed by deep burial. Any equipment removed from the site for disposal should be double-bagged.
- Herbicides could be used to destroy the infected crops or pastures. Infected crops or pastures could be ploughed in.
- Insecticides could be used to destroy the pest.
- Farm machinery used in destruction processes need to be thoroughly washed, preferably using a detergent such as Decon 90.

Decontamination Protocols

If containment, eradication and/or best practice hygiene measures are implemented, machinery, equipment, vehicles in contact with infected plant material or soil or present within the Quarantine Area, should be washed to remove soil and plant material using high pressure water or scrubbing with products such as a farm degreaser disinfectant or a 1% bleach (available chlorine) solution in a designated wash down area. General guidelines for wash down areas are as follows:

- Located away from crops or sensitive vegetation

- Readily accessible with clear signage
- Access to fresh water and power

Site, including entry and exit points should be mud free (e.g. gravel, concrete or rubber matting)

Gently sloped to drain effluent away

Effluent must not enter water courses or water bodies

- Allow adequate space to move larger vehicles
- Away from hazards such as power lines
- Waste water, soil or plant residues should be contained
- Disposable overalls and rubber boots should be worn when handling infected soil or plant material in the field. Boots, clothes and shoes in contact with infected soil or plant material should be disinfected at the site or double-bagged to remove for cleaning.
- If hands, skin or hair have been in contact with infested plant material or soil they should be washed.
- Decon 90 (Enviroequip) is a suitable detergent for using to decontaminate equipment or personnel.
- All chemicals used according to label.

Plants, by-products and Waste Processing

- All infested seedlings and alternate/susceptible host material such as grasses should be destroyed by (enclosed) high temperature incineration, autoclaving or deep burial.
- Infected paddocks should be ploughed in to remove food and decrease larval survival (see 2.7.7).

Also hay, stray or stubble residues should be collected and destroyed after harvesting by burning to reduce carry-over of pest from one season to another.

Disposal Issues

- Once introduced and established, pupae can survive in soils for long periods, even in the absence of plant hosts and thus be difficult to eradicate.
- Particular care must be taken to minimize the transfer of infected soil and trash from the area.
- Raking and burning infected crops is not an option as this procedure is likely to spread the eggs, larvae and pupae greater distances during the raking phase.

Damage Evaluation for Resistance Screening

In the preliminary evaluation of the material (where a large number of lines are to be tested), count shoot fly deadhearts 28 days after crop emergence.

Record the total number of plants and those showing deadhearts separately, and calculate the percentage of plants with deadhearts. Shoot fly damage can also be rated visually on a 1-9 scale (1 = <10%; 2 = 11-20%; 3 = 21-30%; 4 = 31-40%; 5 = 41-50%; 6 = 51-60%; 7 = 61-70%; 8 = 71-80%; and 9 = >80% plants with deadhearts). Select lines with <50% deadhearts or a damage score of < 5 for further testing. For advanced evaluation, sow the test material in 2-3 replications. Record the number and percentage of plants with eggs and deadhearts 21 and 28 days after crop emergence. Genotypes selected in the advanced evaluation can be further screened in cages under multichoice and no-choice conditions.

QUARANTINE AND MOVEMENT CONTROLS

Quarantine Priorities

- Plant material and soil at the site of infection to be subject to movement restrictions.
- Machinery, equipment, vehicles and disposable equipment in contact with infected plant material or soil to be subject to movement restrictions.
- Adult sorghum shoot flies have wings and can move short distances making establishment of quarantine practical.

Movement Control for People, Plant Material and Machinery

Once established sorghum shoot fly will be difficult to eradicate. Therefore, any zoning, quarantine or movement controls will usually pertain to containment and management unless detection occurs soon after establishment.

If Restricted or Quarantine Areas are practical, movement of equipment or machinery should be restricted and movement into the Area only occurs by permit. The industry affected will need to be informed of the location and extent of the pest occurrence.

Movement of people, vehicle and machinery, to and from affected farms, must be controlled to ensure that infected soil or plant debris is not moved off-farm on clothing, footwear, vehicles or machinery.

Examples of movement controls include:

- Signage to indicate quarantine area and/or restricted movement in these zones. Fenced, barricaded or locked entry to quarantine areas.
- Movement of equipment, machinery, plant material or soil by permit only.
- Clothing and footwear worn at the infected site should either be double-bagged prior to removal for decontamination or should not leave the farm until thoroughly disinfected, washed and cleaned.
- All machinery and equipment should be thoroughly cleaned down with a pressure cleaner prior to leaving the affected farm. The clean

down procedure should be carried out on a hard surface, preferably a designated wash-down area, to avoid mud being recollected from the affected site onto the machine.

- Hay / stubble must not be removed from the site or used for feeding stock due to the risk of moving larvae, pupae or eggs.

Post-eradication Surveillance

Specific methods to confirm eradication of Sorghum shoot fly may include:

- Monitoring of sentinel plants using soil from the paddock is undertaken. Sentinel plants are to be grown in pots using soils removed from the affected site that may contain sorghum shoot fly pupae. Plants are to be grown under quarantine containment glasshouse conditions and monitored for symptoms of infection.
- Surveys comprising soil and plant sampling for Sorghum shoot fly to be undertaken for a minimum of 12 months after eradication have been achieved. This pest has short life cycle, hence surveys may need to be repeated every 3-4 weeks.

Balanced fertilizer application, reduce use of organic manure (eg : cattle manure) as is known to attract adult shoot flies.

REFERENCES

Bene G (1986) Notes on the Biology of *Atherigona soccata* Rondani (Diptera Muscidae) in Tuscany and Latium. Redia, 69, 47-63.

Davis JC, Seshu Reddy KV (1981) Shootfly Species and their Graminaceous Hosts in Andhra Pradesh, India. Insect Science and its Application 2, 33-37.

Gahukar RT (1991) Recent Developments in Sorghum Entomology Research Agricultural Zoology Reviews 4, 23-65.

Kundu GG, Jotwani MG, Kishore P (1978) Efficacy of Carbofuran Seed Treatment for the Control of Sorghum Shootfly at Different Levels of Nitrogen Fertilisation. Indian Journal of Entomology 40(3), 346- 347.

IPPC (1995) Requirements for the Establishment of Pest Free Areas. International Standards for Phytosanitary Measures (ISPM) No. 4.

Meksongsee B, Chawanapong M (1985) Sorghum Insect Pests in South East Asia. In: Proceedings of the International Sorghum Entomology Workshop, 15-21 July 1984, pp. 57-64. Texas A&M University and ICRISAT.

Nwanze KF, Nwilene FE, Reddy YVR (1998) Fecundity and Diurnal Oviposition Behaviour of Sorghum Shoot fly, *Atherigona soccata* Rondani (Diptera: Muscidae). Entomon, 23(2), 77-82.

Pont AC (1973) A Review of the Oriental Species of Atherigona Rondani (Diptera, Muscidae) of Economic Importance. In: Jotwani Mg, Young Wr, Eds. Control of Sorghum Shoot Fly. Delhi, India, Oxford and IBH Publishing Company, 27-102.

Pont AC, Magpayo FR (1995) Muscid Shoot-flies of the Philippine Islands (Diptera: Muscidae, Genus *Atherigona* Rondani). Bulletin of Entomological Research Supplement 3, 1-123.

Priyavratha Rao, Narasimha Rao DV (1956) Studies on the Sorghum Shoot-borer-fly *Atherigona indica.*

Mallo ch (Anthomyiidae-Diptera) at Siruguppa. Mysore Agriculture Journal, 31, 158-174.

Seshu Reddy KV (1991) Insect Pests of Sorghum in Africa. Insect Science and its Application 12, 653- 657.

Seshu Reddy KV, and Omolo EO (1985) Sorghum Insect Pest Situation in Eastern Africa. In: Proceedings of the International Sorghum Entomology Workshop, 15-21 July 1984, pp. 31-36, Texas A&M University and ICRISAT.

Sharma, HC (1996) Crop Protection Compendium: Sorghum Shoot Fly, *Atherigona soccata.* Electronic Compendium for Crop Protection. Wallingford, U.K, CAB International.

Sharma M, Kapoor KN, Bharaj GS, 1996. Effect of Seed Treatment of Sorghum with Some New Insecticides for Control of Shoot Fly. Crop Research, 11(1):90-92.

Singh BU, Sharma HC (2002) Natural Enemies of Sorghum Shoot fly, *Atherigona Soccata* Rondani (Diptera: Muscidae). Biocontrol Science and Technology 12(3), 307-323.

Srivastava KP (1985) Sorghum Insect Pests in India. In: Proceedings of the International Sorghum Entomology Workshop, 15-21 July 1984, pp. 65-72, Texas A&M University and ICRISAT.

Swaine G, Wyatt CA (1954) Observations on the Sorghum Shoot Fly. East African Agriculture Journal 20, 45-48.

Taneja SL, Seshu Reddy KV, Leuschner K, 1986. Monitoring of Shoot Fly Population in Sorghum. Indian Journal of Plant Protection 14(2), 29-36.

Agriculture Crops and Food Security
Edited by: Dr. Pawan Kumar 'Bharti' and Alka Chauhan
ISBN: 978-93-5056-881-1
Edition: 2017
Published by: Discovery Publishing House Pvt. Ltd., New Delhi (India)

8 Impacts of Climate Change on Horticulture - Adaptation and Mitigation Strategies for Climate-Resilient Horticulture

[1]Pushpavathi Y., [1]Ashoka Reddy Y.,[1] Thomson T., [1]Surendranath R., [1]Manjunathan R and Rahul N.

ABSTRACT

Global warming and climate change is the greatest concern of mankind in 21st century. Due to climate change, it is projected that rainfall over India will increase by 15–40%, and the mean annual temperature will increase by 3–6°C by the end of 21st century. The established commercial varieties of fruits, vegetables and flowers will perform poorly in an unpredictable manner due to aberration of climate. Melting of ice cap in the Himalayan regions will reduce chilling effect required for the flowering of many of the horticultural crops like Apple, Saffron, Rhododendron, Orchid, etc. Commercial production of horticultural plants particularly grown under open field conditions will be severely affected. Due to high temperature physiological disorder of horticultural crops will be more pronounced eg. Spongy tissue of mango, fruit cracking of litchi, flower and fruit abscission in solanaceous fruit vegetables, etc. Air pollution also significantly decreases the yield of several horticultural crops and increases the intensity of certain physiological disorder like black tip of mango. Hence there is a need to protect these valuable crops for sustainability against the climate change scenario.

Delaying the date of planting can be an adaptation strategy in most of the states of the Indo-Gangetic plains to minimize the yield reductions while for West Bengal and *Kharif* potato-growing regions development of heat tolerant varieties should be the main adaptation strategy. Dogridge (*Vitis champini*) has been found promising for improvement in vigour, yield and quality of seedless grapes as well as tolerance to drought and salinity. The number of disease epidemics has dramatically increased in recent years and also the threat of emerging new diseases and the re-emergence of other diseases. Hence, there is a need to thoroughly understand the potential climate change impacts on host–pathogen interactions, in order to evaluate appropriate

[1] Dr. Y. S. R. Horticultural University, Venkataramanna gudem, West Godavari District-534101, Andhra Pradesh, India

disease management strategies. Horticulture-based farming systems have high potential for sequestering carbon for mitigation of climate change. The perennial trees act as carbon sinks by sequestering the atmospheric carbon. Availability and development of good simulation models for horticultural fruit and vegetable crops is lacking in India with exceptions of potato and coconut where InfoCrop model has been adopted and validated for different agro-ecological regions. For adaptation strategies the emphasis should be on development of production systems for improved water-use efficiency and to adapt to the hot and dry conditions. Strategies like changing, sowing or planting dates, modifying fertilizer application, providing irrigation during critical stages of the crop growth and conservation of soil moisture reserves by mulching with crop residues and plastic mulches are the most important interventions. Development of climate-resilient horticultural crops which are tolerant to high temperature, moisture stress, salinity and climate proofing through genomics and biotechnology would be critically required.

INTRODUCTION

Indian agriculture has made a rapid stride in achieving self sufficiency in food. Albeit horticulture has emerged as a best option for diversification to meet the need for food, nutrition, health care besides providing better returns on farm land and better opportunity for employment, little investment is made in horticulture especially in developing climate resilient models and understanding its impact. Horticultural crops play a unique role in India's economy by improving the income of the rural people. Cultivation of these crops is labour intensive and as such they generate lot of employment opportunities for the rural population provided sufficient charges are paid. Fruits and vegetables are also rich source of vitamins, minerals, proteins, carbohydrates etc. which are essential in human nutrition. Hence, these are referred to as protective foods and assume great importance in maintaining nutritional security of the people. Thus, cultivation of horticultural crops plays a vital role in the prosperity of a nation and is directly linked with the health and happiness of the people.

India is the second largest producer of fruits and vegetables in the world next only to Brazil and China. However, per capita consumption of fruits and vegetables in India is only around 46g and 130g against a minimum of about 92g and 300g respectively recommended by Indian Council of Medical Research and National Institute of Nutrition, Hyderabad. The knowledge about the impact of climate change on horticultural crops is limited. Addressing problems of climate change is more challenging in horticulture crops compared to annual food crops. The issues of climate change and solution to the problems arising out of it requires thorough analysis, advance planning and improved management.

An Insight about Climate Change

Significant variation in either mean state of climate or its variability, persisting for an extended period (typically decades or longer), is referred as climate change, which may be due to natural internal processes or external forcing, or to persistent anthropogenic changes in the composition of the atmosphere or in land use. The earth is the only planet in our solar system that supports life because of unique environmental conditions that are present water, an oxygen-rich atmosphere and a suitable surface temperature. It has an atmosphere of proper depth and chemical composition. About 30% of incoming energy from the sun is reflected back to space, while the rest reaches the earth, warming the air, oceans and land, maintaining an average surface temperature of about 15°C. The chemical concentration in atmosphere for nitrogen is 78%; about 21% is oxygen, which all animals need to survive; and only a small (0.036%) proportion is made up of carbon dioxide which plants use for photosynthesis.

In atmosphere, energy is absorbed by the land, seas, mountains, etc., and simultaneously release some back in the form of infrared waves. All this released heat is not lost to space, but is partly absorbed by some gases present in very small quantities in atmosphere, called greenhouse gases consisting of carbon dioxide, methane, nitrous oxide, water vapour, ozone and a few others. Thus, increased concentration of greenhouse gases leads to increased temperature which in turn has impact on the world climate, leading to the phenomena known as climate change. The earth's climate system constantly adjusts so as to maintain the balance between the energy that reaches it from the sun and the energy that goes from earth back to space. This means that even a small rise in temperature could mean accompanying changes in cloud cover and wind patterns. Some of these changes may enhance the warming, while others may counteract. Cooling effect may result from an increase in the levels of aerosols (small particles of matter or liquid that can be produced by natural or man-made activities). Positive feedback may result from an increase in water vapour due to high evaporation with rise in temperature and can further add to the warming effect. The significant change may impact agriculture/horticulture/fish/livestock and consequently food supply. Climate change per se is not necessarily harmful, but the problems arise from extreme events that are difficult to predict, like more erratic rainfall pattern and unpredicted warm spells shall affect productivity. At the same time, more availability of CO_2 would help in improved yield of root crops, and increased temperature may shorten the period.

Climate Change in Asia

The increase in temperature due to global warming is 0.76°C since 1850. The rate of warming in the last 50 years is double than that for the last century. As many as 11 of the past 12 years were warmest since 1850, when records began. The likely increase in temperature is 1.8–4°C by next century (IPCC, 2007). The threshold value of temperature rise is 2°C for devastating, dangerous and irreversible consequences of warming to manifest world over. Global warming is occurring along with shifting pattern of rainfall and increasing incident of extreme weather events like floods, droughts and frosting. Recent studies suggest clear evidence of reduction in light intensity, rapid melting of glaciers and rise in sea level. The estimates of Indian Institute of Tropical Meteorology, Pune, indicate similar trends in India with slightly higher magnitude. It is projected that rainfall over India will increase by 15–40%, and the mean annual temperature will increase by 3–6°C by the end of twenty-first century. Warming is likely to be more pronounced over land areas with the maximum increase over northern India. The winter and post-monsoon seasons are likely to be more affected by warming. Besides, there would be more fluctuation in temperature, and water availability may decline. The South Asian region is projected to be one of the most vulnerable to climate change. It is attributed to increasing population pressure, extreme poverty and predominance of agriculture and resource crunch in the region. It is projected that by 2020, food requirement in South Asia would be 50% more than the current demand. The challenge is to produce the same from constant or even shrinking land resources due to competition for land from other sectors like infrastructure, industry and housing. Poverty alleviation and food security for teeming millions in India under adverse climate change scenario would be a daunting task. These changes in global environment will have profound effects and serious consequences for agriculture, horticulture, arable ecosystem and society as a whole.

Climate Change and Indian Horticulture

Climate change causes the increased weather variability and mean change in climatic variables such as temperatures and rainfall. There have been instances of loss of horticultural crops due to climate-related extreme events at regional scale such as high temperatures during March 2004 in north India which caused significant losses to horticultural crops such as tomatoes, onion, garlic and other vegetable and fruit crops (Samra and Singh 2004). Cold wave during December 2002–January 2003 caused considerable damage to horticultural crops such as mango, guava, papaya, brinjal, tomato and potato (Samra and Singh 2003). Similarly cold waves in 2006 affected tomato, potato, mango, guava, banana, papaya, tamarind, wood apple, brinjal, etc. In 2007, late snowfall in Srinagar coinciding with full bloom damaged almonds. High rainfall events in 1998, 2005 and 2010 affected kharif and late kharif crop of onion, while untimely heavy rain in March 2008 in west coast of India reduced the cashew yield and nut quality. However, numerous extreme weather events which are localized, but not recorded, have caused immense loss to the farm and rural household income, contributed to fluctuating market price. While above-mentioned examples represent the weather extremes due to increased climatic variability, reported shift in apple cultivation to higher elevations partly due to non-fulfilment of chilling requirement in Himachal Pradesh is an example of impact of climate change and shift in climatic suitability of areas for a given crop. Since growing horticultural crops is seen as an income enhancement activity by a household, it becomes important to provide scientifically tested suitable low-cost and low-carbon adaptation strategies so as to not only improve the livelihood of the farmers but also to make them resilient to climatic risks. This approach will not only help in nutrient, food and livelihood security but also help to improve the overall adaptation of farm, a major foundation for resilient agriculture at national level. Climate change impact assessments provided by global studies indicated a probability of 10–40% loss in crop production in India with increases in temperature by 2080–2100 (Rosenzweig and Parry 1994; Fischer *et al.* 2002; Parry *et al.* 2004; IPCC 2007). Although a number of studies have projected impacts of climate change on field crops, horticulture sector, the major component of agriculture in India, did not receive deserved attention as far as climate change impact assessments are concerned, in spite of it being highly diverse and offers scope for resilience to climatic risks. Apart from this, perennial horticulture has immense potential to play an important role in GHG mitigation through carbon sequestration.

Likely Impact of Climate Change

Global climate change is expected to affect agricultural/horticultural crops through its direct and indirect effects. Scientific evidence suggests a positive effect of increase in atmospheric carbon dioxide in C_3 photosynthetic pathway promoting their growth and productivity. Increased CO_2 will reduce evapotranspiration and thus increase water use efficiency. However, positive effects will be counteracted by increase in temperatures. Rise in temperature will reduce crop duration; increase respiration rate; alter photosynthate partitioning to economic product; alter phenology, particularly flowering, fruiting and reducing chilling unit accumulation; and hasten senescence, fruit ripening and maturity. Cauliflower grows best in cool to warm conditions (15–25°C) with high humidity. Though, some varieties can grow with temperatures over 30°C, but most of the varieties are sensitive to higher temperature. Delayed curd initiation in cauliflower is reported due to increased temperature. Temperature above 30°C induces maximum flower and fruit drop, and high temperatures after pollen release decrease fruit setting, fruit yield and seed setting in tomato.

The sensitivity of individual crop to temperature depends on inherent tolerance and growing habits. Indeterminate crops are less sensitive to periods of heat stress because the time of flowering is extended compared with determinate crops. In onion, warmer temperatures shorten the duration of growth, leading to lower crop yields. Any soil warming would be advantageous for cucurbits, which are generally direct seeded and have a high heat requirement. The rise in temperature will influence survival and distribution of pest population; develop new equilibrium between alternate host crops and pests, hasten nutrient mineralization in soils, decrease fertilizer-use efficiency and increase evapotranspiration with reduced water-use efficiency. The net effect of climate change on horticultural crops will depend on interaction effects of rise in temperature and CO_2 concentration in atmosphere. In general, CO_2 enrichment does not appear to compensate for the detrimental effects of higher temperature on yield. Most importantly, the quality of produce of these horticultural crops is likely to be impacted severely.

The climate change will have many impacts on horticulture and a few examples are given below:

1. A study conducted at IISR, Calicut using GIS models have shown that many areas presently suitable for spices would become unsuitable in another 25 yeas. There would be new areas which are presently unsuitable, become highly suitable for cultivation of spices. This will be applicable in other horticultural crops.
2. Production timing will change due to rise in temperature. Due to rise in temperature, photoperiods may not show much variation. As a result, photosensitive crop will mature faster.
3. The winter regime and chilling duration will reduce in temperate regions affecting the temperate crops.
4. Pollination will be affected adversely because of higher temperature. Floral abortions flower and fruit drop will be occurred frequently.
5. The requirement of annual irrigation will increase and heat unit requirement will be achieved in much lesser time.
6. Higher temperatures will reduce tuber initiation process in potato, reduced quality in tomatoes and pollination in many crops. In case of crucifers, it may lead to bolting; anthocyanins production may be affected in apples and capsicum. Tip burn and blossom end rot will be the common phenomenon in tomatoes.
7. Coastal regions can expect much faster percolation of sea water in inland water tables causing more salinity.

Changing Pattern of Cropping System

Many slow-growing fruit crops require heavy investment on establishment of orchards. Quick alteration/shifting of fruit species or varieties would be difficult and painful loss-bearing exercise under the impact of climate change, which may discourage the development. Recent studies have indicated that in Kullu district of Himachal Pradesh, farmers shifted from apple to vegetables, while in Shimla district at relatively higher altitude, orchards have been replaced from high chilling requiring apple cultivars of apple (Royal Delicious) to low-chilling requiring cultivars and other fruit crops like kiwi, pomegranate and vegetables. In mid-hills of Shimla district, trend is to shift from apple and potato cultivation totally. It is corroborated by declining trend in snowfall and apple productivity in Himachal Pradesh. The mean productivity of apple in 1980–1981 was 7.06 t/ha compared to 4.65 t/ha in 2004–2005. Since many crops with chilling requirements are tree species, moving production areas is difficult. Thus, in replanting orchards and plantations over the next decade, selection of low-chilling requiring types may be advisable. This is just an example of impending impacts of global warming and climate change.

Grape being a temperate crop has very well adapted to tropical regions; under climate change scenario with increase in temperature, there would be change in growing degree days (GDD), which has direct bearing on phenology of the crop (Singh 2010). Hence, under such circumstances, we would have to identify varieties and regions suitable for production of quality fruits. Shift in varietal choice may become necessary in case of grapevines, banana, mango and other important horticultural crops. With global warming, production areas for specific crops and/or timing of planting could be changed, but for many horticultural crops, market windows and infrastructure, such as availability of local packing and distribution facilities, are critical components of the production system. Locations of important production areas are often defined as much by available land, markets and infrastructure as by climatic conditions per se. Thus, as horticulturists we have to ask ourselves and our clientele whether it is realistic to move production areas in response to climate change or whether there are other production practices that can be adjusted to compensate climate change. Climate change and CO_2 are likely to alter important interactions between horticultural plants and pollinators, insect and disease and pests and weeds.

CURRENT STATUS OF IMPACT AND ADAPTATION STUDIES IN HORTICULTURAL CROPS

Vegetables

India is the second largest producer of vegetables in the world (ranks next to China). The current production level is over 165 MT and the total area under vegetable cultivation is around 9.4 million hectares which is about 3% of the total area under cultivation in the country. Environmental stress is the primary cause of crop losses worldwide, reducing average yields for most major crops by more than 50% (Bray *et al.,* 2000). Climatic changes will influence the severity of environmental stress imposed on vegetable crops. The response of plants to environmental stresses depends on the plant developmental stage and the length and severity of the stress (Bray, 2002). Plants may respond similarly to avoid one or more stresses through morphological or biochemical mechanisms (Capiati *et al.*, 2006). Environmental interactions may make the stress response of plants more complex or influence the degree of impact of climate change. Lists of some abiotic stress vegetables and their varieties have been presented in table 8.1 and 8.2 respectively.

Shallow-rooted vegetables are known to be sensitive to moisture deficiency and require frequent supply water of for better yield and quality. Studies have indicated that soil water stress at early stages of onion crop growth caused 26% yield loss. In tomato, water stress accompanied by temperatures above 28°C induced about 30–45% flower drop in different cultivars (Srinivasa, 1995). Chilli, with 60% area under rain fed cultivation, also suffers drought stress, leading to yield loss up to 50–60%. Most vegetables are sensitive to excess moisture stress conditions due to reduction in oxygen in the root zone. Tomato plants under flooding conditions accumulate endogenous ethylene, leading to rapid epinastic leaf response. Onion is also sensitive to flooding during bulbing with yield loss up to 30–40%. Moisture stress has been addressed through the development of varieties tolerant to drought and rainfed conditions. The production technologies like integrated nutrient management practices and in situ soil conservation and polythene mulching have been developed for rainfed chilli production. In tomato, high temperatures can cause significant losses in productivity due to reduced fruit set, smaller size and low-quality fruits. Optimum daily mean temperature for fruit set in tomato has been reported to be 21–24°C (Geisenberg and Stewart 1986) . The pre-anthesis stage is more sensitive in tomato. Post-pollination exposure to high temperature inhibits fruit set in pepper, indicating sensitivity of fertilization process. In cucumber, sex expression is affected by temperature. Low temperatures favour female flower production, which is desirable, and high temperatures lead to production of more male flowers. The duration of onion gets shortened due to high temperature, leading to reduced yields. Though cauliflower is a temperate crop, with development of tropical Indian cauliflower, it became possible to cultivate in hot and humid tropical conditions and throughout the year in north Indian plains. Now, India is second highest producer after China with a share of 33% of the world production. In Karnataka, Maharashtra and in plateau areas of Madhya Pradesh, Jharkhand and Orissa where *Kharif* crop is taken, the temperature constraint is primarily due to high night temperatures, which are already bordering the critical temperature for tuber initiation and good bulking. Preliminary simulation studies indicate reductions in productivity from 6% to 18% in the different states are likely by 2020 if no adaptation strategy is adopted. Studies indicate that delaying the date of planting can be an adaptation strategy in most of the states of the Indo-Gangetic plains to minimize the yield reductions, while for West Bengal and *Kharif* potato growing regions, development of heat-tolerant varieties should be the main adaptation strategy.

Plant sensitivity to salt stress is reflected in loss of turgor, growth reduction, wilting, leaf curling and epinasty, leaf abscission, decreased photosynthesis, respiratory changes, loss of cellular integrity, tissue necrosis, and potentially death of the plant. Most of the vegetable crops are highly sensitive to flooding and genetic variation with respect to this character is limited. Flooded crops especially in tomato plants accumulate endogenous ethylene that causes damage to the plants (Drew, 1979). Under low oxygen levels stimulate an increased production of an ethylene precursor, 1-aminocyclopropane-1-carboxylic acid (ACC), in the roots. The severity of flooding symptoms increases with rising temperatures; rapid wilting and death of tomato plants is usually observed following a short period of flooding at high temperatures (Kuo *et al.,* 1982). During the last 40-50 years air pollution level increasing at an alarming rate in the developing countries and causing potential threat to the crop production. Sulphar dioxide, nitrogen oxide, hydrofluride, ozone and acid rain are the primary air pollutant. Ozone has adverse effect on vegetable production in terms of reducing growth, yield and quality. Risk of the air pollution is more when vegetable crops grown close to the densely populated areas. A recent study indicated that the ambient air pollution significantly decreased the yield upto more than 50 percent incase of Brassica oleracia, Lactuca sativa and Raphanus sativus. Many vegetable crops namely tomato, water melon, potato, squash, soyabeans, cantaloupe, peas, carrot, beet, turnip, etc are more susceptible to air pollution damage. Yield of vegetable can be reduced by 5-15 percent when daily ozone concentrations reach to greater than 50 ppb (Raj Narayan 2009).

Table 8.1: List of Some Abiotic Stresses Vegetable Crops

Sl. No.	Tolerant	Crop
1.	Drought tolerant	Chilli, melons, tomato, onion
2.	Heat tolerant	Peas, tomato, beans, Capsicum
3.	Salinity tolerant	melons, peas, onion
4.	Flooding/ excess moisture tolerant	tomato, onion, chilli

Source: Rai and Yadav (2005)

Table 8.2: List of Some Variety and Advanced Line Tolerant to Abiotic Stress

Sl.No	Tolerant	Crop	Variety	Advanced Line
1.	Drought/rainfed	Tomato	Arka Vikas	RF- 4A
		Onion	Arka Kalyan	MST-42 and MST-46
		Chilli	Arka Lohit	IIHR Sel.-132

2.	Photo insensitive	Dolichos	Arka Jay, Arka Vijay,arka Sambram, ArkaAmogh, Arka Soumya	IIHR-16-2
		Cow pea	Arka garima, ArkaSuman, Arka Samrudhi	
3.	High temperature	Capsicum		IIHR Sel.-3
		French bean		IIHR-19-1
		Peas		IIHR-1 and IIHR-8
		Cauliflower		IIHR 316-1 and IIHR-371-1

Source: Hazra and Som (1999) and Rai and Yadav (2005)

Tuber Crops

In India, potato is grown in a thermally suitable window, and the availability of suitable growing period in India is likely to be affected seriously by climate change. The heat-sensitive potato crop is mostly confined to Indo-Gangetic plains (about 80% of the area) under irrigated conditions due to climatic constraints. Higher temperature at the start of the growing season would lead to shortening of the effective growing season. The preliminary results of the simulations studies show that the productivity is likely to improve in Punjab, Haryana and Western UP by 7% and 4% in the year 2020 and 2050, respectively (Singh *et al.*, 2005 and 2008). In these areas, currently the growing period is short due to the occurrence of frost and due to the warming up of winters, frost situations may become infrequent and consequently longer growing period could be realized, leading to improved productivity. In states like Bihar, West Bengal Gujarat, the productivity is likely to decrease by 2–19% and 9–55% in the year 2020 and 2050, respectively, since in these areas, the winters are already milder and further rise in winter temperatures would adversely affect the productivity (Singh *et al.*, 2010).

Although cassava and sweet potato are considered to be tolerant to drought conditions, significant reduction in tuber yield as well as in starch content occurs and varieties vary in their response to water deficit stress/high-temperature stress conditions. Mild water-deficit stress (WDS) is favourable for tuber growth. In cassava, drought during first 3 months delays tuber initiation and bulking. Studies have shown that about 28–42% of tuber yield was found to be reduced under drought conditions during last 4 months of crop growth period (Ramanujam 1990). Sweet potato yields decreased when the available soil moisture decreases below 20% and the tuber initiation period is the most sensitive to due to its effect on tuber number. Water stress during tuber initiation period induces lignification of tubers and hampers tuber growth. Sweet potato variety "Sree Bhadra" tolerant to drought conditions has been released by Central Tuber Crops Research Institute, Trivandrum. Although cassava may sustain vegetative growth and biomass at high temperatures (33–40°C) under adequate soil moisture, sucrose synthesis and export from the leaves and starch synthesis in tubers will be affected at temperatures >30°C. Simulation studies at CTCRI on increase in temperature on sweet potato yield using SPOTCOMS model showed that tuber yield increased by 1.26 t/ha due to 1°C rise in mean temperature between 19.24°C and 20.24°C and yield decreased by 0.12 t/ha due to 1°C rise in mean temperature between 28.24°C and 29.24°C.

Fruit Crops

India is the second largest producer of Fruits after China, with a production of 89.51 million tonnes of fruits from an area of 6.2 million hectares. A large variety of fruits are grown in India, of which mango, banana, citrus, guava, grape, pineapple and apple are the major ones. Due to rise in temperature, crops will develop more rapidly and mature earlier. For example, Citrus, grapes, melons etc. will mature earlier by about 15 days. Strawberries will produce more runners at the expense of fruits. Specific chilling requirements of pome and stone fruits will be affected hence dormancy breaking will be earlier. Delay in monsoon, dry spells of rains, and untimely rains during water stress period, supra-optimal temperatures during flowering and fruit growth, hailstorms are some of the most commonly encountered climatic conditions experienced by the citrus growers over the past decade or so. The climate change increases the atmospheric temperature and change of rainfall pattern, as a result, banana cultivation may suffer from high temperature, soil moisture stress or flooding/water logging. High temperature and moisture stress also increase sunburn and cracking in apples, apricot and cherries and increase in temperature at maturity will lead to fruit cracking and burning in litchi (Kumar and Kumar 2007). Air pollution also significantly reduced the yield of several horticultural crops and increases the intensity of certain physiological disorders like black tip of mango which is induced by coal fume gases, sulphur dioxide, ethylene, carbon monoxide and fluoride. Leaf production increases by one leaf per month for every 3.3 to 3.7°C rise in minimum or mean temperature from 10-20°C or 13.5 to 25°C respectively. Higher temperature (31-32°C), in general, increases the rate of plant maturity in annual species, thus shortening the growth stages, during which developing fruits and suckers absorb photosynthetic products. The temperature below 10°C leads to impedance of inflorescence and malformations of bunches. Chilling symptoms on leaves are not seen immediately but it may take 2 to 4 days to appear. The production of apple has gradually increased but the productivity has fallen from 10.8 to 5.8 t/ha (Awasthi *et al.*, 2001). The reasons attributed to it are climate variability, soil, crop improvement etc. Among all the productivity reducing factors, climate is difficult to manage. The changes in climate in the form of erratic precipitation, increase in temperature, lesser days serving as the chilling period have started affecting the mountain agricultural production systems and ultimately the food security of the people.

Perennial fruit crop orchards are established with large investments; the stresses imposed due to climate variability would influence the production on year-to-year basis, influencing the farmers' income drastically and his decision to continue growing such crops in the long run. Continuous losses for few years would force the farmers to give up growing such crops altogether. In Himachal Pradesh, the rise in average temperature, long spells of drought during summers and less snowfall during winters have rendered large area supposed to be marginally suitable for apple cultivation unfit, thereby forcing farmers to shift to cultivation of other cash crops. Apple cultivation has been adversely affected in lower areas of Kullu and Mandi districts, and as a result of this, the farmers in the state have shifted to cultivation of vegetables like tomato and peas. In Rajgarh area of Sirmaur district, apple area has been diverted to peach. Mango has vegetative bias, and this becomes stronger with increase in temperature, thus influencing the flowering phenology. Temperature is reported to have influence on flowering, and the percentage of hermaphrodite flowers was greater in late emerging panicles, which coincided with higher temperatures (Singh *et al.*, 1966). The extreme weather events of hot and cold wave conditions have been reported to cause considerable damage to mango and guava. Delay in monsoon, dry spells and untimely rains during water stress period imposed for inducing flowering, higher temperatures during flowering and fruit growth are most commonly encountered climatic conditions by the citrus crop. Higher temperature (31–32°C), in general, increases the rate of plant maturity in banana, thus shortening the bunch development period (Turner *et al.*, 2007). High air temperatures (usually greater than 38°C) and bright sunshine cause sunburn damage on exposed fruits. Choking of bunches is also caused by high temperatures (above 38°C) and drought (Stover and Simmonds, 1972). The soil moisture deficit stress in banana during vegetative stage causes poor bunch formation, lower number and small sized fingers. Waters stress during flowering causes poor filling of fingers and unmarketable bunches. Water stress reduces the bunch weight and other growth parameters. Bananas subject to flooding by stagnant water for more than 48 h are severely stunted. Though grape originated in temperate regions, modifications in production system, taking up two prunings and one crop, have enabled it to adapt to tropical conditions. Under climate change conditions there would be changes in availability of growing degree days (GDD), leading to hastening of the phonological processes. Dogridge (*Vitis champini*) has been found promising for improvement in vigour, yield and quality of seedless grapes as well as tolerance to drought and salinity.

Table 8.3: List of Some Variety Tolerant Abiotic Stress

Sl. No.	Crop	Variety	Tolerant
1	Pomegranate	Ruby	Drought tolerant
2	Annona	Arka Sahan	Drought tolerant
3	Fig	Deanna and Excel	Drought tolerant
4	Grape (rootstock)	Dogridge	Salinity tolerant
5	Mango	Bappakai	Salinity tolerant
6	Lime	Rangpur lime and Cleopatra mandarin	Salinity tolerant

Source: Bose and Mitra (1996)

Plantation Crops

Cashew requires relatively dry and mild winter coupled with moderate dew during night for profuse flowering. High temperature (>34.4°C) and low relative humidity of <20% during afternoon cause drying of flowers, resulting in yield reduction. Cashew, being grown mostly under rainfed conditions, is vulnerable to climatic variability and drought conditions caused due to shifts in rainfall pattern. Unseasonal rains and heavy dew during flowering and fruiting period aggravate the incidence of pests and diseases, and pollinating insect activities also reduced to the minimum resulting in poor setting of nuts. Further the rains received during harvesting period result in soaking of nuts and affecting shelf life of nuts and quality of kernels. Unseasonal rains at ripening stage lead to blackening of nuts as well as rotting of apples on trees (Yadukumar *et al.*, 2010).

Studies conducted on "Impact of climate change in cashew" at Directorate of Cashew Research, Puttur, India indicated that the rainfed cashew crop is highly sensitive to changes in climate and weather vagaries, particularly during reproductive phase. Cashew requires relatively dry atmosphere and mild winter (15-200C) coupled with moderate dew during night for profuse flowering. High temperature (>34.4 0C) and low relative humidity (<20%) during afternoon causes drying of flowers, resulting in yield reduction. Unseasonal rains and heavy dew during flowering and fruiting period aggravated the incidence of pests and diseases. All these situations resulted in reduction yield upto 50 to 65%.

The studies conducted at Central Plantation Crops Research Institute, Kasaragod, indicate the general warming trend is in most of the coconut growing areas (Naresh Kumar *et al.*, 2007). Coconut productivity increased over the past 50 years except recent declining trend in Maidan area of Karnataka, Coimbatore of Tamil Nadu state, due to consecutive droughts. The production was reduced by about 3,00,000 nuts/year for 4 years. Productivity loss was to the tune of about 3500 nuts/ha/year. Apart from drought, other natural calamities like cyclone have impacted the crop production and productivity. For instance, the decline in crop production due to1996 cyclone in Godavari district of Andhra Pradesh was to the tune of 220 million nuts/year in 6 years. Apart from drought other natural calamities like cyclone etc have impacted the crop production and productivity. In coconut, arecanut and cocoa increased CO_2 led to higher biomass production. But a slight decline in biomass production was apparent at elevated air temperature. All three crops responded differentially under elevated air temperature. In coconut, net photosynthesis rate has reduced but increased that of arecanut and cocoa. However, TDM was slightly decreased in all three crops.

Increase in temperature during the last decade appears to be adversely affecting the tea productivity (Gopakumar 2011). Therefore, warming across the tea-growing area is a threat to tea productivity. Similar was the case in coffee productivity also in the absence of blossom and backing showers. Crop growth simulation models outside the country indicated that a rise of 2°C in temperature is likely to affect the area under tea and coffee adversely. However, detail studies need to be carried out on regional scales to establish the impact of global warming and climate change on tea as well as coffee productivity for which various agencies involved in the industry should take initiatives as a part of climate resilient horticulture. Climate projections in different scenarios indicated that Maidan parts of Karnataka, eastern Tamil Nadu, coastal Andhra Pradesh, Pondicherry, West Bengal and Assam in decreasing order are found to be hot spots as per different HadCM3 model scenarios.

Spice Crops

In general due to increase in maximum and minimum day temperature and decreasing the annual rainfall the productivity showed decreasing trend in most of the black pepper growing areas of India. In black pepper, Accs 1380(IC 316801), 1387(IC 316803), 1410(IC 316817), 1423(IC 316825) and 1430(IC 316832) were identified as relatively tolerant to drought. In cardamom, RR1(IC 349591), CL-893 (IC 349537), Green Gold (IC 349550) were found relatively tolerant under Kerala, India condition. Kashmir's prized saffron crops have suffered a 40% drop in production, one of the three places in world-besides Iran and Spain-most famous for its saffron, water shortages are straining the crops. Some of the saffron farmers who traditionally relied on rainwater are now looking at irrigation measures to save their rare and labour intensive crop.

The spice crops generally grown as intercrop in plantation crops are also equally influenced by climate change. Studies have shown that many suitable areas of spices will become marginally suitable, or new areas, which are presently unsuitable, become highly suitable for cultivation of spices. Geographic information system (GIS) was used at Indian Institute of Spices Research, Calicut, to analyse the effect of change in the climatic parameters on black pepper and ginger. The Eco-crop model of DIVA GIS indicated that with an increase of 2°C, most of the areas where these crops are being cultivated may become unsuitable and some new areas may become suitable for cultivation (Krishnamurthy *et al.*, 2010). Seed spices are winter season crops and commonly grown in arid and semi-arid track of Rajasthan and Gujarat, requiring certain period of low temperature for optimum vegetative growth. The arid zone ecosystem is very fragile and is prone to serious imbalances even with the slightest disturbance. Heavy losses have been observed due to combined effect of chilling and frost injury. Cumin, coriander, nigella, ajowan are the crops which are very sensitive to frost. Incidence of frost causing serious loss in yield almost reaches up to zero. Fennel and fenugreek are also affected by frost but growth stage plays an important role. So far no efforts have been made to identify the source of resistance against low temperature injury in available germplasm of seed spices crops. Drought is a recurrent phenomenon in arid region, and among abiotic stresses, water stress and occurrence of low temperature during critical growth stage affect seed spices.

Flower Crops

Melting of ice cap in the Himalayan regions will reduce the chilling requirement for the flowering of many of the ornamental plants like Rhododendron, Orchid, Tulipa, Alstromerea, Magnolia, Saussurea, Impatiens, Narcissus etc. Some of them will fail to bloom or flower with less abundance while others will be threatened. Plant species requiring high humidity and water may find them under difficult conditions for survival. Plains of India will also have similar kind of problems and will be affected either by drought or excessive rains, floods and seasonal variations. Commercial production of flowers particularly grown under open field conditions will be severely affected leading to poor flowering, improper floral development and colour. Chrysanthemum is a short day plant. So flowering round the year in open field condition is not possible. Low temperatures shut down flowering in Jasmine (<19°C) and lead to reduction in flower size. Flowers do not open up fully in tropical orchids wherever temperatures <15°C. High temperature leads to flower bud drop and unmarketable spikes in tropical orchids when temperature remains >35°C.

Impact of Climate Change on Outbreak of Diseases and Pests

Studies have indicated that under climate change conditions, elevated carbon dioxide concentrations, altered temperature and precipitation regimes may alter growth stages and rates of development in the life cycle and pathogenicity of pathogens, as well as modify the physiology and resistance of host plants. Based on assessment of important diseases of horticultural crops in India, impacts of climate change are felt in epidemic out breaks of fruit rot (*Phytophthora meadii*) and leaf spot (*Phyllosticta arecae* and *C. gloeosporioides*) of areca nut, bud rot (*Phytophthora palmivora*) of coconut, yellow rust, *Alternaria* bunch rot, *Botryodiplodia* dieback and *Grenaria* leaf and fruit rot in grapes, *Macrophoma* in banana, *Cercospora* and wilt in chillies, blossom blight in mango and wilt and nodal blight in pomegranate in certain locations. Although Phytophthora blight was a serious limiting factor in potato in India since 1952, these diseases never posed any threat to other vegetable crops. Since 2008, severe outbreaks of Phytophthora diseases such as late blight on potato and tomato (*P. infestans*), fruit rot on brinjal (*P. parasitica*), wilts in chilli and capsicum (*P. capsici*), blights in cucurbits (*P. capsici*), fruit rot in okra (*P. parasitica*) and root rot in cabbage and cauliflower (*P. megasperma / P. drechsleri*) have been noticed (Chowdappa 2010). The detailed analyses of *P. infestans* populations associated with late blight of tomato indicated emergence of new population that differed from the "old" US-1 lineage that dominated the *P. infestans* population worldwide prior to 1980 and IN-1 and IN-2 genotypes on potato in India. This new population triggered severe epidemics on tomato in India since 2009. As result, 10–15 fungicide applications from as early as June through October are taken in Karnataka state to manage late blight on tomato. This causes a significant expenditure to farmers and a significant environmental risk. Studies elsewhere have predicted that for each 1ºC increase in temperature, late blight can occur 4–7 days earlier, and the susceptibility period extended by 10–20 days.

The incidence of Sigatoka leaf spot disease was first reported by the All India Coordinated Research Project (tropical fruits) Jalgaon Centre during the year 1997–1998. As a case study the relationship between the weather parameters (2000–2007) and the incidence of Sigatoka leaf spot disease clearly shows a positive correlation with an increasing trend in the afternoon relative humidity and the increase in rainfall over the corresponding years. Changing climate conditions can contribute to a successful spread of newly introduced viruses or their vectors and establishment of these organisms in areas that were previously unfavourable. For example, tobacco streak virus was introduced in India in 1997 and now it is adapted to chilli, cucurbits, ornamentals and okra. The most important vectors such as aphid, white fly, thrip and leaf-hoppers, which are associated with potyviruses, begomoviruses, tospoviruses and phytoplasma, have emerged during the last two decades. Recent observations have shown that resistance to Bhendi yellow vein mosaic virus tends to break when okra is grown at higher temperatures. The number of disease epidemics has dramatically increased in recent years and also the threat of emerging new diseases and the re-emergence of other diseases. Some recent examples are incidence of thrips-transmitted tospoviruses and white fly-transmitted begomoviruses in chilli, cucurbits, okra and tomato. Hence, there is a need to thoroughly understand the potential climate change impacts on host–pathogen interactions, in order to evaluate appropriate disease management strategies (Krishna Reddy 2010).

Climate Change and Pollinators

The Intergovernmental Panel on Climate Change (IPCC) reports an approximate temperature increase ranging from 1.1°C to 6.4°C by the end of this century and that the increases in temperature will be greatest at higher latitudes (IPCC 2007). The biological impacts of rising temperatures depend upon the physiological sensitivity of organisms to temperature change. Deutsch *et al.,* (2008) found that an expected future temperature increase in the tropics, although relatively small in magnitude, is likely to have more deleterious consequences than changes at higher latitudes. The reason for this is that tropical insects are relatively sensitive to temperature changes (with a narrow span of suitable temperature) and that they are currently living in an environment very close to their optimal temperature. Deutsch *et al.* (2008) point out that in contrast, insect species at higher latitudes – where the temperature increase is expected to be higher – have broader thermal tolerance and are living in cooler climates than their physiological optima. Warming may actually enhance the performance of insects living at these latitudes. It is therefore likely that tropical agroecosystems will suffer from greater population decrease and extinction of native pollinators than agroecosystems at higher latitudes. Coope (1995) gives three possible responses of species to climate change, viz., adaptation to the new environment, migration to another suitable area and extinction. The first response is unlikely since expected climate change occurs too rapidly for populations to adapt by genetic change. With increase in temperatures, many species move towards poles and higher altitudes. Tropical pollinators may respond to different temperature cues than pollinator species at higher latitudes. Temperature-induced activity patterns may also differ, depending on pollinator size, age and sex. Winter temperature might also be of importance for pollinators. The effects of climate change on pollinators depend upon their thermal tolerance and plasticity to temperature changes. There is an urgent need to investigate the thermal tolerance of important crop pollinators and differences in thermal tolerance among *Apis* species and subspecies. Environmental cues controlling the phenology of important pollinators might include maximum daily temperature, lack of frost, number of degree days (number of days with a mean temperature above a certain threshold), day length and snow cover.

Bees are the most important group of pollinators, and like other insects, they are ectothermic, requiring elevated body temperature for flying. The temperature of their surroundings determines their activity (Willmer and Stone 1997). The high surface-to-volume ratio of small bees leads to rapid absorption of heat at high ambient temperatures. All bees with body weight above 35 mg (*Apis, Bombus, Xylocopa* and *Megachile*) are capable of endothermic heating (Bishop and Ambruster 1999). Behavioural responses of pollinator insects to avoid extreme temperatures have the potential to significantly reduce pollination services (Corbet *et al.*, 1991). Shifts in climate are bound to cause changes in behaviour of pollinators. The time taken for thermoregulation at higher temperatures comes at the cost of foraging. With increase in temperatures, the efficiency of pollen removal and deposition will change, and pollinators are at risk of overheating, especially in regions where ambient temperatures are high and climatic conditions are stable. It is important to investigate the taxonomic differences in pollinator's ability to regulate body temperature and avoid overheating (Hegland *et al.*, 2009).

Table 8.4: Economic Impacts of Insect Pollination of the World Agricultural Production Used Directly for Human Food and Listed by the Main Categories Ranked by their Rate of Vulnerability to Pollinator Loss

Crop category	Average value of a production unit	Total production economic value (EV)	Insect pollination economic value (IPEV)	Rate
	€per metric tonne	10^9€	10^9€	%
Stimulant crops	1225	19	7.0	39.0
Nuts	1269	13	4.2	31.0
Fruits	452	219	50.6	23.1
Edible oil crops	385	240	39.0	16.3
Vegetables	468	418	50.9	12.2
Pulse	515	24	1.0	4.3
Spices	1003	7	0.2	2.7
Cereals	139	312	0.0	0.0
Sugar crops	177	268	0.0	0.0
Roots and tubers	137	98	0.0	0.0
All categories		1618	152.9	9.5

Modelling to Predict the Likely Impact of Climate Change

We need quick and clear understanding of impact of climate change on horticultural crops for making sound action plan because horticulture based farming systems have high potential for sequestering carbon for mitigation of climate change. The perennial trees act as carbon sinks by sequestering the atmospheric carbon. The carbon credits could be earned under the clean development mechanism (CDM). The horticultural waste could be composted locally instead of dumping in the land fills, which can reduce the release of methane that is involved in global warming. The organic waste could also be used for generating biogas as an alternate energy source. There are considerable uncertainties about agronomic implications of horticultural crops. Predicting impact of climate change on horticultural crops accurately on regional scale is a big problem. It can be accomplished only by a modelling approach through well validated robust crop simulation models. These crop simulation models incorporate the effect of various factors of growth and yield in a mathematical model processed by computers to give results quickly for specific situation. Well validated simulation tools developed for cereal crops have been helpful in predicting of impact of climate change. Availability and development of good simulation models for horticultural fruit and vegetable crops are lacking in India probably with exception of potato and coconut where InfoCrop model has been adopted and validated for different agro-ecological regions. Controlled experiments for perennial crops with large-size trees are difficult for quantifying the direct effect of various abiotic stresses on growth, development and yield. We need to develop methodologies to quantify the adverse impacts of climate change on perennial crops like mango, grapes, apple, orange, citrus, litchi, guava and others on priority. Similarly annual vegetable crops like capsicum, cucurbits, cauliflower and root and tubers and flower crops urgently need crop simulation models. Once these simulation models are available, prediction of impacts and vulnerability of existing areas under these horticultural crops under climate change scenario can be examined, and new target areas for possible shifting of species and varieties for cultivation can be identified. Possible adaptation measures to reduce the impact of climate change can also be studied through simulation models for suggesting changes in management practices. Development of crop simulation models for horticultural crops in India is now a priority area of research.

Uses of Crop Models for Managing Horticulture

A better informed crop management can significantly reduce the yield loss. There is an urgent need for decision support system (DSS) for better management of agriculture at farm and regional level for a sustainable climate resilient crop production. Since a farmer need answers to several questions related to crop production and marketing, crop models are of immense use not only from climate change perspective but also from crop management point of view.

The major applications of crop simulation models include:

1. Crop management
2. Environmental characterization and agro ecological zoning
3. Estimating potential production and yield gap analysis
4. Strategic and anticipatory decision making
5. Developing breeding strategies
6. Crop potential zones for land use planning
7. Indoor crop management, hi-tech horticulture
8. Crop insurance

9. Weather-based horti-advisory
10. Research priority setting
11. Local and regional planning
12. De fining research priorities
13. Technology transfer
14. Policy support

Crop modelling becomes particularly important in research and development of perennial plantation crops, since it takes a lot of time for conducting research experiments. The lag period for recovery of plantations in the event of prolonged stress such as droughts is also very long, and crop modelling can act as a decision support system for managing the plantations. As any approach, simulation modelling also has limitations and uncertainties attached to it. Hence, use of ensemble of models, model integration, becomes important. Use of more than one strategy and coupling of strategies provide more robust information and assessments. Not only the growth simulation models but the plant architectural models play an important role in managing the horticultural crops. Plant architecture is modelled for grapes, palms, apple, olives, etc., using the ARCHIMED, ALEA platforms. Exploitation of models and modelling techniques for managing horticultural crops in changing climates is essential for integrating the scientific, technological and socioeconomic knowledge in pursuit of minimizing the adverse impacts and maximizing the potential benefits of climate change.

Research Thrusts for Horticultural Crops in Climate Change Watershed

Since very little information is available from India in horticultural crops with respect to response of crops to elevated CO_2, temperature and extreme events, there is a need to conduct focused research to generate information for modelling impacts of climate change and derive adaptation and mitigation strategies. Some of the thrust areas for research include:

- Development of crop coefficients for growth and development
- Quantification of sensitivity and sensitive stages of crops to weather aberrations Quantification of impacts of elevated CO_2 and change in temperature and rainfall on growth, development, yield and quality of horticultural crops
- Monitoring the phenology of perennial crops under changing climates, etc.
- Development of crop simulation models for horticultural crops
- Development of eco-friendly low-carbon adaptation technologies and their deployment in large areas
- Assessment of the impacts at regional level for more horticultural crops

- Assessment of potential adaptation strategies (for evolving targeted no regret low-carbon adaptation strategies)
- Quantification of carbon sequestration potential of perennial horticultural systems
- Weather-based pest-forecasting system
- Location-specific weather forecast based on eco-friendly horti-advisory and real-time crop monitoring
- DSS for horti-advisory and use of ICT for bridging research-stakeholder communication
- Quantification of ecological goods and ecosystem services provided by various sectors of horticulture

There is a lot of scope to improve the institutional support systems such as weather-based agro-advisory, input delivery system, development of new land use patterns, community storage facilities for horticultural perishable produce, community-based natural resource conservation and training farmers for adapting appropriate technology to reduce the climate related stress on crops. All these measures can make the horticultural farmer more resilient to climate change.

Adaptation Strategies

To address the adverse impacts of climate change on productivity and quality of horticultural crops, we need to develop sound adaptation strategies. The emphasis should be on development of production systems for improved water-use efficiency and to adapt to the hot and dry conditions. Strategies like changing sowing or planting dates in order to combat the likely increase in temperature and water stress periods during the crop-growing season. Modifying fertilizer application to enhance nutrient availability and use of soil amendments to improve soil fertility for enhancing nutrient uptake. Providing irrigation during critical stages of the crop growth and conserving soil moisture reserves are the most important interventions. The crop management practices like mulching with crop residues and plastic mulches help in conserving soil moisture. In some instances, excessive soil moisture due to heavy rain becomes a major problem and it could be overcome by growing crops on raised beds. In addition to employing modified crop management practices, the challenges posed by climate change could be tackled by developing tolerant varieties. Several institutions have evolved hybrids and varieties, which are tolerant to heat and drought stress conditions. They must be used very effectively to combat the effect of climate change depending upon their performance in a given agro-ecological region. Efforts should be intensified to develop new varieties suitable to different agro-ecological regions under changing climatic conditions. In comparison to annual crops, where the adaptation strategies can be realized relatively fast using a wide range of cultivars and species, changing the planting dates or season, planting and rearrangement of orchards requires a consideration of the more long-term aspects of climate change. Therefore, before resorting to any adaptation option, a detailed investigation on the impact of climate change on perennial crops is necessary.

Mitigating Climate Change

The long-time horizon of perennial crops creates situations like favourable areas may become unfavourable during the life of a single orchard. The choice of a variety is complicated by the risk that the best variety for the current climate may be poorly suited for future climates. Thus, while adaptations such as planting new varieties and shifting to new areas may reduce impacts in the long-term, short-term losses may largely be unavoidable. In wine grape, each grape variety grows in a range of temperatures, and for each variety it is possible to de fi ne climates for premium wine production. The physiological and morphological differences between varieties (genotypes) enable production over a relatively large range of climates and depending upon the suitability to different growing areas the cultivars may be adopted.

In situations where there is a strong consumer preference for a select cultivar and also the suitable varieties are not available to adapt to the changing climate of a particular growing region, the option of using rootstocks for better performance of the scion cultivars could be explored. Although climate change is a reality, CO_2 and methane are likely to increase which may cause impact in terms of increased temperature, more demand for water and increased biotic and abiotic stresses. Mid-hill chilling will not be enough to induce flowering in apple, and high temperature may cause desiccation of pollen, shrivelling of fruits resulting in reduced yield and more failure of the crops. These are the likely impact which causes the concerns. But there are innumerable examples to cite that climate has been changing and the technologies have helped in mitigating the problem. As a matter of fact, grape is a temperate fruit, which has been largely grown under cool climate, be it for table purposes or for winemaking. But the technological change in plant architecture and production system management has helped to produce grape in tropical situation, with highest productivity in the world. Salinity and alkalinity were a great problem for successful growing of grape, but identification of suitable rootstocks has made it highly productive. If we look to potato, tomato, cauliflower and cabbage, these are thermo-sensitive crops and were productive only under long-day conditions in temperate climate. But development of heat tolerant cultivars and adjustment in production system management has made it possible with very high productivity, even in subtropical and mild subtropical and warmer climates. These are the past experiences, which clearly bring home the point that through innovative research, threat of climate change could be converted into the opportunity, but will need visualization of likely change, its impact and planning to mitigate its bad impact. Now, available tools of biotechnology could add for speedier delivery of research results.

Critical Gaps

Based on the studies conducted in various institutes so far for understanding, the impacts of climate change on horticultural crops and adaptation options following critical gaps have been identified and listed here:

- The database on present climatic conditions, future climate scenarios and likely climatic risks associated with different agro-ecological regions growing horticultural crops needs top priority.
- The information on impacts of high temperature, limited and excess moisture stresses, elevated CO_2 concentrations and their interaction at critical stages of crop growth of horticultural crops under Indian conditions is scarce and needs urgent attention.
- The vast historic data available with AICRP centres on different crops across the country on weather, crop performance, phenology, yield and incidence of pest and diseases needs thorough analysis.
- The documentation on the emergence and incidence of pests and diseases under climate variability and climate change conditions in horticultural crops in different growing regions at the national level across the institutes is very much essential in devising new strategies in the management of pest and diseases.
- The integrated resilient adaptation strategies for specific critical stages of crops, seasons and agro-ecological regions under climate change situations need to be developed not only for sustaining but for enhanced production of horticultural crops.
- Quantification of the carbon emission through the production, protection and post-harvest management of horticultural crops and sequestration potential of perennial crops and horticulture production systems needs priority.
- There is need to develop ecofriendly and green technologies for production, protection and post-harvest management of horticultural crops and landscaping practices to mitigate the emission of greenhouse gases.

Future Strategies

Depending on the vulnerability of individual crop and the agro-ecological region, the crop-based adaptation strategies need to be developed, integrating all available options to sustain the productivity. Developing strategies and tools to comprehensively understand the impact of climate change and evolve possible adaptation measures in horticultural crops is less understood. To enhance our preparedness for climate change and to formulate a sound action plan, we need to identify gaps in vital information and prioritize research issues from point of view of farmers, policy planners, scientists, trade and industry. It is imperative to deliberate upon the likely changes which can happen in next 50–100 years; how these changes could affect growth, development and quality of horticultural crops; what are the technologies which shall help to mitigate the problem; and what kind of innovative research should be done to overcome the challenges of climate change. Thus, policy issues, adaptation strategies and mitigation technologies could be worked out, and challenges could be converted into opportunity with the updating of following:

- Priority of education, research and development and policy implications for enhancing adaptive capacity of Indian horticulture to climate change
- Capacity assessment of Indian horticulture for mitigation of greenhouse gases
- Appropriate short- and long-term action plan to mitigate the impact of climate change in horticulture

Conclusions

Climate change per se will have impact on horticultural crops due to erratic rainfall, more demand for water and enhanced biotic and abiotic stresses. However, the changes will not be only harmful, as enhanced CO_2 concentration may enhance faster photosynthesis and increased temperature may hasten the process of maturity. However, measures to adapt to these climate change-induced changes are critical for sustainable production. Increased temperature will have more effect on reproductive biology and reduced water may affect the productivity, but adaptive mechanism like time adjustment and productive use of water shall reduce the negative impact. The strategies must have to identify the gene tolerant to high temperature, flooding and drought, nutrient efficient cultivars and production system for efficient use of nutrient water. Strategies have to address the enhanced water-use efficiency and cultural practices that conserve water and promote crop. Development of climate-resilient horticultural crops which are tolerant to high temperature, moisture stress, salinity and climate proofing through genomics and biotechnology would be essentially required. This would need highly prioritized research to address the impact of climate change. Enhancing the adaptation of tropical production system to changing climatic condition is a great challenge and would require integrated efforts and an efficient and effective strategy to be able to deliver technologies that can mitigate the effects of climate change on diverse crops and production systems. Knowledge of carbon sequestration, especially through perennial horticulture, needs to be enhanced, which could be utilized for enhancing the income through trading of carbon. Research must address all the strategies which can convert the challenges into the opportunity. Concerted and integrated efforts with effectiveness and efficiency would definitely make us stronger to face the challenges and meet the ever increasing demand for food.

REFERENCES

Awasthi RP, Verma HS, Sharma RD, Bhardwaj SP and Bhardwaj SV (2001) Causes of Low Productivity in Apple Orchards and Suggested Remedial Measures: Productivity of Temperate Fruits. Jindal, K.K. and Gautam, D.R. (Eds), 1-8.

Bose TK and Mitra SK (1996) Fruits: Tropical and Subtropical. Nayaprakash, Kolkata, India.

Bray EA (2002) Abscisic Acid Regulation of Gene Expression during Water-deficit Stress in the Era of the Arabidopsis Genome. Plant Cell Environ 25: 153-161.

Bray EA, Bailey-Serres J and Weretilnyk E (2000) Responses to Abiotic Stresses: Biochemistry and Molecular Biology of Plants. Gruissem, W., Buchannan, B. and Jones, R. (eds). ASPP, Rockville, MD 1158-1249.

Capiati DA, País SM and Téllez-Iñón MT (2006) Wounding Increases Salt Tolerance in Tomato Plants: Evidence on the Participation of Calmodulin-like Activities in Cross Tolerance Signaling. Journal of Experimental Botany 57: 2391-2400.

Chowdappa P (2010) Impact of Climate Change on Fungal Diseases of Horticultural Crops. In: Singh HP, Singh JP, Lal SS (Eds) Challenges of Climate Change-Indian Horticulture. Westville Publishing House, New Delhi

Coope GR (1995) Insect Faunas in Ice Age Environments: Why so Little Extinction? In: Lawton J, May R (eds) Extinction rates. Oxford University Press, Oxford, UK

Corbet SA, Williams IH, Osborne JL (1991) Bees and the Pollination of Crops and Wild Flowers in the European Community. Bee World 72:47–59

Deutsch CA, Tewksbury JJ, Huey RB, Sheldon KS, Ghalambor CK, Haak DC, Martin PR (2008) Impacts of Climate Warming on Terrestrial Ectotherms Across Latitude. Proc Natl Acad Sci U S A 105: 6668–6672

Drew MC (1979) Plant Responses to Anaerobic Conditions in Soil and Solution Culture. Curr. Adv. Plant Sci 36: 1-14.

Fischer G, Shah M, van Velthuizen HV (2002) Climate Change and Agricultural Vulnerability. International Institute for Applied Systems Analysis, Laxenburg

Geisenberg C, Stewart K (1986) Field Crop Management. In: Atherton JG, Rudich J (eds) The Tomato Crop, A Scientific Basis for Improvement. Chapman and Hall, New York

Gopakumar CS (2011) Impacts of Climate Variability on Agriculture in Kerala. Dissertation, Cochin University of Science and Technology

Hazra P and Som MG (1999) Technology for Vegetable Production and Improvement. Naya Prokash, Kolkata, India.

Hegland SJ, Nielsen A, Lázaro A, Bjerknes AL, Totland Ø (2009) How does Climate Warming Affect Plant Pollinator Interactions? Ecol Lett 12:184–195

IPCC (2007) Climate Change 2007: Fourth Assessment Report of the Intergovernmental Panel on Climate Change (IPCC), WMO, UNEP

IPCC (2007b) Climate Change 2007: Climate Change Impacts Adaptation and Vulnerability Summary for Policymakers. Inter-Governmental Panel on Climate Change, Geneva

Krishna Reddy M (2010) Climate Change and Virus Diseases of Horticultural Crops. In: Singh HP, Singh JP, Lal SS (eds) Challenges of Climate Change-Indian Horticulture. Westville Publishing, New Delhi

Krishnamurthy KS, Kandiannan K, Chempakam B, Parthasarathy U, Parthasarathy VA (2010) Climatic Influence on Growth and Productivity of Balack Pepper. In: Singh HP,

Singh JP, Lal SS (eds) Challenges of Climate Change-Indian Horticulture. Westville Publishing, New Delhi

Kumar R and Kumar KK (2007) Managing Physiological Disorders in Litchi. Indian Horticulture 52 (1): 22-24

Kumar R and Kumar KK (2007) Managing Physiological Disorders in Litchi. Indian Horticulture 52 (1): 22-24

Kuo DG, Tsay JS, Chen BW and Lin PY (1982) Screening for Flooding Tolerance in the Genus Lycopersicon. Hort Science 17(1): 6-78.

Naresh Kumar S, Rajagopal V, Siju Thomas T, Cherian vinu K, Ratheesh Narayanan MK, Ananda KS, Nagawekar DD, Hanumanthappa M, Vincent S, Srinivasalu B (2007) Variations in Nut Yield of Voconut (Cocos nucifera L.) and Dry Spell in Different Agroclimatic Zones of India. Indian J Hortic Sci 64:309–313

Parry ML, Rosenzweig C, Iglesias Livermore AM, Fischer G (2004) Effects of Climate Change on Global Food Production under SRES Emissions and Socio-economic Scenarios. Glob Environ Change 14:53–67

Rai N and Yadav D S (2005) Advances in Vegetable Production. Researchco Book Centre, New Delhi, India.

Raj Narayan (2009) Air Pollution–A Threat in Vegetable Production. In: Sulladmath, U. V. and Swamy, K.R.M. International Conference on Horticulture (ICH-2009) Horticulture for Livelihood Security and Economic Growth, 158-159

Ramanujam T (1990) Effect of Moisture Stress on Photosynthesis and Productivity of Cassava. Photosynthetica 24:217–224

Rosenzweig C, Parry ML (1994) Potential Impact of Climate Change on World Food Supply. Nature 367:133–138

Samra JS, Singh G (2003) Cold Wave of 2002–2003: Impact on Agriculture. ICAR Pub, New Delhi

Samra JS, Singh G (2004) Heat Wave of March 2004: Impact on Agriculture. ICAR Pub, New Delhi

Singh HP (2010) Impact of Climate Change on Horticultural Crops. In: Singh HP, Singh JP, Lal SS (eds) Challenges of Climate Change-Indian Horticulture. Westville Publishing, New Delhi

Singh JP, Govindakrishnan PM, Lal SS, Aggarwal PK (2005) Increasing the Efficiency of Agronomy Experiments in Potato using INFOCROP-POTATO Model. Potato Res 48:131–152

Singh JP, Govindakrishnan PM, Lal SS, Aggarwal PK (2008) Infocrop-potato a Model for Simulating Growth and Yield of Potato in the Sub-tropics. Central Potato Research Institute, Shimla, Technical Bulletin No 87

Singh RN, Mujumder PK, Sharma DK (1966) Sex Expression in Mango (Mangifera indica L.) with Reference to Prevailing Temperature. Proc Am Soc Hortic Sci 89:228

Srinivasa Rao NK (1995) Management of Heat Moisture and Other Physical Stress Factors in Tomato and Chilli in India. In Collaborative Vegetable Research in South Asia, Proceedings of the SAVERNET Midterm Review Workshop, AVRDC, Tainan

Stover RH, Simmonds NW (1972) Bananas. Longman, London

Turner DW, Fortescue JA, Thomas DS (2007) Environmental Physiology of the Bananas (Musa app.). Braz j Plant Physiol 19:463–484

Yadukumar N, Raviprasad TN, Bhat MG (2010) Effect of Climate Change on Yield and Insect Pests Incidence on Cashew. In: Singh HP, Singh JP, Lal SS (eds) Challenges of Climate Change-Indian Horticulture. Westville Publishing, New Delhi

Index